# Intelligence on the Frontier Bet[...] and Civil Society

*Intelligence on the Frontier Between State and Civil Society* shows how today's intelligence practices constantly contest the frontiers between normal politics and security politics, and between civil society and the state.

Today's intelligence services face the difficult task of managing the uncertainties associated with new threats by inviting civil actors to help, while also upholding their own institutional authority and their responsibility to act in the interest of the nation. This volume examines three different perspectives: Managerial practices of intelligence collection and communication; the increased use of new forms of data (i.e. of social media information); and the expansion of intelligence practices into new areas of concern, for example cybersecurity and the policing of (mis-)information. This book accurately addresses these three topics, and all the chapters shine more light on the inclusion, and exclusion, of civil society in the secret world of intelligence.

By scrutinizing how intelligence services balance the inclusion of civil society in security tasks with the need to uphold their institutional authority, *Intelligence on the Frontier Between State and Civil Society* will be of great interest to scholars of Security Studies and Intelligence Studies. The chapters were originally published as a special issue of *Intelligence and National Security*.

**Karen Lund Petersen** is Professor (with special responsibilities) at the University of Copenhagen and Director of the Centre for Advanced Security Theory. Her primary research interests are security and risk governance, with a particular focus on political risk, corporate security management and intelligence.

**Kira Vrist Rønn** is Lecturer at University College Copenhagen, section for Emergency and Risk Management. Her primary research interests are ethical issues related to policing and security.

# Intelligence on the Frontier Between State and Civil Society

*Edited by*
**Karen Lund Petersen and Kira Vrist Rønn**

Routledge
Taylor & Francis Group

LONDON AND NEW YORK

First published 2020
by Routledge
2 Park Square, Milton Park, Abingdon, Oxon, OX14 4RN

and by Routledge
52 Vanderbilt Avenue, New York, NY 10017

*Routledge is an imprint of the Taylor & Francis Group, an informa business*

First issued in paperback 2021

Chapters 1–4 & 6–7 © 2020 Taylor & Francis

Chapters 5 & 8 © 2019 Didier Bigo and Hedvig Ördén. Originally published as Open Access.

*British Library Cataloguing in Publication Data*
A catalogue record for this book is available from the British Library

ISBN13: 978-0-367-44168-5 (hbk)
ISBN13: 978-1-03-208409-1 (pbk)

Typeset in Myriad Pro
by Newgen Publishing UK

**Publisher's Note**
The publisher accepts responsibility for any inconsistencies that may have arisen during the conversion of this book from journal articles to book chapters, namely the inclusion of journal terminology.

**Disclaimer**
Every effort has been made to contact copyright holders for their permission to reprint material in this book. The publishers would be grateful to hear from any copyright holder who is not here acknowledged and will undertake to rectify any errors or omissions in future editions of this book.

# Contents

# Citation Information

The chapters in this book were originally published in *Intelligence and National Security*, volume 34, issue 3 (November 2019). When citing this material, please use the original page numbering for each article, as follows:

For any permission-related enquiries please visit:
www.tandfonline.com/page/help/permissions

# Notes on Contributors

**Didier Bigo** is Professor of International Political Sociology at Sciences-Po Paris-CERI, France, and part-time Professor at King's College London, Department of War Studies Research. He is additionally Director of the Centre for Study on Conflicts, Liberty and Security (CCLS) and Editor of the quarterly journal *Cultures & Conflicts*, published by l'Harmattan.

**Kristoffer Kjærgaard Christensen** received his PhD from the University of Copenhagen, Department of Political Science. His research is on the significance of cybersecurity for contemporary security politics, looking at how cybersecurity involves new security actors and contributes to creating new political spaces and understandings of (security) politics and democracy. He now works with cybersecurity in the Danish Ministry of Health.

**Adam Diderichsen** is Assistant Professor of Emergency and Risk Management at the University College Copenhagen.

**Myriam Dunn Cavelty** is Senior Lecturer for Security Studies and Deputy for Research and Teaching at the Center for Security Studies (CSS) at ETH Zürich. Her research focuses on the politics of risk and uncertainty in security politics and changing conceptions of (inter-)national security due to cyber issues (cybersecurity, cyberwar, critical infrastructure protection) in specific.

**Mark Daniel Jaeger** is a postdoctoral researcher at the Centre for Advanced Security Theory at the University of Copenhagen. He specializes in the sociology of conflict and risk in the area of societal disputes involving ICT and in the area of international sanctions.

**Tobias Liebetrau** is a postdoctoral researcher at the Center for Military Studies, University of Copenhagen. His research focuses on the implication of ICT for security politics and theory, examining how cybersecurity plays out in the context of EU security governance. Prior to his enrolment in the PhD programme, he worked at the Danish National Centre for Cybersecurity under the Danish Defence Intelligence Service.

**Hedvig Ördén** is a PhD candidate in Political Science at Stockholm University. Her main research interests concern political theory, intelligence analysis and EU security policy on the information threat.

**Karen Lund Petersen** is Professor (with special responsibilities) at the University of Copenhagen and Director of the Centre for Advanced Security Theory. Her primary research interests are security and risk governance, with a particular focus on political risk, corporate security management and intelligence.

**Kira Vrist Rønn** is Lecturer at University College Copenhagen, section for Emergency and Risk Management. Her primary research interests are ethical issues related to policing and security.

**Rune Saugmann** is an Academy of Finland postdoctoral researcher at Tampere University. His interdisciplinary research on the visual mediation of security has appeared in *Security Dialogue, EJIR, Journalism Practice, European Journal of Communication, Global Discourse, JOMEC, Int'l Journal of Arts & Politics* as well as numerous edited collections in IR and media studies.

**Sille Obelitz Søe** is a postdoctoral researcher in philosophy of information in the Department of Information Studies at the University of Copenhagen. At the core of her research lies the concepts of information, misinformation and disinformation and their pragmatic nature – with connections to big data, algorithms, information ethics and privacy.

# Introduction: Bringing in the public. Intelligence on the frontier between state and civil society

Karen Lund Petersen and Kira Vrist Rønn

**ABSTRACT**

This special issue is based on the observation that today's intelligence services stand before a difficult task of, on the one hand, having to manage the uncertainties associated with new threats by inviting civil actors in to help, while also, on the other hand, having to uphold their own institutional authority and responsibility to act in the interest of the nation. In balancing this task, we show how today's intelligence practices constantly contests the frontiers between normal politics and security politics and between civil society and the state. In this introduction we argue that these changes can be observed at three different levels. One is at the level of managerial practices of intelligence collection and communication; another is in the increased use of new forms of data, i.e. of social media information; and a third is the expansion of intelligence practices into new areas of concern, e.g. cybersecurity and the policing of (mis-) information.

Complex and uncertain threat environments, with terrorism, cybersecurity and global financial crisis, have made many traditional management tools unfit and profoundly transformed the ways in which intelligence services deal with threats to the nation and its citizens. In this special issue, we argue that intelligence agencies today stand before a defining gap between an increasing demand from society and politicians to provide security and the organization's ability to fulfil those demands and needs. In order to manage this gap between expectations and possibilities for management, new methods, coalitions and partnerships are considered pertinent.

These practices include the use of new technologies for collection and analysis as well as arrangements to increase cooperation and partnerships between national and foreign intelligence and security services, between intelligence and police services, between intelligence and security services and the public, and between intelligence and private companies and 'other potentially uneasy bedfellows'.[1] While these practices help to manage the gap and thus meet public expectations, they also confront and challenge a long-established role of intelligence agencies in society: as institutions which are able to make well-informed judgements and decisions on how to protect national interests.

The engagement of new methods might seem an unavoidable consequence of having to meet new challenges and manage uncertainty; however, some of these methods challenge both our vision of democracy and privacy and the organizational identity of the services. The organizational identity is challenged by the inclusion of new partnerships and collaborations. Almost paradoxically the intelligence services need on the one hand to manage uncertainties and in the course of that to invite new actors in to help, while they also need to assume authority and responsibility to act in the interest of national security. This organizational reality, the articles in this special issue argue, creates not only new managerial concerns but – and far more importantly – it also challenges our most fundamental democratic values, namely freedom and protection.

The articles in this special issue analyse this new role of intelligence services and show how today's management practices and alliances contest the frontiers between normal politics and security politics and between civil society and the state. As Rune Saugmann Andersen argues in his analysis of the intelligence use of amateur photographs, images taken by civilians are increasingly turned into military imagery and used for the purpose of conceptualizing conflicts zones. Yet, in doing so, the 'normality' associated with that of taking private photos and sharing these on social media becomes an object of security politics. Thereby, security comes to invade the very idea of 'citizenry' and privacy. In similar terms, Adam Diderichsen shows how intelligence work has come to define core tasks in what we used to think of as 'normal' bureaucratic governmental institutions, challenging the bureaucratic logic of governmental agencies.

In a broad perspective, this special issue raises the most intrusive question of them all: namely what role intelligence services have or should have in a globalized democratic society, where threats are hard to pin down and manage by normal means of control and where new means of control are deemed necessary. In the words of Didier Bigo, we ask, 'What happens when intelligence services are demonopolized?'

## The de-monopolizing of intelligence practices

Within the larger aim of understanding current attempts to demonopolize intelligence, the articles especially focus on three dimensions. First, the managerial practices of intelligence collection and communication and how those new practices redefine the role of the public in security affairs and affect the management structures and the organizational identity of intelligence services. Second, how the performance of different forms of data mining, i.e. of social media information, challenges fundamental rights of citizens – e.g. the right to privacy – both nationally and globally. Third, the expansion of intelligence practices into new areas of concern, e.g. cybersecurity and the policing of (mis-) information in the context of the EU.

The term 'civil society' is generally applied in a broad sense, as a gathering of concepts of non-state actors, including individuals, groups and private companies. While 'the public' has similar connotations, traditionally referring to the role of individual citizens in the national political community, the articles also show that the concept of public becomes more blurry when addressing new types of security threats. Accordingly, Christensen and Liebetrau argue that when it comes to cybersecurity 'it becomes much more opaque who has a right to security and a legitimate say in holding those responsible to account'. Hence, a main aim of the issue is to flesh out and question how the public is currently being put into play in new and different ways in the context of security. Later, we will specify the three dimensions/themes and group the articles under the following sections.

### New practices of communication and intelligence collection

The first theme concerns the communication between intelligence services and the wider public. Communication is here understood as a way to cope with pressing public and political expectations and thus a way to *manage management* that prescribes certain roles for the public. Two articles address the issues of organizational identity of intelligence services by discussing how new forms and means of communication render the public active actors in the identification and collection of intelligence. This inclusion of the public raises some new democratic and managerial dilemmas.

In her article 'Three concepts of intelligence communication: awareness, advice or coproduction', Petersen shows how the role of communication vis-à-vis the public has changed from being primarily concerned with creating awareness and advice to that of finding an institutional form that supports communication for the purpose of co-production. This change, she argues, assigns an active role to the public where they are made co-responsible for identifying security threats and risks to society. Hence, Petersen argues that this communication strategy functions as a way to manage the uncertain threat and risk environment facing society and the intelligence services as such. Hence, including the public in the reply to the often illusory public demand for security in an absolute sense can be viewed as a legitimacy-enhancing endeavour on the part of the services. By navigating the complexity facing the services via increased public inclusion, the services seem to manage the 'performativity gap' which arises when organizations face complex, if not impossible, tasks such as the management of current security risks and uncertainties on one hand and the political and public demands for (absolute) security on the other hand.

Co-production of intelligence is likewise a keyword in the article 'From madness to wisdom: intelligence and the digital crowd'. In this piece, Cavelty and Jaeger scrutinize how crowd sourcing increasingly becomes a crucial part of intelligence practices. They understand crowd sourcing as an element of the Big Data wave influencing an ever-increasing range of societal functions, and they argue that the inclusion of the crowd raises new types of question concerning how voluntary and involuntary security communication is changing the relationship between intelligence agencies and the public due especially to Internet and Communication Technologies (ICT). The authors argue that whereas the crowd was previously something to be neutralized and controlled, the crowd increasingly participates in the coproduction of security and of a resilient society. This new endeavour and role of the crowd raises new dilemmas such as increased inclusion of privately owned and designed social media platforms in security governance. Hence, the privately mediated information from and on the crowd potentially creates conflicting interests between the ICT companies, the intelligence services and the public.

### Social media, the Internet and privacy

A second group of articles study how the mere idea of 'privacy' is challenged in a world where new technologies allow for a different engagement with citizens. Thus, by considering the frontiers between public and private in the current security landscape, we also hint to the emerging discussions concerning ownership, control, access and exploitation of personal information and photos on social media platforms in the name of security and public safety. Hence, the importance of open sources and information from social media is increasing rendering discussions on the nature and exploitation of such information pertinent.

Saugmann Andersen argues in his article 'Open-source intelligence and individual security' that photos taken in conflict and war zones by citizens are extensively exploited by intelligence services via social media platforms. He argues that the use of such images 'changes not only media practices and the representation of conflict, but are increasingly part of the logics of conflict itself'. Furthermore, this undertaking potentially turns citizens into active actors in a specific conflict. Along with this usage of online amateur photos in conflicts, the citizens providing such images unwillingly become endangered, since the photos can be tracked back to the specific individuals by digital traces. Saugmann Andersen explores how open-source intelligence was used in the context of investigating the downing of MH17 over eastern Ukraine and argues that this investigation relied heavily on citizens' images. Saugmann Andersen concludes that this new tendency 'creates a new kind of individual security dilemma in which citizens are endangered if they voice everyday concerns visually because the digital traces of their everyday visual practices are appropriated by conflict actors.'

In line with the paper by Saugmann Andersen, Rønn and Søe argue in their article 'Is social media intelligence private?' that the exploitation of social media information in the name of security and public safety is often regarded as unproblematic by the services themselves, since the majority of such information is publicly available. In this article, Rønn and Søe however argue against this claim also reflected by Omand, Bartlett and Miller (2012) stating that openly available SOCMINT is non-intrusive. Social media platforms are similar to public spaces; however, this in the view of the authors does not mean that governmental bodies should randomly access such information in order to provide societal security and public safety. The authors argue that the concept of privacy is somewhat unfit for the context of social media due to difficulties concerning control over information and the flaws concerning an adequate concept of informed consent. Hence, the authors argue that systematic exploitation of social media platforms potentially creates a negative chilling effect where citizens will avoid certain types of communication via such platforms due to the fear of being watched. Thus, Rønn and Søe conclude that the services should take the democratic virtues (freedom of speech and expression) rendered possible by social media platforms into account before randomly exploiting information from such platforms.

On the practice of data mining in the context of intelligence, Bigo likewise provides a comprehensive and thought-provoking analysis of the logics embedded in the cross-national sharing of secret information, especially between national SIGINT bodies. Bigo argues that 'marginal' digital behaviour often becomes the marker for suspicion for the intelligence services and the warrant for the inclusion of individuals on lists which are shared between a large number of security authorities worldwide. Bigo calls this phenomenon a 'mass production of "shared secrets"'. He further argues that a range of challenges arise in the wake of such sharing of secret digital information, which is further boosted by this cross-national sharing of such information. First of all, the individuals have no right to know why they are included in such lists and thus why they became suspects, which in his words 'creates a problem regarding the rule of Law and democratic principles, and suppose new discussions about the boundaries between secrecy, security, publicity and scrutiny.' Secondly, the cross-national sharing of secret SIGINT leads to a destabilizing of the dichotomies 'public and private, internal and foreign, shared and (national) secret distinctions.' Bigo calls for further attention on the fact that the increased sharing of secrets between states, leads to a new type of global suspicion where individuals can also be followed worldwide via digital traces, due to 'marginal digital behaviour' and this, Bigo argues, creates new challenges regarding the legal certainty concerning these individuals.

### New conceptual practices: intelligence, misinformation and cybersecurity

The third and final group of articles look at how new conceptual developments work to establish an identity of security management within the intelligence services, which enforces old structures of secrecy and authority in a range of new domains, which challenge those same structures of knowledge and fundamentally redefines the mere meaning of the public. Hence, this part of the issue is organized around a concern about what happens when the traditional area of expertise of intelligence services expands and furthermore what happens when fundamental democratic conventions are challenged by seemingly new security needs.

The traditional notion that some intelligence work is 'inherently governmental' is more challenged now than ever. As Petersen and Tjalve state, even 'the collection of intelligence has drifted outside the purview of the agencies themselves'.[2] New actors such as partners in banks, industry, social institutions, hospitals, prison guards and citizens are main players in the intelligence context. Hence, the relationship between the state and civil society is radically different now and this is especially obvious in the context of cybersecurity where the public/private dependency is somewhat turned around.

In the article 'A new role for "the public"?', Christensen and Liebetrau argue that the relationship between state and civil society, i.e. private companies, is not simply characterized by 'mutual cooperation and mutual benefit'. On the contrary, the state is becoming more and more dependent on the companies and their willingness to inform, cooperate, etc. Furthermore, companies are not, like most intelligence services, delimited by national borders and often they may simply consult cooperate security departments instead of state security agencies when they face security challenges. In the article, Christensen and Liebetrau introduce some of the new challenges related to accountability and oversight in the context of cybersecurity. Applying WannaCry as the starting point for discussions, they argue that 'the public' in the case of cybersecurity cannot be neatly defined in terms of 'a national political community'. Furthermore, they argue that who has a right to security and a legitimate say in holding those responsible to account becomes much more opaque in the context of cybersecurity. They call for a redefinition of 'security publics' in the context of cybersecurity, since these publics become more context sensitive and in-flux in the case of cybersecurity. This fact affects the notion of whom intelligence services are accountable towards and to some degree also the task of identifying responsible and accountable actors in the case of cybersecurity.

The second article in this part of the issue is titled 'Spreading intelligence', and here Diderichsen addresses another context where traditional intelligence practices are changing. Diderichsen argues that by increasingly applying the concept 'intelligence' to, for example, policing, public administration or risk management, the institutions adhere to what could be termed a specific 'intelligence' or 'adversarial logic', where the presence of an enemy is presumed. The general endorsement and spreading of intelligence could intuitively be understood as unproblematic since it simply reflects an urge to be increasingly knowledge-based. Diderichsen, however, argues that more is at risk in the spreading of intelligence, and his analysis shows that the adoption of intelligence in traditional non-intelligence practices entails a problematic transformation in the nature of 'the social relationships founded in and by these various institutions', for example, in the presumption of an enemy instead of a client, a colleague, a citizen, etc.

Finally, in the article 'Deferring substance', Ördén provides a comprehensive analysis of EU policies addressing so-called 'information threats'. Such threats are understood as threats from misinformation and fake news and in the article Ördén argues that it is not clear what the subject of these policies are – that is – who is considered relevant for protection and against what? Furthermore, the article shows how intelligence and security practices of the EU are expanding into new areas not previously understood as in need of protection by EU bodies. Hence, in this sense Ördén scrutinizes how 'information threats' are being *securitized* and considered as an urgent issue of EU security policies even though the main concepts – information threats, security etc. – are unclear and diverging in the chosen EU policies. The complexity of the threat spelled out by Ördén in her search for a 'referent object of security' in current EU policies addressing 'information threats' seems to suggest that there is no clear understanding of what security means in this regard and thus neither of who and what should be protected and by whom.

Generally, this special issue seeks to create a stronger dialogue between intelligence and security studies; two disciplines which increasingly share readers. In security studies, many of the security practices we have just described have been captured by the term 'management of unease' – describing a seeping spread of the security logic to the everyday risk practices of bureaucracies, governmental agencies and companies.[3] Where security traditionally was considered an exception to the law, today's politics of 'resilience' seem to rewrite or even suspend the difference between 'normal politics' and 'security politics' – between war and peace – altogether. This development is in many ways troubling as it fundamentally calls into question the classical understanding of the sovereign state as the guarantor of security and thereby individual freedom (cf. Skinner 1989). By bringing this perspective into intelligence studies, we aim and hope to spur a wider debate about the role of intelligence services in society; a debate on managerial realities that are co-constitutive of our wider society and its values.

## Notes

1. Richards, "Intelligence Dilemma," 773; Aldrich, "Global Intelligence"; Petersen & Tjalve, "Intelligence Expertice"; and Petersen, *Coporate Risk*.
2. Petersen and Tjalve, "Intelligence Expertice," 23.
3. Huysmans, *The Politics of Insecurity*; Bigo, "Globalized In-Security" & "Liason Officers in Europe"; Neal, "Normalization and Legislative Exceptionalism"; and Petersen & Tjalve, "(Neo)Republican Security Governance".

## Disclosure statement

No potential conflict of interest was reported by the authors.

## Bibliography

Aldrich, R. "Global Intelligence Co-Operation versus Accountability: New Facets to an Old Problem." *Intelligence and National Security* 24/1 (2009): 26–56. doi:10.1080/02684520902756812.

Bigo, D. "Liaison Officers in Europe: New Officers in the European Security Field." In *Transnational Policing*, edited by J. W. E. Scheptycki, 67–99. London and New York: Routledge, 2000.

Bigo, D. "Globalized-In-Security: The Field and the Ban-Opticon." In *Translation, Biopolitics, Colonial Difference*, edited by N. Sakai and J. Solomon, 109–156. Hong Kong: University of Hong Kong Press, 2006.

Huysmans, J. *The Politics of Insecurity. Fear, Migration and Asylum in the EU*. London: Routledge, 2006.

Neal, A. W. "Normalization and Legislative Exceptionalism: Counterterrorist Lawmaking and the Changing Times of Security Emergencies." *International Political Sociology* 6, no. 3 (2012): 260–276. doi:10.1111/j.1749-5687.2012.00163.x.

Petersen, K. L. *Corporate Risk and National Security Redefined*. London: Routledge, 2012.

Petersen, K. L., and V. Schou Tjalve. "Intelligence Expertise in an Age of Information Sharing: Public-Private "Collection" and Its Challenges to Democratic Control and Accountability." *Intelligence and National Security* 33/1 (2018): 21–35. doi:10.1080/02684527.2017.1316956.

Petersen, K. L., and V. S. Tjalve. "(Neo)Republican Security Governance? US Homeland Security and the Politics of "Shared Responsibility"." *International Political Sociology* 7, no. 1 (2013): 1–18. doi:10.1111/ips.12006.

Richards, J. "Intelligence Dilemma? Contemporary Counterterrorism in a Liberal Democracy." *Intelligence and National Security* 27, no. 5 (2012): 761–780. doi:10.1080/02684527.2012.708528.

# Three concepts of intelligence communication: awareness, advice or co-production?

Karen Lund Petersen

**ABSTRACT**

Communication aimed at the public has been an almost absent topic in intelligence studies. This is despite a growing recognition of the importance of communicating towards the public in preventive security, counterterrorism, cyber security and organized crime prevention. This article attends to the practice of communicating intelligence to the public. It does so in order to show the diversity of communication practices in Western intelligence today. By investigating how the intelligence community communicates about 'communication' to the public, the article identifies three different concepts of communication, that each exposes different understandings of the public and democratic concerns.

In intelligence studies, the question of security communication has mainly been treated as a matter of providing information and estimates to governments on current and evolving threat levels. Especially, the Second Gulf War generated an increased political and academic focus on the nature of intelligence communication and the so-called potential 'political role' of intelligence advisors. Security communication became the subject to public scrutiny, as the idea of the intelligence agency as a politically independent institution was questioned.[1] In effect, security communication came to frame new debates on parliamentary control, oversight and the executive's ability to make informed decisions on national security.[2]

In the aftermath of the war, the legitimacy of the system was linked to the need for redefining the relation of communication between the services and the political system, both by installing more oversight, implementing new institutional reform and by sharpening the methods and 'language policies' of the agencies. Although it is recognized that there are huge uncertainties involved in providing probabilities on security threats, numeric value scales (such as Bayesian statistics) were and are most frequently seen as the solution to prevent political bias. Using these numeric values, probabilities and impact levels to convey analytical results are often argued to be preferable due to the fact that it makes advice seem 'value-free' and 'non-politicized'.[3] This debate is interesting for many reasons, not least because it reflects how the line between intelligence expertise and that of political practice is negotiated: on what it means to give non-biased and non-politized advice, and what this does to the managerial behaviour of the agencies.[4]

In this article, I will shed light on a slightly different, yet somehow similar, kind of intelligence communication – namely the communication directed towards the public. Communication aimed at the public is a rather recent topic in intelligence studies – though increasingly important to practice. It engages the public through websites, apps, community programmes and partnerships; it asks for awareness, for advice and even sometimes for action. Like traditional intelligence communication, the aim is to the find a format for communication that on the one hand upholds the authority of the organization as experts in the field, while also making it possible to navigate in a context where solutions are increasingly complicated and expectations are high. In describing such a bureaucratic challenge, scholars talk about a late modern 'performativity gap': a gap between the outside's expectations of control and effective solutions and the capacity of institutions and administrations to actually satisfy those expectations. This gap, scholars argue, may create a legitimatization crisis, and, following on from that, an increased need for documentation, evaluation and inspection of management procedures.[5]

Communication can, in this way, be seen as a tool that helps to manage this 'performance gap' between the organization and its outside. It helps to establish the authority of the services and define the meaning of security expertise – in a world where the relation between the desired ends of control and the means of mitigation is considered limited. Communication has, in other words, become an organizational label for a number of the current institutional pressures on intelligence services, encompassing 'a space' for dealing with societal expectations.

Communication towards the public is, however, much more than just a matter of managing this gap between expectations and possible performance. While public communication at one level works to justify and make visible what is being done to control and protect against current and unknown threats, it also functions as a means to mobilize this same public to act on its behalf. Communication practices are, I will argue in this article, organizational practices that work as instruments for steering as well as working to define legitimate authority, action and responsibility.

In this article, I study how communication embodies 'a particular intention', and how it consequently addresses 'the solution of a particular problem'.[6] Following the conceptual historians Quentin Skinner and Reinhart Koselleck, it becomes possible to observe many different ways in which the concepts of communication are used in today's debate on the role of intelligence in society; concepts that each define and confine what can possibly be considered meaningful organizational action. In other words, by studying the use of the term 'communication', we get to understand how some managerial practices and solutions become possible and others impossible, as well as get to understand how intelligence services perceive their authority in relation to the public.

The article will thus present a study of how the concept(s) of communication, when employed by intelligence experts, constructs the meaning of expertise and legitimate action. The countries in focus are mainly the A and the UK, while examples from Denmark are also brought in. The results are based on a thorough analysis of the intelligence studies literature, speeches, reports and website presentations on intelligence communication.

The argument will proceed as follows. The first part will examine how the intelligence community communicates about 'communication'. The first section of the article identifies three different concepts of communication in the current debates on intelligence. I argue that each of these concepts (communication as awareness, advice or co-production) constructs the role of the public differently and evokes different organizational forms. The analysis draws on risk communication studies to understand and discuss how control and authority have been written and rewritten in these approaches to communication: how new forms of security organizations are consolidated, how new understandings of secrecy are generated and how the traditional authority of the services in society are challenged. The second part of the article discusses how these three concepts of communication mirror different organizational risk cultures, which each define different needs for institutional reform.

## Communicating 'communication' to the public

There are commonly two ways in which the intelligence literature has understood 'communication' in relation to the public. One is 'communication as awareness' and refers to speaking, publishing and making actions visible (e.g., at the homepage) in the name of democratic accountability. Communication thus serves the democratic civil society's possibility of scrutinizing the actions of the state.[7] The second way is communication as advice through warnings and threat assessments, meant for the public to undertake collective or individual action.[8] While these two concepts are the ones we usually think of when talking about communication between a 'sender' (the institution) and a 'receiver' (the public), we have recently witnessed a third concept of communication that challenges these previous rather conventional understandings of communication. In this article, I have termed the third concept 'communication as co-production', denoting an expressed need for the public to engage in the definition of new threats. Openness is, in this instance, not simply about transparency, oversight, or about directing behaviour. Rather, it is a matter of how to mobilize and engage a wide range of societal groups, organizations and businesses to share information, be prepared and better recover.

While these three concepts coexist they do, however, appear with some degree of historical succession, going from what the intelligence analyst Bowman Miller (2011) calls a 'need to know' to a 'need to share' culture.

Also, while this article shows that all three concepts are present in Danish, American and British intelligence practices, one must recognize a cultural diversity in the use of these concepts of communication: diversity with respect to the different organizational cultures of the intelligence services – foreign or domestic – and with respect to differences in national cultures.

In what follows I will not go into detail about the cultural differences, but rather focus on how each of the three concepts has a distinctive character: how they politically function to write, rewrite and challenge conventional understandings of the authority relation between the services and civil society.

### First concept: communication as awareness

The first concept of *communication as awareness* is, contrary to the other concepts treated below, not aimed at spurring civil action or mobilizing the public to the management of new threats. Rather, this conceptual discourse describes communication as a means to create accountability in the institutions by creating a general democratic public awareness. Openness and secrecy are the defining counter-concepts, as the concept of communication relies on the classical dilemma between the need for securing the national interest against the need for democratic debate. The concept of communication comes, in this way, to describe a solution to a classical dilemma between that of upholding the ability of the state – in the face of threats to the nation – to act authoritatively versus a general democratic need for civil society to hold the state accountable for its actions. This discourse on communication you can find almost everywhere in the Western world. Typically, we see it in executive speeches published by the services, where information sharing typically is explained as a matter of 'understanding' or 'trusting' the actions of the authorities.

A review of the Danish and British security intelligence practice on information-sharing demonstrates an approach to counter-terrorism and other security threats that rely strongly on such notions of openness, secrecy and trust. The former director of the British Secret Intelligence Service (SIS or MI6), Sir John Sawers, argues,

'Secret organisations need to stay secret, even if we present an occasional public face, as I am doing today... Without the trust of agents, the anonymity of our staff, the confidence of partners, we would not get the intelligence. The lives of everyone living here would be less safe. The United Kingdom would be more vulnerable to the unexpected, the vicious and the extreme'.[9] Similar examples can be found in the Danish and American debates. As a former naval intelligence officer and historian, Warren F. Kimball, writes in a note about the 'CIA and openness': 'But why worry about openness and declassification at all? Why take even the slightest risk in order to satisfy the curiosity of historians or journalists supposedly looking for something bizarre and sensational? Simply put, the United States of America is a democracy, and democracies cannot survive in secret...How can the American government be accountable to its public without jeopardizing the security of the nation? The answer is simple and profound – common sense'.[10] Again, the value of democracy becomes the underlying argument for communication vis-à-vis the public.

In the case of Denmark, the security intelligence agency compares itself to a 'normal' bureaucratic institution, stating that: 'Like other public authorities, the Danish Security Intelligence

Agency, must be prepared to be accountable to the public with regard to the way in which the business is exercised and, not least, the use of public funds.' This quote, like in the one on the CIA (from Kimball, above), witnesses an institution that sees openness as bound by a Weberian logic of legal procedures and democratic rules. The argument is thus formalistic and communication fits into the story of what a bureaucracy can and should do.

Yet, this understanding of 'communication as awareness' does more than just describing a respect for democracy, it also works to defend a 'need' for secrecy. Intelligence services are not entirely 'normal' bureaucracies, as the main emphasis in these debates on openness is on the limits of that openness: on the need for secrecy. The concept of secrecy plays a prominent role in this discourse on communication, as the concept works to justify why core political democratic bureau-cratic ethical principles of control must be constrained – in the name of national security. Rather than concerning itself with what information to share and whom to share it with, the material tends to document a security communication practice based on little or no sharing.

Very much in line with this kind of thinking, the public are presented with threat assessments 'in order to meet the public's large interest in the topic and, at the same time, to avoid myths and misunderstandings', as stated in an official Danish intelligence publication.[11] In the UK, we find a very similar discourse. Here, SIS explains that '(p)art of sustaining public confidence in the intelligence services is debate about the principles and value of intelligence work. And the purpose of today is to explain what we in SIS do and why we do it. Why our work is important, and why we can't work in the open. A lot is at stake'.[12] This is in line with the arguments of many intelligence scholars, who argue that the entire profession is defined by secrets. 'They live in a world of secrets while the rest of society does not', Uri Bar-Joseph (2010) argues.

The intelligence bureaucracy is thus not presented as 'just' an ordinary bureaucracy, but rather as one that understands the 'exception': one that has to operate with a constant need for judgement. As Petersen and Tjalve 2018 write in their discussion on intelligence expertise, this ethos of judgement is a 'less formalistic and more elusive dimension to bureaucratic accountability' than the Weberian rule-driven ethos. As Warren Kimball states in his post on the CIA, decisions on what to share are all about judgement or 'commonsense'.

To sum up, one can see this discourse on communication (awareness) as an attempt to strike a balance between a rule-bound logic of procedures on the one hand and the constant need for judgement on what is safe to share on the other.

## Second concept: communication as advice

Where this first concept of communication ('communication as awareness') tends to assume a subtle and historically bound relation between the agency and the public, having trust and secrecy as its main defining concepts, the second concept ('communication as advice') designates the public as an agent that can act on the requests of the agency. We thus turn from a discourse of democratic openness and awareness, to one on effectiveness and action.

One good empirical example on 'communication as advice' is the US advisory system. On the first page of the Department of Homeland Security (DHS) guide for the National Terrorism Advisory System (NTAS) it is stated that '…all Americans share responsibility for the nation's security and should always be aware of the heightened risk of terrorist attack in the United States and what they should do'.[13] Thus, dissemination of knowledge through this system is closely related to that of sharing responsibility for protection. As further explained in a report evaluating the risk commu-nication of the DHS, 'the purpose of warnings, regardless of the threat, is to provide information to citizens and groups that allow them to make informed decisions about actions to take to prevent and respond to threats'.[14]

Intelligence information is portrayed as expert knowledge clearly divorced from the *receiving* public, yet, as something that makes the public able to 'make informed decisions'. As the US risk communication report concludes, threat information should be provided through multiple methods to ensure that dissemination of the information is comprehensive and that people receive the information regardless of their level of access to information'.[15] We are here presented with a classical risk communication effort of making the public understand the data and information produced by the agency. It presents what risk communication experts have labelled a 'source-receiver' understanding of communication – an understanding of information as something that can be 'handed over'.[16] In similar terms, in his analysis of the 9/11 environment, Gregory F. Treverton (2009) argues that the whole idea of 'sharing' implies that the meaning of information is owned by the agencies and that the flow only goes in one direction – from the agency to the public. Comparable to the above-discussed concepts of awareness and secrecy, also here a clear hierarchy of knowledge is maintained.

Similar examples on the use of threat assessments can be found in the UK and Denmark. Yet, in the UK, we see a more modest appeal as attention here is directed towards certain sectors rather than the general public at large. At MI5's homepage, they explain: 'They (the threat assessments) are a tool for security practitioners working across different sectors of the Critical National Infrastructure (CNI) and the police to use in determining what protective security response may be required.'[17]

Other programmes are set-up to activate the public by asking citizens to report 'suspicious activity' (USA) or to use the 'Anti-Terrorist Hotline' (UK). Others again engage and responsibilize the public (mainly private businesses within the so-called critical infrastructure) by the use of public–private partnerships.[18]

In the language of risk communication, we see an expression of a rather realist understanding of security communication: a belief in the possibility of correcting public opinion by adjusting bureaucratic risk communication practices. We are witnessing an understanding of threats and risks as something that can be objectively mapped and properly communicated to erase possible errors in the public perceptions of risk.[19] This same sender-receiver understanding of communication is also present in the scholarly literature on warnings systems and alarm standards. The core question in this debate has been: 'how much and what type of information is needed for the public to make informed decisions?' Here, the central question is how to balance the need for providing information against the risk of creating false alarms, losing public trust in the system and creating unnecessary fear i.e., avoiding the 'crying wolf'.[20] This discourse expresses a vision of the intelligence agencies as providers of knowledge and assumes a great trust in the public's ability to handle and manage the information provided. Thus, the public is assumed to be capable of processing the information for the benefit of the nation.

Although the two concepts of communication, treated so far (communication as *awareness* and *advice*), differ, they share a sender-receiver understanding of communication – and thus an understanding of information as expert knowledge, possessed by intelligence agencies and disseminated to the public. Thus, both, in their own way, establish an expert-amateur hierarchy between the services and the public. While it might read as a 'responsibilization' of the public to direct action, I will argue that this is not the case. The management solutions are kept in a rather traditional language as expertise, establishing the agency as the managing expert. In this approach, the so-called performativity gap between a demand from the outside to find solutions to the many uncertainties and the (im)possibility of the agencies to satisfy those demands, is not recognized or present. On the contrary, in the communication discourses on awareness and advice, new and existing threats are treated as tangible and, therefore, manageable within the current setup.

Another similarity to the discourse on awareness is found in a profound concern about how to balance the need for providing information against the risk of compromising national security.[21] Threat assessments are often less about the substance of the actions needed to be undertaken than a description of a managerial process. Like in the previous discourse on communication as awareness, the 'practice of secrecy' is highlighted as fundamental to the intelligence practice. As the psychologists Vermeir and Margócsy write in their study on the practice of secrecy: 'they want to keep the secret, but they also want to indicate that they have a secret, to veil and unveil at the same time.'[22] This psychodynamics of secrecy, they argue, creates an aura of superiority, as the social structure of secrecy works effectively to establish a hierarchy between those who have and those who do not have access to information.[23] In similar terms, private sector partnerships and other structures of information-sharing, institutionalized by intelligence agencies, are controlled channels of information.

In Jack Bratish's historical review of the concept of 'secrecy', he shows how the concept traditionally has been regarded as a counter-concept to 'the public', and in this way was used to establish a hierarchy between the intelligence services and its outside.[24] Secrecy works to manifest what has been termed, 'democratic elitism': a vision of public participation that rests on a notion of citizenry which is distinct from the intelligence experts, who are generally better-equipped make judgements in the common interest.[25] Yet, as this discourse on communication as advice shows, this vision of participation is under increasing pressure today, and the traditional hierarchy of knowledge increasingly challenged. While this discourse on advice does open up the possibility for public participation in the management of new threats, it, however, also struggles to cope with rather settled structures of authority and secrecy.

While these understandings of communication are strong, they have, I will argue, become under increasing pressure in another and more recent discourse on public responsibility and participation in the definition of new threats.

### Third concept: communication as co-production

Following from the discourse on advice, we can observe a third concept of communication becoming forceful in intelligence work: namely a concept that stresses civic participation. While the concept of communication as advice enforced a clear separation between sender and receiver, this third concept of communication (as co-production) goes beyond such an understanding of communication and challenges the boundary of the institution. In a broader historical perspective, one could argue that this turn to 'communication as co-production' reflects a shift from government to governance, from a centralized to a decentralized understanding of security expertise. In other words, it recognizes the importance of the security management being made outside the jurisdiction of nation-state bureaucracies, in a fragmented public and private sphere. The emphasis is on social networks, professional networks, economic and even criminal networks,[26] tightly or loosely organized in communities of knowledge.

A good example of such communication policy is found in the management of cyber security where we very often see a call for private companies to chip-in and help define possible threats. In an opinion piece written for the *Sunday Times*, the Director of GCHQ, Jeremy Fleming, calls for a much closer collaboration between the intelligence services and the private sector. Under the heading 'New technologies are opening the door to cyber-rogues; you can help shut it', he argues that intelligence services should be included in the corporate development of new technologies in order to 'ensure that we protect our right to privacy and maximize the tremendous upsides inherent in the digital revolution.'[27] Hence, communication is not so much about giving advice and setting direction, as it is about learning: about the inclusion of new 'private' knowledge from the civil and private sector – and encouraging self-governance within the sector. The MI5 and GCHQ-led Cyber Security Information Sharing Partnership (CISP) and the American FBI-led 'InfraGuard' are examples of an institutionalization of this kind of thinking and collaboration with the private sector on critical infrastructure protection.[28]

A different example of such 'communication as co-production' is found in the descriptions of well-known US Suspicious Activity Reporting (SAR), undertaken by FEMA. 'Preventing terrorism is a responsibility of every American, and requires an alert and informed citizenry that is ready to report suspicious activity that may be indicative of a terrorist act or terrorism planning', it is argued.[29] In similar terms, the public are, at the front page of FBIs homepage, asked to 'Submit a Tip' on threats and crimes, using the 'if you see something, say something' campaign slogan as the catch phrase to enrol the public in the national security effort.[30] In the UK, MI5 calls for the public to report 'Suspected threats to National Security'[31] and in Denmark, the current effort against cyber attacks express a similar need for private reporting on national security.[32] Common to all these efforts is their open invitation to the public to anticipate new threats.

Risk scholars have for years done research on the different institutional frameworks to better facilitate understanding, representation and dialogue.[33] Where the previous two forms of communication (awareness and advice) envision a rather traditional sender-receiver structure, these new institutional forms in security politics can be characterized as constructivist, as this form of communication opens up for participation in the interpretation of present and future risks to society. In the current institutional setup of partnerships and reporting systems, security communication is considered a necessary tool for morally engaging and activating private companies and citizens; aiming not only to collect information but also to educate the public to self-governance.

This question of how society participates and becomes a co-creator of risk and security knowledge defines our understanding of where the boundary of the institution itself goes and thus the understanding of what security management actually is.[34] As mentioned in the introduction, communication is to a large extent about managing uncertainty; about meeting the social and political expectation of what should be delivered (e.g., security in cyber space). Visibility is an important way to show the public how the institution works to meet these demands. Yet, this discourse on co-production is doing more than just meeting a public demand for efficiency and solutions. By institutionalizing 'communication as co-production' (fusion cells, partnerships, reporting systems), modern intelligence services also come to recognize their limited institutional capacity and ability to meet those demands in a world of uncertainty (e.g., cyber and terrorism etc.). It is a practice that in many ways diffuses responsibility by including a wide range of actors in the intelligence work – making everybody, and then nobody, responsible in the case of a major event.

In other words, intelligence agencies find themselves in what sociologists have termed a late modern risk society: in a world where full control is considered impossible. While the answer logically is to open up to society's own identification and management of new threats, this development challenges the institutional setup based on expertise. Rather than communicating 'actual risks' (as with the concept of 'communication as advice'), policy improvement comes to lie in the institutional framework for participation.

Many scholars have pointed to how the understanding of secrecy has changed and is challenged by this new framework of communication. One can even repeat William E. Colby's words from 1976, saying that: 'If "national security" is discredited as a catch-all justification for total secrecy, a new theory of legitimate secrecy must replace it.'[35] Yet, where Colby, like many scholars, points to legal arrangements for the protection of personal information and freedoms, the situation today is fundamentally different.[36] In this discourse on communication as co-production, secrecy can no longer be considered something for only the agencies to manage. Rather, citizens and private companies are constituted as managers of secrecy.

This concept of communication thus admits to the fact that further improvement of national security lies in the participation of the public, and therefore that citizens and companies might become the new experts. In effect the 'public' is no longer constituted as the 'counter-concept' to secrecy, and in effect as that which will oppose or counter the world of secrets.[37] The public has itself become a management body of those secrets.

The fundamental idea that intelligence expertise resides within a small elite, who can act on behalf of the public interest, is thereby questioned, as the realist vision of communication (that facts can be communicated and acted upon) is dismissed. The intelligence expert and the elitist vision behind the western national security setup are questioned, as it accepts a post-modern vision of knowledge as co-created and not exact.

This development creates new political and democratic concerns about authority in security politics: who should be provided a seat at the table and engaged in decisions on national security? Who should decide what counts as national security knowledge? And on what criteria and who should decide whom to engage? In short, how is and can co-production be managed and democratically defended?

## Cultures of control: from a hierarchical to egalitarian security organizations?

The above discussion of current trends in security communication involves a description of a development from a hierarchical vision of knowledge to an egalitarian one. The first two approaches to communication highlighted what could be termed a consensus-based security order, as they assume a large degree of consent and homogeneity among societal groups with respect to national security priorities. Such consent made it rather easy for the institution to remain in a hierarchical position and assume authority in relation to the public to which the communications were directed. This is contrary to the kind of egalitarianism expressed in the concept of communication as co-production, which stresses the need for broader public participation in the selection and definition of risks. This understanding of communication relies strongly on the self-governance of the many.

With the development towards co-production, it is often difficult to uphold direction and ideas of common interest, as egalitarian principles and not hierarchy become the main culture of selecting risks. As anthropologist Mary Douglas shows in her writings on cultures of risk, one way of creating unity and identity within such egalitarian cultures of self-governance is to call for a common enemy: to create a vision of that threatening Other which everyone can unite against.[38] In such a security culture, unity is based on necessities and truisms, rather than on clear structures of authority between state and civil society – the structure upon which we used to base our democratic institutions. Co-production will thus come with some rather worrying democratic consequences.

How can these consequences be managed? While it is still too early to evaluate the scale of the consequences, scholars working on risk communication have long been concerned about this development in communication strategies of organizations and have discussed different managerial 'coping' strategies. In their work on risk communication, Jasanoff (1998) and Ferree et al (2002) observe how different approaches to communication are supported by different political systems. The first approach is termed a realist approach and stresses the ability of the few to know what is best for society. This approach is normally linked to the traditional bureaucratic state with trust in science and exact truths. The second, constructivist, approach emphasizes the quality of weighting all valuable arguments in the selection of risk and is supported by a political system resting on public participation. A last one, termed 'discursive', sees communication as a means to encourage public debate and possibly resistance. In other words, it is an approach to communication which is supported by political institutions that foster pluralism and political debate about the selection of risk.[39]

The communication strategies described above witness a current development away from a realist understanding of communication as a matter of communicating real truths towards a constructivist one based on broader participation and coproduction in the definition of new risks. In the literature on risk communication such constructivist modes of thinking, however, are often supported by institutions that rest on equal representation.

Applying this to the world of intelligence, this would mean that communication as co-production, in order to be democratically sound, should be based on an institutional framework, which ensures equal representation. Instead of merely 'privatizing' responsibility in the hands of private citizens and businesses, it is possible to see intelligence services as facilitators of a network of information; something that is sometimes recognized in the setup of PPPs.

In a liberal-democratic society, a complete decentralization of knowledge production (and thus responsibility) would be detrimental to the system. The metaphor 'supervision state'[40] works well here to describe this dilemma: the need for the intelligence community to give citizens the opportunity to act on the one hand and the need to remain strong enough to define where the line should be drawn between essential and non-essential information, to select the threats important to national security, on the other.

If representation is taken into consideration, it becomes possible to imagine a security culture based on a pluralistic ideal that works in a highly institutionalized bureaucratic setting i.e., a bureaucratic organization that supports dialogue, inclusion and active participation, and therefore accepts 'negotiation' as a baseline for any authoritative selection of security risk.

## Conclusion

Public communication is much more than a new tool of management; it is a cognitive framework for conceptualizing a new vision of the relation between the intelligence organization and its surroundings.

This article has identified three concepts of communication in the intelligence debate. One stresses the need for public awareness and another engages in the business of giving advice. Both of these concepts stress the possibility of adjusting bureaucratic risk communication strategies to manage public action and erase possible errors in the perceptions of risk. The third concept of communication, the article showed, rests on a much more constructivist understanding of communication, an understanding of risks as mediated and co-produced in society. In this vision, policy improvement mainly lies in the institutional framework for participation and thereby in the representation of interests.

One could argue that intelligence studies has come a long way in reviving the classical realist debate about openness, transparency and national interest.[41] Yet, the classical focus on national interest still seems to be a black box that hides away the critical questions of who actually, in a policy based on *co-production*, responsibilization and mobilization of the public, comes to represent the public? The question of representation is today more important than ever for understanding security politics.

Institutionalization and representation are, however, not doing away with authority and power. On the contrary, power relations might just become more subtle. We, therefore, need to introduce a fourth concept of communication into intelligence work: one that addresses the power-knowledge relation implied in the communication of expert knowledge. In this model, policy improvement must lie in the possibility of resistance and criticism. A model of communication should be supported by political institutions that foster pluralism and political debate about risk.

In conclusion, we need to understand the full implications of this constructivist turn in intelligence communication. We need to understand the full content of these constructions of communication and their relation to the institutional modes of control, and make sure that they become a substitute for openness and oversight via public debate.

## Notes

1. Scott and Jackson, "The Study of Intelligence in Theory and Practice," 139.
2. Betts, *Enemies of Intelligence*; and Treverton, *Intelligence for an Age of Terror*.
3. Weiss, "Communicating Uncertainty in Intelligence"; Kent, "Words of Estimative Probability".
4. The similarities to other social science debates on what constitutes expertise and knowledge (c.f Jasanoff *Science at the Bar*) are striking, yet, the democratic challenges are different, as intelligence communication takes place in a sphere of secrecy (appealing to a national interest) and thus excludes any kind of public scrutiny.
5. Power et al, "Reputational Risk."
6. Skinner, "Meaning and Understanding," 50. Or as the German conceptual historian, Reinhart Koselleck, argued: 'The concept is bound to a word, but is at the same time more than a word: a word becomes a concept when the plenitude of a politico-social context of meaning and experience in and for which a word is used can be condensed into one word' (Koselleck, *Futures Past*, 84). Thus, as concepts are 'concentrates of meaning', they are more than words (Ibid. 84); concepts embody the meanings of the political and social experience.
7. See note 2 above.

8. E.g. Freedman, "The Politics of Warning"; and Altheide, *Terrorism and the Politics of Fear*.
9. Guardian, "Sir John Sawers's Speech."
10. Kimball, "Openness and the CIA."
11. Danish Security and Intelligence Service, "Om Trusselsvurdering."
12. The Guardian, "Sir John Sawers's Speech." For a similar understanding of communication, see also the remarks made by the chair of the Intelligence and Security Committee, Rifkind, in the Guardian 2013 "We are making intelligence accountable."
13. Department of Homeland Security, "NTSA Guide."
14. Government Accountability Office, "Communication Protocols," 15.
15. Ibid., 16.
16. Kasperson et al., "The Social Amplification of Risk."
17. MI5, "Threat Levels."
18. Christensen and Petersen, "Public-Private Partnerships on Cyber Security."
19. Jasanoff, "The Political Science of Risk perception"; and Fischoff "Risk Perception and Communication Unplugged."
20. Shapiro and Cohen, "Color Bind"; and Fischhoff et al., *Risk Communication*.
21. Morgan et al, *Risk Communication*.
22. Vermeir and Margócsy, "States of Secrecy."
23. Blank, "Two Schools of Secrecy."
24. Bratish, "Public Secrecy and Immanent Security."
25. Bachrach, *The Theory of Democratic Elitism*.
26. Sørensen and Torfing, "Network Governance"; and Rhodes, "The New Governance."
27. Fleming, "New Technologies are Opening the Door to Cyber-Rogues."
28. Within the framework of the DHS, a wide and highly complex net of partnerships, coordinating councils, cross-sector councils and working groups have been set-up to provide this basis for outreach and collaboration. Similarly the FBI has set-up a huge net of partnerships most of which aim to advise private companies on security within and outside the USA. It is almost impossible to count the current number of arrangements, but a conservative estimate would be around 100 private-public partnerships within the DHS and the FBI alone.
29. FEMA, "Improving the Public's Awareness."
30. As argued by Petersen and Tjalve, the meanings of 'suspicious', or the 'something', is referred to as just out of the ordinary, and is, therefore, a call for a co-creation of the mere meaning of threat. Petersen and Tjalve, "(Neo)Republican Security Governance."
31. MI5, "Suspected Threats to National Security".
32. Despite many discursive similarities and transatlantic collaboration on these matters, the UK and Danish governments seem to have a stronger emphasis on government responsibilities and legal regulation, installing a more realist notion of communication as awareness. See e.g., The Guardian report on war games, The Guardian, "US and UK Plan Cyber 'War Games' to Test Resilience."
33. Palenchar and Heath, "Strategic Risk Communication"; Plough and Krimsky, "The Emergence of Risk Communication Studies."
34. Petersen and Tjalve, "(Neo)Republican Security Governance."
35. Colby, "Intelligence Secrecy and Security in a Free Society," 4.
36. In a similar fashion a report from the European Parliament on national security and secrecy points to the lack of 'independent and effective juridical accountability'. The report thereby stays within a traditional discourse on how to balance the concern for the legal protection of individual freedom versus that of national security. European Parliament, *National Security and Secret Evidence*.
37. See note 24 above.
38. Religiously based political systems or sectarian communities are however good examples of such security cultures (e.g., ISIS); societies where God is the object of either fear or hope. In such security culture, destiny rather that control of the future is the ruling vision, in the last instance leaving communication as means of control rather unnecessary. Douglas and Wildavsky, *Risk and Culture*; Douglas, "Risk as a forensic resource."
39. Jasanoff, "The Political Science of Risk Perception"; and Ferree et al., "For Models of the Public Sphere in Modern Democracies."
40. Andersen, "Supervisionsstaten og den politiske virksomhed."
41. Good "The National Interest."

## Disclosure statement

No potential conflict of interest was reported by the author.

# Bibliography

Altheide, D. L. *Terrorism and the Politics of Fear*. New York: Rowman & Littlefield Publishers, 2006.

Andersen, N. Å. "Supervisionsstaten Og Den Politiske Virksomhed [The Supervision State and the Political Reality]." In *Den politiske virksomhed* [The Political Company], edited by C. Frankel, 231–260. Copenhagen: Samfundslitteratur, 2004.

Bachrach, P. *The Theory of Democratic Elitism: A Critique*. Boston: Little Brown, 1967.

Bar-Joseph, U. "The Professional Ethics of Intelligence Analysis." *International Journal of Intelligence and Counterintelligence* 24, no. 1 (2010): 22–43. doi:10.1080/08850607.2011.519222.

Betts, R. *Enemies of Intelligence: Knowledge and Power in American National Security*. New York: Columbia University Press, 2007.

Blank, L. "Two Schools for Secrecy." In *Government Secrecy: Classic and Contemporary Readings*, edited by J. Goldman and S. Maret, 59–68. Westport: Libraries Unlimited, 2009.

Bratich, J. "Public Secrecy and Immanent Security: A Strategic Analysis." *Cultural Studies* 20 (2006): 493–511. doi:10.1080/09502380600708937.

Christensen, K. K., and K. L. Petersen. "Public-Private Partnerships on Cyber Security: A Question of Loyalty." *International Affairs* 93, no. 6 (2017): 1435–1452. doi:10.1093/ia/iix189.

Colby, W. E. "Intelligence Secrecy and Security in a Free Society." *International Security* 1, no. 2 (1976): 3–14. doi:10.2307/2538496.

Danish Security and Intelligence Service. "Om Trusselsvurdering [On the Threat Assessment]." 2011. Accessed 19 April 2016. https://www.pet.dk/default.aspx.

Department of Homeland Security. *NTSA Guide. National Terrorism Advisory System Public Guide*, April 2011. Accessed October 2018. http://www.dhs.gov/xlibrary/assets/ntas/ntas-public-guide.pdf

Douglas, M. "Risk as a Forensic Resource." *Daedalus* 119, no. 4 (1990): 1–16.

Douglas, M., and A. Wildavsky. *Risk and Culture: An Essay on the Selection of Technical and Environmental Dangers*. Berkeley: University of California Press, 1982.

European Parliament. *National Security and Secret Evidence in Legislation and before the Courts: Exploring the Challenges*. EU: Directorate-General for Internal Policies, 2014.

Ewald, F. "The Return of Descartes' Malicious Demon: An Outline of a Philosophy of Precaution." In *Embracing Risk*, edited by T. Baker and J. Simon, 273–301. Chicago, IL: University of Chicago Press, 2002.

FEMA. "Improving the Public's Awareness and Reporting of Suspicious Activity: Key Research Findings from Literature Review, Household Survey, Focus Groups and Interviews." 2012. Accessed October 2018. http://www.fema.gov/media-library/assets/documents/24355.

Ferree, M. M., W. A. Gamson, J. Gerhards, and D. Rucht. "Four Models of the Public Sphere in Modern Democracies." *Theory and Society* 31 (2002): 289–324. doi:10.1023/A:1016284431021.

Fischhoff, B. "Risk Perception and Communication Unplugged: Twenty Years of Process." *Risk Analysis* 15, no. 2 (1995): 137–145.

Fischhoff, B., P. Slovic, S. Lichtenstein, S. Read, and B. Coms. "How Safe Is Safe Enough? A Psychometric Study of Attitudes." *Policy Science* 9 (1978): 127–152. doi:10.1007/BF00143739.

Fleming, J., "GCHQ Director: New Technologies are Opening the Door to Cyber-Rogues; You Can Help Shut It." *Sunday Times*, August 2018.

Freedman, L. "The Politics of Warning: Terrorism and Risk Communication." *Intelligence and National Security* 20 (2005): 379–418. doi:10.1080/02684520500281502.

Good, R. C. "The National Interest and Political Realism: Niebuhr's "Debate" with Morgenthau and Kennan." *Journal of Politics* 22 (1960): 597–619. doi:10.2307/2126924.

Government Accountability Office. "Communication Protocols and Risk Communication Principles Can Assist in Refining the Advisory System." *Report for the Department of Homeland Security*. Washington DC: GAO, June 2004.

The Guardian. "Sir John Sawers's Speech – Full Text." *The Guardian*, October 28, 2010. http://www.theguardian.com/uk/2010/oct/28/sir-john-sawers-speech-full-text

The Guardian. "US and UK Plan Cyber 'War Games' to Test Resilience." *The Guardian*, January 16, 2015. https://www.theguardian.com/technology/2015/jan/16/cyber-war-games-uk-us-intelligence

Homeland Security Council. "National Strategy for Homeland Security 2007." 2007. Accessed October 2018. http://www.dhs.gov/xlibrary/assets/nat_strat_homelandsecurity_2007.pdf

Jasanoff, S. *Science at the Bar. Law, Science and Technology in America*. Harvard: Harvard University Press, 1995.

Jasanoff, S. "The Political Science of Risk Perception." *Reliability Engineering and System Safety* 59 (1998): 91–99. doi:10.1016/S0951-8320(97)00129-4.

Kasperson, R. E., O. Renn, H. S. Paul Slowic, J. E. Brown, J. X. K. Robert Goble, and S. Ratick. "The Social Amplification of Risk: A Conceptual Framework." *Social Analysis* 8, no. 2 (1988): 177–187.

Kent, S. "Words of Estimative Probability." *Studies in Intelligence* (1964). https://www.cia.gov/csi/books/shermankent/6words.html

Kimball, W. F. "Openness and the CIA." Center for the Study of Intelligence, CIA (2007). https://www.cia.gov/library/center-for-the-study-of-intelligence/kent-csi/vol44no5/html/v44i5a08p.htm

Koselleck, R. *Futures Past*. Massachusetts: MIT Press, 1985.

Lund, P. K., and V. S. Tjalve. "(Neo)Republican Security Governance? US Homeland Security and the Politics of 'Shared Responsibility'." *International Political Sociology* 7, no. 1 (2013): 1–18. doi:10.1111/ips.12006.

MI5 Homepage. "Threat Levels." Accessed October 2018. https://www.mi5.gov.uk/threat-levels

MI5 Homepage. "Suspected Threats to National Security." Accessed October 2018. https://www.mi5.gov.uk/contact-us

Miller, B. H. "The Death of Secrecy: Need to Know…With Whom to Share." *Studies in Intelligence* 55, no. 3 (2011): 1–6.

Morgan, M. G., B. Fischhoff, A. Bostrom, and J. A. Cynthia. *Risk Communication: A Mental Models Approach*. Cambridge: Cambridge University Press, 2002.

Palenchar Michael, J., and R. Heath. "Strategic Risk Communication: Adding Value to Society." *Public Relations Review* 33, no. 2 (2007): 120–129. doi:10.1016/j.pubrev.2006.11.014.

Petersen, K. L., and V. Schou Tjalve. "Intelligence Expertise in the Age of Information Sharing: Public-Private "Collection" and Its Challenges to Democratic Control and Accountability." *Intelligence and National Security* 33, no. 1 (2018): 21–35. doi:10.1080/02684527.2017.1316956.

Plough, A., and S. Krimsky. "The Emergence of Risk Communication Studies: Social and Political Context. Science." *Technology & Human Values* 12, no. 3/4 (1987): 4–10.

Power, M., T. Scheytt, K. Soin, and K. Sahlin. "Reputational Risk as a Logic of Organizing in Late Modernity." *Organization Studies* 30, no. 2–3 (2009): 301–324. doi:10.1177/0170840608101482.

Rhodes, R. A. W. "The New Governance: Governing without Government." *Political Studies* 44 (1996): 652–667. doi:10.1111/j.1467-9248.1996.tb01747.x.

Rifkind, M. "We are Making Intelligence Accountable." *The Guardian*, March 3, 2013. https://www.theguardian.com/commentisfree/2013/mar/03/justice-and-security-bill-intelligence-agencies

Scott, L., and P. Jackson. "The Study of Intelligence in Theory and Practice." *Intelligence and National Security* 19, no. 2 (2004): 139–169. doi:10.1080/0268452042000302930.

Shapiro, J. N., and D. K. Cohen. "Color Bind: Lessons from the Failed Homeland Security Advisory System." *International Security* 32, no. 2 (2007): 121–128. doi:10.1162/isec.2007.32.2.121.

Skinner, Q. "Meaning and Understanding in the History of Ideas." *History and Theory* 9, no. 1 (1969): 3–53. doi:10.2307/2504188.

Slovic, P. "Baruch Fischhoff and Sara Lichtenstein. 'Facts and Fears: Societal Perception of Risk'." *Advances in Consumer Research* 8, no. 1 (1981): 497–502.

Sørensen, E., and J. Torfing. "Network Governance and Post-Liberal Democracy." *Administrative Theory & Praxis* 27, no. 2 (2005): 197–237. doi:10.1080/10841806.2005.11029489.

Treverton, G. *Intelligence for an Age of Terror*. Cambridge: Cambridge University Press, 2009.

Vermeir, K., and D. Margoscy. "States of Secrecy: An Introduction." *British Society for the History of Science* 45, no. 2 (2012): 153–164. doi:10.1017/S0007087412000052.

Weiss, C. "Communicating Uncertainty in Intelligence and Other Professions." *International Journal of Intelligence and CounterIntelligence* 21 (2007): 57–85. doi:10.1080/08850600701649312.

# From madness to wisdom: intelligence and the digital crowd

Mark Daniel Jaeger and Myriam Dunn Cavelty

**ABSTRACT**
This article sheds light on the complexity and sensitivity of crowd-based intelligence in security governance. The 'crowd' as special manifestation of 'the public' is both challenging and enabling new forms of intelligence practices. As a spontaneous eruption of collective activity, the crowd is a notion of great versatility. Sometimes considered mad/dangerous, sometimes wise/useful, the crowd's drivers are a context-dependent collage of (affective) group engagement, projection from the outside and the workings of digital technologies. The article traces how the existence of crowds in its variations is connected to how they are approached by security agents and their intelligence practices.

## I. Introduction

In 2004, James Surowiecki published a popular book entitled 'The Wisdom of the Crowd: Why the Many are Smarter than the Few',[1] in which he shows how groups are better at making certain types of decisions or predictions than individuals, even if they are experts. The title of his book is an allusion to a 19th century study on crowd psychology by Charles Mackay called 'Extraordinary Popular Delusions and the Madness of Crowds',[2] in which the author eloquently exposes the pitfalls of herd mentality, group mania, and religious mass folly. Two very different accounts: how can they be explained?

This special issue addresses the role of civil society in the practices of intelligence. Our contribution aims to understand the notion of the 'crowd' as a special manifestation of 'the public' and its role in both challenging and enabling new forms of intelligence practices. In contemporary security practices, the crowd is sometimes considered mad and dangerous and sometimes considered wise and even necessary to solve certain contemporary security problems, like in the two publications mentioned above. We explain the assumptions behind these two conceptions and shed light on their consequences in terms of two opposing roles of crowds for intelligence practices: Sometimes, the crowd is an *object* of intelligence, but sometimes it is also a *vehicle* to intelligence.

We depart from the existing literature in two ways. First, a distinction between two meanings of intelligence can be made, a narrow and a broad one.[3] The narrow one is focused on organizations or individuals 'whose task it is to gather, analyse and convey information' (p.2) for foreign and security policy purposes. The second, broader meaning of intelligence looks to the more general ability of any social entity to make sense of its environment, in order to act in informed ways. Most contributions in intelligence studies follow the first definition, with a focus limited to intelligence agencies and the professionals in these organizations that have relatively stable tasks and roles in the foreign policy of states. We purport here that by adopting a more flexible meaning of intelligence towards the second understanding, and taking it beyond the organizations that are immediately tasked to do intelligence as part of the state apparatus, we can understand changing concepts and practices of intelligence better.

Second, we claim that intelligence collection practices and the formation and dissolution of crowds are interlinked through technology. The literature tends to take intelligence agencies as stable entities with predefined tasks and looks at their particular activities in given national contexts, even if new types of intelligence collection are considered.[4] Here, we first consider the larger scientific and technological trends behind the move from crowds as 'mad' to crowds as 'wise', to highlight how the technological possibilities of collecting, storing, analysing and distributing information made new forms, new conceptions and, ultimately, new engagements of the crowd possible. The proliferation of ICT and, especially, social media, led to the rise of new crowd phenomena and the advancements in algorithmic data analysis provide the means to exploit a new comprehensive source of information for intelligence purposes.

Based on this, we suggest a typology of crowd-based intelligence practices in the digital age. We point out that the crowd is now a regular element in intelligence practices, echoing larger structural changes in intelligence and security governance that broadened the scope to non-traditional adversaries and blur the distinction between foreign and domestic, state and non-state. Departing from simply representing an object or a target of intelligence, the crowd has not only become a valuable source of information in intelligence, but is sometimes actively contributing as an intelligence agent to security governance.

We find that crowd-based intelligence practices are never neutral or value-free. Rather, the crowd is co-created by intelligence activities. These activities establish and modulate relations between on the one hand the public as well as the crowd as source and of intelligence and on the other hand the agencies themselves. Crowd-based intelligence practices have a political dimension that does not only blur the distinction between 'crowd' and 'citizen' or vehicle and object, but also deeply implicates the technologies and their owners in the process, raising important questions about transparency, proportionality and accountability. This more dialectical conception of surveyor and surveilled will help scholars and practitioners of intelligence understand how their practices might influence crowd behaviour in potentially unexpected, even undesirable ways; and more importantly, how the interaction between civil society and intelligence is affected and shaped by these practices.

This article has three parts: In the first section, we trace the changes in notions of the crowd, from when the crowd was mostly conceived as a danger to the existing social order, to this day, when it has become a collaborator in dealing with crises in certain contexts. We pay special attention to the technological changes involved in the evolution of crowd-based intelligence practices. In the second part, we discuss three modes of crowd-based intelligence practice. In particular, we will show in what way the emergence of crowds as a social entity with particular attributes ascribed to it depends on how it is referred to and addressed in specific, often value-laden ways in political discourse and what the consequences of this are for the intersection between intelligence and civil society.

## II. Changing notions of the crowd

One of the perhaps best-known concepts in the study and practice of intelligence is the 'intelligence cycle'. Though the number of the steps in this cycle differ,[5] the portrayals of the cycle have in common a phase in which intelligence is *collected*, a second in which this collected material is turned into *analysis*, and a third during which these produces are *disseminated* (or communicated) to different consumers of intelligence. 'The crowd' as social phenomenon can play a significant role in all three phases of the intelligence cycle: The crowd can be a specific source to *collect* information from, it can be used to provide *analysis* (and solutions), and it can become a direct *addressee* in security communication. This signifies that it can be *passive* as a mere source for intelligence or it can become an *active* part of security governance. Importantly, whether the crowd is used as purely passive information provider or is given a more active role in finding solutions often depends on how the crowd is conceptualized: as 'mad' or 'wise'.

In order to understand the different nuances of characterizing the crowd and how it related to intelligence practices, we trace the development of three different conceptions of the crowd in a first part. Alterations in perspectives on and understandings of the crowd in academic research closely align to cultural and socio-economic changes in society more generally.[6] Even back in the 19th century, the particular way of gathering exhibited in crowd form was seen to be tied to a 'particular moment in history, to a set of technologies and environmental changes and to hypothesized features of human behaviour'.[7] In a second step, we therefore illustrate how recently evolving notions of the crowd are connected to developments in digital technologies. Embedded in broader socioeconomic changes, these technological developments reinforce important aspects of crowd alterations and are complicit in making possible new conceptions of the crowd.

### Three crowd variations

Ever since it was first discovered in the 19th century as spontaneous eruption of collective social activity has the crowd been of interest to security governance, but also to academia. Though highly diverse in its focus on conclusions, the literature shares an interest in describing the attributes driving this social phenomenon throughout the decades. A distinctive factor used to understand crowd manifestations has been the role ascribed to (individual and collective) *emotion*, in opposition to a more 'rational' inclination. On the extreme end of the spectrum, the crowd is seen as mad and dangerous. Prominently for this view, Le Bon[8] depicted the crowd as a (racially) deranged, irrational, affect-ridden riff raff in France in the late 19th century. Others established a distinction between 'the crowd' as affective (temporal) phenomenon which sparks uncertainty in its dynamic, and 'the public', the rational citizen that acts prudently and comprehensively and represents a calculating and calculable political actor that can be managed from a security governance perspective.[9] The characterization of the crowd as explosive, emotional, and unfathomable mass existing in opposition to its rational counterpart easily leads to its perception as a threat to social order and security.

As part of the behavioural turn in social sciences, sociologists and social psychologists developed an alternative notion of the crowd from about the 1960s. Neil Smelser carefully dissected collective crowd behaviour as belief-guided mobilization that seeks to engage with, and change, prevailing values and norms.[10] Scholars like Ralph Turner, Charles Tilly, Henry Tajfel, Stephen Reicher and Clark McPhail demonstrated that crowd behaviour was not irrational but rational in its choices.[11] At this time, citizens turned activists, became immersed in crowds pursuing civil rights, protesting against environmental destruction and nuclear re-armament. Such crowd behaviour was considered logical and rule-guided, even allowing game-theoretical models to be applied to the phenomena.[12] Being rational in its actions yet still emotionally driven in its formation, the crowd thus changes from being seen as an unequivocal threat to society to being a rather neutral object of security governance. It becomes an expression of society that might need to be controlled in certain circumstances (when it crosses thresholds of violence, for example) but not 'neutralized',[13] since it is a legitimate political expression of discontent.

The third and latest iteration of social scientific research into crowds casts them in a positive light – in fact, it even describes them as superior to other forms of social collectives. This favourable conception builds upon complex systems research, a result from various new theoretical, epistemological, and mathematical developments, supported by advances in computing for ever more complex calculations to better understand the developing technological society.[14] A focus on systems – a set of mutually dependent components or variables that stand in interrelation with every other component in the set and in interaction with the system environment[15] – opened up a new conception of the crowd. The irrationality sometimes attributed to it was no longer seen as the result of emotions, but rather as an expected behaviour of a complex system, which behave contra-intuitive due to parallel occurrences happening at different speeds, irregularities, and non-linear cause/effect relationships.[16] From here, it was not far to 'the wisdom of crowds' and to other popular conceptions such as collective intelligence or swarm intelligence.

These latter concepts give rise to a belief in the superiority of crowd performance, one that suggests crowds may actually contribute to intelligence and security governance in hitherto unimagined ways. Collectively, crowds may possess information that cannot be gained from individual members. The 'wise' crowd thus can outperform conventional methods of analysis and provide insight where more linear approaches fail. In turn, developments in ICT that carry and represent such crowd-based information provide means for effectively accessing such information that did not exist previously.

## Specificities of the digital crowd

Societal and technological changes are closely intertwined, occurring in an interdependent relationship.[17] This means that the developments giving rise to crowd wisdom cannot be fully grasped without understanding how its formation, organization, but also its analysis is inter-twined with technology.[18] For reasons of simplicity, we will call these technologies 'information and communication technologies' (ICT) and the type of crowd they are intertwined with 'digital crowd'.

The advent of ICT, especially mobile devices and the ability to exchange information through social media, adds a new aspect to mobilization and therefore crowd formation – and also to the possibilities and limits of intelligence. There are mainly two factors: the temporal and the spatial implications of adding ICT as means of communication. As Stephanie Alice Baker observed,[19] ICT as a 'social phenomenon reorganizes and extends temporal and spatial boundaries' of the crowd, which can now 'simultaneously occupy both geographic and virtual public arenas'. ICT support the emergence of such crowds gone virtual/digital across a wide range of different contexts. At the same time, well-known traits traditionally associated with crowds apply in these settings, as emotions are often amplified in social media contexts, potentially increasing the likelihood of an eruption of social discontent.

The digital crowd rises from specific material-discursive arrangements[20] that help the phenom-ena to transcend time and space. Instead of appearing only in local hotspots, ICT enable crowds to transcend traditional geographical limits. Technology supports the quick formation of loose social ties across a geographically dispersed population. One example in the West are the crowd action patterns by Occupy Wall Street, which realized an activism that was transnational in its idea yet local in its physical manifestation.[21] Largely organized through social media, it represented a quickly growing globalized crowd with no hierarchy, its volatility supported by an open, loosely defined agenda that made it easy to connect with. On a geographically more limited scale but still transcending the hyper-localism of traditional crowds, Arab Spring crowd action united geogra-phically and socio-economically dispersed groups in a dialectic between online and offline action.[22] Social media and ICT more generally greatly facilitated information sharing and mobilization[23] supported the recognition that grievances were shared across and beyond local contexts and thus enabled collective action.[24]

Another important aspect in many of these crowd instantiations is their globalizing of resources. Through the proliferation of ICT, crowd networks do not only quickly expand beyond local contexts, but, through their geographical transcendence, may also globalize the influx of resources. Uprisings may profit from logistical, material or informational support from dislocated 'outsiders' whether Diaspora members or activists supporting the cause.[25] In social protest and uprisings, networks extend beyond local confines and even beyond national boundaries.[26] Indeed, by helping to bridge the gap between local and global, ICT help the constitution of movements and at the same time seem to provide a horizontal connective 'carrier' function for local empowerment when traditional traits of civil society are absent.[27]

In addition to breaking with geographical confines, ICT also support the redefinition of the temporal dimension of crowd existence. Instead of a spontaneous eruption that exists entirely in the moment and dissolves again quickly, some contemporary crowds become much more enduring and stable. Behind the daily fluctuations of protest crowds in the Arab Spring, the digital crowd had a stable existence that lasted for many weeks. Occupy Wall Street, meandering in its existence between movement (with a more stable agenda and structure) and crowd, lasted for years. This is not to say that it was the same individual members that kept with the crowd for that prolonged period, rather, it lived on through its heterogeneity and thematic openness, which endured any fluctuation in membership.[28] However, even if dispersed geographies and stretched temporalities are special characteristics of digital crowds, they are not necessary traits of contemporary crowds. Spontaneous upheavals, crowds existing for just a couple of hours or days, may also thrive on the availability and the technical possibilities provided by ICT.

From the viewpoint of security practitioners, the digital crowd comes with new uncertainties but also new opportunities. Quite clearly, there are different types of crowds – while all of them are formed through spontaneous collective action with a specific goal, these goals differ widely. This raises several questions: If time and place are transcended, where and when do crowds even exist? How can they be found and observed? These individual questions point to a larger, overarching issue of what actually constitutes a crowd, but also how security agents and intelligence practices contribute to it. This focuses our attention on new types of intelligence collection practices and how they related to different notions of the crowd next.

## III: a typology of crowd-based intelligence practices

In this section, we put the practice of a certain mode of collecting information, along with social agents referring to crowds, at the conceptual centre. More specifically, we are interested in different types of online, distributed problem-solving models that leverage the collective information production of online communities to serve specific organizational goals.[29] We discuss three cases, loosely following the three steps of the intelligence cycle, situated on a continuum from active to passive participation: crowds used to collect information from, crowds formed through specific analysis purposes, and crowds in their most active form, to help gather and disseminate information.

ICT enable all forms of crowd-based intelligence, through promoting the quick formation of social ties, globalization of resources and redefinition of the temporality of crowds. Their social role however is much different across forms of crowd-based intelligence, illustrating that the use and meaning of technologies depends on context.[30] They support intelligence practices that give rise to much different visions of crowds, from benign to adversarial – ICT are not simply neutral instruments.

### The crowd as passive information provider

Digital crowds produce large amounts of data that allow particular collection practices to emerge. One of them, Social media intelligence (SOCMINT), builds on the abundant availability of personal information on social media platforms. The switch from 'analogous' exchange to digital and online forms of interaction amounts to creating a giant paper trail of individual and mass behaviour. Social media typically integrate multiple dimensions of social life of individual users, private, socioeconomic, cultural and others.[31] As a result, these different dimensions become mapped into one profile, providing an encompassing view that hitherto could only be assembled under substantial effort to the gaze of surveyors. As a subset of Open source intelligence (OSINT) – which also includes more 'classical' sources such as press or research articles – SOCMINT takes advantage of crowd-sourced information, pooled by social media, for near real-time situational awareness, insight into group relations and even an identification of criminal intent through following online interactions.[32] Along with the advent of big data and the use of new types of algorithms, inferences can be drawn from fragmented data that used to be difficult to translate into useful intelligence.

Exploiting the crowd as passive information provider serves a range of intelligence tasks, ranging from more general, longer-term purposes to intelligence that is short-term and event-specific. Communication tools like Twitter and instant messaging services can be used for near real-time situation reconnaissance and monitoring.[33] To the extent that communication occurs in an accessible/unencrypted manner, SOCMINT may also permit identifying unlawful intent. But even when contents of communication are not accessible, SOCMINT may offer a certain remedy, as social media in particular can provide so-called metadata from the analysis of social network structure and topography.[34] Crowd-based intelligence from social media thus reveals the relations between users, i.e. who interacts with whom, when and how frequently.

One of the big promises of crowd-sourced SOCMINT thus is insight into members of the crowd, either directly from communicated content, or indirectly by inferring from interaction and other data. Intelligence and security agents seek utility from such crowd-based intelligence however far beyond the vicinity of current events. Transcending the temporal immediacy traditionally associated with crowds, the long-term surveying of a crowd through OSINT and SOCMINT seeks to uncover events in the making, with the aim of predicting and potentially preventing developments before they fully unfold, from crime to social unrest.[35]

Whereas classical open source information is explicitly made available with the purpose of general public accessibility in mind, interaction on social media is typically among groups of users only. Even if users do not seek to restrict access, they generally do not expect that their content and personal information is completely public (see Kira Vrist Rønn and Sille Obelitz Søe, this issue), let alone serving as a source for intelligence. There is thus a marked tension between public and private information on social media, which effectively creates an OSINT 'grey zone', wherein the legitimacy if not legality of collecting and exploiting information can be an open question.[36] This tension exists across all kinds of SOCMINT and, arguably, may even extend to digitized OSINT. The point is that in any of such exercises, the crowd participates *involuntarily* (passively) in intelligence practices, even if it contributes information.

The manifestation of such crowds that most strongly resonates with traditional views like Le Bon's of crowds as a threat to social order is in riots, such as the one occurring in London in 2011. Social media but also closed, that is encrypted messenger systems were used for organization and coordination, as well as for real-time event updates.[37] This type of crowd communication forcefully excludes, and is deliberately directed against, state security agents. However, a key aspect in this exampled was the accompanying of the riots by a crowd-based intelligence campaign that was pursued by state authorities and directed against the rioting crowd.

Contemporary activism often appears in crowd form too, at least initially: Information becomes quickly distributed among crowd members, from near real-time data on events, mobilization, to tactical coordination for realizing activities. ICT have an important role as carriers of information that help in spreading the message and recruiting new members into the crowd. Ahead of the dawn of social media, ICT were already instrumental in crowd-sourced information production. During the Seattle protests against the WTO in 1999, for example, ICT-based information collection and tactical coordination were key instances of crowd-based intelligence that strengthened the activist's cause.[38] Social media soon replaced the list servers used in these days, and further enhanced real-time event monitoring and coordination of rapid response action networks.

While the Seattle protests were highly focused geographically, the crowd was a transnational occurrence. A similar local focus with a transnational component, activist crowds during the Arab Spring formed a crucial backbone of the uprising. Social media and ICT similarly reinforced real-time monitoring of events, coordinated action among protesters, and more generally greatly facilitated information sharing and mobilization.[39] With the Occupy Wall Street phenomenon, the intensity of transnationalism further intensified.

Across the discussed contexts, crowd-based intelligence in contemporary activism can be characterized as falling into 'three elemental modes of peer-production that operate together to create organization in crowds: the production, curation, and dynamic integration of various types of information content and other resources that become distributed and utilized across the crowd'.[40] Crucially, this kind of crowd-behaviour engaged in as part of contemporary activism occurs at best in a neutral relation, but most often in outright opposition to state authorities. While in some occasions there may be limited collaboration between activists and state security agents, crowd-based action and information exchange is not part of this. Rather, it represents an instance of crowd behaviour that takes place apart and, often, in opposition of intelligence agencies.

### Analysis and the crowd

This type of crowd manifests as spontaneous crowd formation in the face of disaster events, with the purpose to provide analysis of crisis situations. The exemplary case is the Haiti earthquake in 2010, after which so-called 'crisis mapping' occurred. Formed at the intersection of emergent behaviour, social activism, citizen journalism and the democratization of geospatial information, crisis mapping is both a process and an outcome that combines various streams of 'crowdsourced' information that is verified, categorized and visualized by volunteers using satellite imagery and open source mapping platforms. Based on the information provided by affected people on the ground, an international 'online crowd' translated the data into information that fed into an 'interagency map', which served as an intermediary for relief agencies seeking to address the needs of the public.[41] Horizontal data flows from community networks also contributed to the mapping exercise. In the emerging crowdsourcing setup, a second layer of volunteers, who were not on the ground but recruited online, analysed the data and condensed it into systematic information.[42]

As a bottom-up phenomenon, crisis maps are signs of a type of social behaviour that can offer relevant insight for discussions on building community resilience. As a tool, crisis mapping should be seen as a contribution to the larger crisis management toolbox. It is a source for information gathering, crisis response planning, and crisis communication that can provide states with an additional dynamic, low-cost way of engaging the broader population as well as seeing and analyzing the terrain both during and after a crisis.[43]

Crisis maps are best understood by focusing on the specific context in which they emerge. First, people tend to use new media to communicate the effects of a disaster (when and where possible). On the one hand, new communication media and the interaction they enable are thus complicit in making the crisis environment more complex. On the other, they also provide new solutions for dealing with complexity. Crisis mapping leverages the innate desires of people to share information during emergencies. Rather than letting this information get 'lost', it captures, verifies and structures it to help with crisis management efforts.

This technique of pooling together disparate information is known as 'crowdsourcing'. The neologism stands for the trend of leveraging the mass collaboration enabled by Web 2.0 technologies to achieve certain goals, often in the business context. Somebody – the crowdsourcer – broadcasts a problem to a community and requests its assistance in finding a solution. The community works autonomously or in some loosely coordinate fashion to volunteer ideas and feedback. It is rewarded via soft or hard benefits, the former referring to intellectual recognition or satisfying some type of volunteering or philanthropic desire whereas the latter refers to (monetary) compensation.

Second, as today's crises are increasingly complex, they have disproportionate effects and toggle between extremes – involving multiple actors, phenomena and speeds. They often challenge the ability of states to sufficiently protect their citizens by creating more and different damage than anticipated as well as overwhelming the capacities of first responders. Also, national and international audiences mercilessly dissect governments' performance in crisis situations.

A common reflex of some state officials has been to react defensively to these shifts, as such tools challenge the traditional information dominion of governments, can come with explicit or implicit calls for democratization of information or increased transparency, or are used to 'blame and shame' governments for their actions or inactions respectively.

Crisis mapping efforts are initiated and managed by non-state actors with governments having a varied and minor role in the process. Information flows occurred mostly from the bottom up: Affected people provide the initial data on their own initiative; the resulting model was governed by the relief agencies. The (local) crowd, being mostly a source of information and a target of relief intervention, amends and even amplify state agency capacities that were disabled by the disastrous event.

Crowdsourcing is of course greatly enabled and sped-up by technology. But the underlying pattern in behaviour when people are confronted with crisis situations deserves attention in its own right. Rather than just wait for crisis responders, individuals are increasingly using ICT tools to be more active in the crisis response phase. This spontaneous behaviour can be seen as an expression of the adaptive and resourceful nature of human beings – and as a trait related to the inherent resilience of some groups and communities.

## Dissemination and beyond

This type of crowd-based intelligence is an open collaboration between state authorities and *the public*. For certain intelligence tasks that are part of security governance, state authorities build on the support of *citizens*. These tasks range from information seeking to analysis and even predicting future situations. Collaborative crowd-based intelligence thus occurs in concrete crisis situations as well as in times where collaboration purposes are of a more abstract nature. A first kind of collaborative crowd-based intelligence takes place as part of crisis responses.

Another instance of this kind of crowd-based intelligence occurred in lieu of the Boston marathon bombing in 2013. After two bombs exploded near the finishing line, killing several and injuring hundreds of people, authorities issued calls for public assistance in investigating and tracking down the perpetrators. However, these open calls for crowdsourcing intelligence met an already ongoing parallel investigation by an active multitude organized through social media. Crowd-sourced information from the scene spread within minutes,[44] followed by a crowd-sourced investigation that rather paralleled the one by public authorities than being led by it.[45] Initial support to police forces through providing crowd-sourced information turned into a crowd-driven amateur investigation that went separate from the official one.[46] Also, during the London riots in 2011, the London Metropolitan Police and others engaged in crowd-based intelligence through social media recruiting the public's support in information gathering. In particular, reporting on events and information on offenders was sought.[47]

A second kind of collaborative crowd-based intelligence in security governance takes place independent of immediate crises. Geared towards scouting information and surveillance, campaigns like the 'If You See Something, Say Something' of the US Department of Homeland Security, or similar approaches taking place at public transportation hubs across the world outsource basic security work a generalized crowd, or members of the public who purportedly have responsibility to identify and escalate pre-defined suspicion indicators such as abandoned bags.[48] The scope of the campaign of the US Department of Homeland Security is quite broad; however, ranging from terrorism related activities to ordinary crime, hacking and vandalism.[49]

While the two preceding kinds of collaborative crowd-based intelligence in security governance aim for information gathering, a third kind is about information analysis for foresight purposes. It taps the 'wisdom of the crowd' to forecast political events, often based on open source information. Exemplary of this approach is the Good Judgement Project, pursued by psychologists Philip Tetlock and Barbara Mellers and sponsored by the Intelligence Advanced Research Projects Activity (IARPA) of the US Office of the Director of National Intelligence. In the research, thousands of nonexperts were asked to make probability estimates on political developments and scenarios for up to 12 months in the future.[50] Results showed that certain groups of individuals ('superforecasters') after receiving some basic training consistently outperformed even trained intelligence analysts.[51]

This third type of crowd-based intelligence practices casts the crowd into an optimistic light. Information is not sought on the crowd, but through the active support of the crowd, which is less adversary, less capricious, less unreliable mass, but more the public composed of citizens, who are invited to actively participating in intelligence work. It also effectively reinterprets security into a task that extends beyond the traditional confines of state agents and rather encompasses society as a whole.

## IV: performing the crowd

As the preceding sections illustrate, 'the crowd' is a notion of great versatility, in theory and in practice. Since its beginnings, the term's meanings changed, developed, and multiplied. Its drivers are as much a collage of (affective) group engagement, projection from the outside and the workings of technology, as it is defined by evolving contexts. In short, the crowd is not a simple, straightforward term. It is complex and multifaceted – and its meaning is always political.

In fact, there is often a direct relation between intelligence judgments about a crowd's attributes from a security governance perspective and the way its behaviour is observed – the more irrational and disruptive it appears, the more likely such an emergence will be considered a threat. Although events such as protests against the negative repercussions of neo-liberal globalization to vandalism and burglary-focused riots represent wildly different contexts, from the perspective of the crowd-observing intelligence, these crowds appear fundamentally similar.

Of course, in reality, different types of crowds sometimes morph into each other so that the categorization is often less clear in practice. Also, crowd-sourced intelligence regarding a specific event may evoke more generalized crowd-sourced surveillance; insights from generalized crowd-sourced intelligence may lead to a specific, event-focused intervention. For example, events during the Arab Spring triggered a reaction by security authorities that was at first event-specific and focused in its reactions on the on-going situation, but then became more general; it was crude in the beginning, but grew in time more sophisticated.

Crowd-based intelligence in turn, in its various incarnations, embodies, represents and replicates these traits. Moreover, crowd-based intelligence is a practice that performs the crowd. Different ways of crowd-based intelligence give rise to different meanings of 'the crowd'. The crowd, as an agent in responding to crises and catastrophes, as the revolutionary crowd, may appear as the active, networked multitude. It may become manifest locally only momentarily or it may transcend time and space, beyond borders and the ephemerality of singular events. Crowd-based intelligence may describe a phenomenon that is driven by its members or one that enacts a passive, virtual crowd by surveying and simulating them.

In the following, we would like to critically reflect on the politics of crowd-based intelligence in security governance. We focus on two main themes: First, on the use of 'the crowd' against other kinds of terms such as 'the public' and how these terms continue to reflect a difference in meaning in contemporary crowd-based intelligence; and on crowd-based intelligence as a way of performing such difference. Second, we link this to the role of ICT in crowd-based intelligence, seeking to highlight how ICT are implicated in the politics of crowd-based intelligence.

### Politics of the crowd

Over time, the notion of the crowd, while showing tensions in its meaning from early onwards, became more differentiated, but kept much of its political sensitivity. Referrals to crowds that are unsettling social order, that are close to violence, or resembling a mob stand against crowds supporting police action and security governance and even the 'wisdom of the crowd'. In crowd-based intelligence practices, this tension lives on. It is reflected in the acting multitude that seeks to realize what it deems public goods in its own initiative, whether this is then taken up by security actors such as in crisis response, or viewed by them with suspicion, as in case of Occupy Wall Street.

The tension becomes more forcefully apparent through the different connotations of crowd-based intelligence in security governance that is collaborative, building on open calls for support, such as during the London riots in 2011. Here, the crowd becomes 'the public'. The call is on the *citoyen* to partake and take up responsibility in securing the common good. In fact, the opposition to the violent mob again is on full display. Referring to the exercise as 'crowd-based intelligence', similar to the paralleling practice of surveying social media for communication of 'the mob', just blurs the terms' boundaries and lends them to absurdity.

The tension represents two quite different sides of the crowd-based intelligence coin that existed ever since the masses became a phenomenon of interest to social science and security governance. The crowd is a vehicle of information gathering as well as an object of it. While in certain contexts, such as open call crowd-based intelligence, a clear distinction still comes through, for the surveyed, simulated crowd of OSINT/SOCMINT it collapses entirely. The vehicle becomes the object. It is as much an involuntary collaborator in security governance as it is the target of suspicion.

In intelligence, as Adam Diderichsen points out in this special issue, information is always gathered on a (potential) adversary. Crowd-based intelligence, then, is not a neutral exercise. For some of its instances, the original designation of the crowd as 'the Other' continues to exist, at least as a latent possibility. The meaning of the term in its concrete context thus matters politically. Indeed, the theory one utilizes for looking at an object usually determines its shape, something that also applies to governing the crowd.[52] This matters for communicating with and about the crowd – for example in open call collaborating in a security event. It can be a challenge to avoid statements that appear prejudicial to legal proceedings.[53]

Yet the theories guiding/making the gaze also play in more subtly, but no less consequentially: When crowd-based intelligence becomes mediated, such as with OSINT/SOCMINT, this adds an additional layer of observation. In other words, ICT, and their various configurations, become implicated in politics and so do the *owners* of these technologies. When crowd-sourced information becomes collected and curated by privately owned social networking platforms, when large swathes of Big Data get dissected by privately owned algorithms, then these technologies and their owners become a part of intelligence and security governance.

### Dissolution of boundaries

ICT become intermingled in the politics of crowd-based intelligence, through the coalescence of vehicle and object, the blurring of the notion of public and private information, the break-down of topographical and temporal limits. Social media bear many of these traits in an exemplary fashion. For the owners of social media platforms, the mentioned collecting and mapping of multiple dimensions of social life and the curating of this data into one profile rests on the rationale of data maximization for economic exploitation. Coincidentally, the technology already provides the bases for SOCMINT. It is an inconvenient but irrefutable truth that in effect, these ICT are dual-use goods. It is not a coincidence that there are export restrictions in place for certain components, which are treated as sensitive goods due to their potential to support surveillance by authoritarian and totalitarian regimes.[54]

Social media platform owners profit from the blurring of public and private information and so do intelligence agents. Yet by extending what Hribar, Podbregar and Ivanusa call the 'grey zone' of published but not quite meant-to-be public information, by making the crowd of consumers also into a product, social media companies reinforce the collapse between vehicle and object of crowd-based intelligence. Expanding the 'grey zone' for economic exploitation also reinforces the SOCMINT rationale. In the end, there is a trilateral constellation of partially overlapping, partially conflicting interests between ICT companies, intelligence agencies and consumer/product/citizens/surveyed crowd.

The synergies of utilizing ICT that were designed for commercial exploitation of user data for intelligence purposes come with its own drawbacks though. Whereas information garnered from social media may appear reasonably straightforward, the means of inferring from large quantities of data are much less so. The algorithms built for this task are not only made, usually, with commercial purposes in mind, they are also private intellectual property. It remains in doubt to what extent algorithms bought from the private industry for security governance purposes are audited or transparent in their workings or rather stay essentially a black box.[55]

In the end, the utility of any crowd-based intelligence exercise, including those that are OSINT/SOCMINT related, as well as its political implications, remain highly context dependent. It is influenced by the kind of crowd involved, by its technological carrier, and how the crowd is represented on that carrier. Decisions what to focus upon, how and by what means thus remain important. It is the privilege and the responsibility of the intelligence agencies to make these kinds of decisions. However, the complexity and sensitivity of crowd-based intelligence in security governance requires special considerations for appropriate rules, oversight and accountability.

## V: conclusion

Since their coming into existence, crowds have been an object of security governance and of interest to intelligence. Different notions of the crowd relate to different intelligence information interests: from an image of the crowd as society's 'Other' that needs to be surveyed in order to neutralize it, through citizen activists-become-crowds that need to be controlled, to crowds as partaking in security governance. Based on a sociology of crowd-sourcing practices in intelligence and security governance, we identified different categories of crowd-sourcing that are clearly distinguishable in an ideal-typical fashion. In practice though, different kinds of crowd-sourcing can intermingle and occur simultaneously.

Seemingly, different kinds of crowds evoke clearly defined, differing intelligence practices. However, a closer analysis reveals that this simple cause-effect assumption does not hold. Academic theories of the crowd developed closely in line with the appearance of the crowd in societies. During LeBon's times, some may have questioned his conclusions, but the 'nature' of the phenomenon as affect-driven, de-individuating mass was hardly questioned. Later, along with a gradual change in perceptions of mass engagement in lieu of the 1968 civil rights protests towards citizen activism, academic theories provided a vision of the crowd as rational, interest-guided group action. Similarly, responses in security governance to the phenomenon of the crowd build on this variety of perspectives. After 1968, direct state-violence against crowds became controversial; de-escalation strategies now built on anticipating and controlling behaviour, and on communication.

This demonstrates not only that theory is an important guide to behaviour but, more importantly, that theory to a significant extent *defines the phenomenon* in the first place. Although political circumstances, and conceptions of what represents acceptable behaviour for seeking political impact (or for neutralizing it) obviously vary across time and space, there is no reason to believe that the 'nature' of the crowd actually changed. Which means that the other option is the plausible one, namely that changing theories of the crowd led to changing perceptions of the phenomenon. The events of 1968, and its governance efforts from a security perspective provide ample evidence of a struggle of perceptions of the nature of the phenomenon. In fact, research evidence suggests that the crowd theory held by security actors indeed guides their practices.[56]

In the double function of theory in defining the phenomenon and practice as an expression of theory thus lies the key to the politics of the crowd. When the crowd is the mad Other that practices seek to neutralize this reflects the classical friend/enemy distinction, with its problematic implications of Schmittian sovereign exceptionalism disabling established processes of account-ability and democratic control. The active, rational crowd, systematically participating in provision of security in turn reflects an image of citizens constantly on the watch, of society as a whole working towards resilience.

When in OSINT/SOCMINT the crowd is vehicle and object of intelligence practices that, in principle, seek to gather information on an adversary, then the specific arrangements through which such practices are performed ultimately contribute to defining the society we are living in. Crowd-based intelligence thus is more than an innocent practice that does no more than serving its immediate aims, such as SOCMINT. Questions about proportionality, legitimacy and account-ability deserve a convincing answer from security governance policymakers and practitioners.

## Notes

1. Surowiecki, *The wisdom of crowds*.
2. Mackay, *Extraordinary popular delusions*.
3. Jervis, "Intelligence and International Politics".
4. Coultas, "Crowdsourcing intelligence to combat terrorism:"; and Omand et al., "Introducing Social Media Intelligence (SOCMINT)".
5. cf. Lowenthal, *Intelligence*.
6. Reicher, "The Psychology of Crowd Dynamics".
7. Kelty, "Preface: Crowds and Clouds".
8. Le Bon, *The crowd*.
9. Blumer, "Collective behavior"; and Park, *The Crowd and the Public and Other Essays*.
10. Smelser, *Theory of Collective Behavior*.
11. Tajfel, *Differentiation between social groups*; Reicher, "Crowd behaviour as social action"; McPhail, *The Myth of the Madding Crowd*; and Tilly und Wood, *Social Movements 1768–2012*.
12. Granovetter, "Threshold Models of Collective Behavior".
13. Della Porta und Fillieule, "Policing Social Protest".
14. Bertalanffy, Ludwig von, *General Systems Theory: Foundations, Development, Applications*; Rapoport, *General System Theory*; and Axelrod, *The Complexity of Cooperation*.
15. Bertalanffy, *Perspectives on General System Theory: Scientific-Philosophical Studies*, 154.
16. Forrester, *Industrial Dynamics*.
17. Winner, "Do artifacts have politics?".
18. see also Warner, "Reflections on Technology and Intelligence Systems".
19. Baker, "From the criminal crowd to the 'mediated crowd'", 44.
20. Aradau und Blanke, "The Politics of Digital Crowds".
21. Juris, "Reflections on #Occupy Everywhere"; Conover u. a., "The Digital Evolution of Occupy Wall Street"; Bennett et al., "Organization in the crowd".
22. Aouragh und Alexander, "The Arab Spring| The Egyptian Experience".
23. Tufekci und Wilson, "Social Media and the Decision to Participate".
24. Howard und Hussain, *Democracy's Fourth Wave?*.
25. Lim, "Clicks, Cabs, and Coffee Houses".
26. Starbird und Palen, "(How) will the revolution be retweeted?".
27. Khondker, "Role of the New Media in the Arab Spring".
28. Bennett und Segerberg, "The logic of connective action".
29. The definition paraphrases Brabham's *Crowdsourcing*, xix., but is less predetermined with respect to agency.
30. Brabham, *Crowdsourcing*; Hosseini u. a., "Crowdsourcing: A taxonomy and systematic mapping study"; see also Bartlett und Miller, "The state of the art".
31. Fuchs und Trottier, "Towards a theoretical model of social media surveillance".
32. Omand, Bartlett, und Miller, "Introducing Social Media Intelligence (SOCMINT)".
33. Omand et al., 805f.; and Hribar et al., "OSINT", 532f.
34. Bartlett und Miller, "The state of the art".
35. Wang et al., "Automatic Crime Prediction Using Events Extracted from Twitter Posts"; Bogomolov u. a., "Once Upon a Crime"; Cadena u. a., "Forecasting Social Unrest Using Activity Cascades".
36. Hribar et al, "OSINT".
37. See note 19 above.
38. Smith, "Globalizing Resistance"; and Garrett, "Protest in an Information Society".

39. See note 23 above.
40. Bennett et al., "Organization in the crowd", 232.
41. Munro, "Crowdsourced translation for emergency response in Haiti"; and Gao u. a., "Harnessing the Crowdsourcing Power".
42. Starbird und Palen, "Voluntweeters".
43. Heinzelman und Waters, *Crowdsourcing crisis information in disaster-affected Haiti*; Shklovski, Palen, und Sutton, "Finding Community Through Information and Communication Technology in Disaster Response".
44. Cassa u. a., "Twitter as a Sentinel in Emergency Situations".
45. Nhan e6t al., "Digilantism".
46. Tapia et al., "Run amok".
47. Dene et al., "Social Media and the Police"; and Panagiotopoulos et al., "Citizen–government collaboration on social media", 354.
48. Reeves, "If You See Something, Say Something".
49. See https://www.dhs.gov/see-something-say-something/campaign-materials/indicators-infographic-full (accessed 4 July 2018).
50. Tetlock u. a., "Forecasting tournaments"; and Mellers u. a., "The psychology of intelligence analysis.".
51. Mellers u. a., "Identifying and cultivating superforecasters"; and Tetlock und Gardner, *Superforecasting*.
52. Hoggett und Stott, "The role of crowd theory".
53. Bartlett und Miller, "The state of the art", 49.
54. E.g. Council Regulation (EU) No 264/2012, Annex III. Swiss State Secretariat for Economic Affairs (SECO), Ordinance of Measures against the Islamic Republic of Iran (946.231.143.6), Article 5 and Annex 4.
55. Dencik et al., "Prediction, Pre-Emption and Limits to Dissent", 1140.
56. See note 52 above.

## Disclosure statement

No potential conflict of interest was reported by the authors.

## Bibliography

Aouragh, M., and A. Alexander. "The Arab Spring| The Egyptian Experience: Sense and Nonsense of the Internet Revolution." *International Journal of Communication* 5, Nr. 0 (September 2 2011): 15.
Aradau, C., and T. Blanke. "The Politics of Digital Crowds." *Lo Squaderno*, 33 (2014): 9–12.
Axelrod, R. *The Complexity of Cooperation: Agent-Based Models of Competition and Collaboration*. Princeton: Princeton University Press, 1997.
Baker, S. A. "From the Criminal Crowd to the "Mediated Crowd": The Impact of Social Media on the 2011 English Riots." *Safer Communities* 11, Nr. 1 (2012): 40–49. doi:10.1108/17578041211200100.
Bartlett, J., and C. Miller. "The State of the Art: A Literature Review of Social Media Intelligence Capabilities for Counter-Terrorism." *Demos* 4 (2013): 1–69.
Bennett, W. L., and A. Segerberg. "The Logic of Connective Action: Digital Media and the Personalization of Contentious Politics." *Information, Communication & Society* 15, Nr. 5 (2012): 739–768. doi:10.1080/1369118X.2012.670661.
Bennett, W. L., A. Segerberg, and B. S. Walker. "Organization in the Crowd: Peer Production in Large-Scale Networked Protests." *Information, Communication & Society* 17, Nr. 2 (2014): 232–260. doi:10.1080/1369118X.2013.870379.
Bertalanffy, L. V. *General Systems Theory: Foundations, Development, Applications*. New York: George Braziller Publishing, 1968.

Bertalanffy, L. V. *Perspectives on General System Theory: Scientific-Philosophical Studies*. New York: George Braziller Publishing, 1975.

Blumer, H. "Collective Behavior." In *New Outline of the Principles of Sociology*, edited by Alfred McClung Lee and Robert Ezra Park, 2nd ed., 166–222. New York: Barnes & Noble, 1951.

Bogomolov, A., B. Lepri, J. Staiano, N. Oliver, F. Pianesi, and A. Pentland. "Once upon a Crime: Towards Crime Prediction from Demographics and Mobile Data." In *Proceedings of the 16th International Conference on Multimodal Interaction*, 427–434. ICMI '14. Bogazici University, Istanbul, Turkey. New York, NY: ACM, 2014. doi:10.1145/2663204.2663254.

Brabham, D. C. *Crowdsourcing*. Cambridge, MA: MIT Press, 2013.

Cadena, J., C. J. Gizem Korkmaz, A. M. Kuhlman, N. Ramakrishnan, and A. Vullikanti. "Forecasting Social Unrest Using Activity Cascades." *PLOS ONE* 10, Nr. 6 Juni 19 (2015): e0128879. doi:10.1371/journal.pone.0128879.

Cassa, C. A., R. Chunara, K. Mandl, and J. S. Brownstein. "Twitter as a Sentinel in Emergency Situations: Lessons from the Boston Marathon Explosions." *PLoS Currents* 5, Juli 2 (2013). doi:10.1371/currents.dis. ad70cd1c8bc585e9470046cde334ee4b.

Conover, M. D., E. Ferrara, F. Menczer, and A. Flammini. "The Digital Evolution of Occupy Wall Street." *PLOS ONE* 8, Nr. 5 Mai 29 (2013): e64679. doi:10.1371/journal.pone.0064679.

Coultas, B. T. "Crowdsourcing Intelligence to Combat Terrorism: Harnessing Bottom-Up Collection to Prevent Lone-Wolf Terror Attacks". Master's thesis. Monterey, CA: Naval Postgraduate School, 2015.

Della, P. D., and O. Fillieule. "Policing Social Protest." In *The Blackwell Companion to Social Movements*, edited by David A. Snow, Sarah A. Soule, and Hanspeter Kriesi, 217–241. Oxford: Blackwell Publishing, 2008.

Dencik, L., A. Hintz, and Z. Carey. "Prediction, Pre-Emption and Limits to Dissent: Social Media and Big Data Uses for Policing Protests in the United Kingdom." *New Media & Society* 20, Nr. 4 April 1 (2018): 1433–1450. doi:10.1177/1461444817697722.

Denef, S., S. B. Petra, and N. A. Kaptein. "Social Media and the Police: Tweeting Practices of British Police Forces during the August 2011 Riots." In *Proceedings of the SIGCHI Conference on Human Factors in Computing Systems*, 3471–3480. CHI '13. New York, NY: ACM, 2013. doi:10.1145/2470654.2466477.

Forrester, J. W. *Industrial Dynamics*. Cambridge, MA: MIT Press, 1972.

Fuchs, C., and D. Trottier. "Towards a Theoretical Model of Social Media Surveillance in Contemporary Society." *Communications* 40, Nr. 1 (2015): 113–135. doi:10.1515/commun-2014-0029.

Gao, H., G. Barbier, R. Goolsby, and D. Zeng. "Harnessing the Crowdsourcing Power of Social Media for Disaster Relief", Januar 2011.

Garrett, R. K. "Protest in an Information Society: A Review of Literature on Social Movements and New ICTs." *Information, Communication & Society* 9, Nr. 2 April 1 (2006): 202–224. doi:10.1080/13691180600630773.

Granovetter, M. "Threshold Models of Collective Behavior." *American Journal of Sociology* 83, Nr. 6 Mai 1 (1978): 1420–1443. doi:10.1086/226707.

Heinzelman, J., and C. Waters. *Crowdsourcing crisis information in disaster-affected Haiti*. US Institute of Peace Washington, DC, 2010. http://dspace.africaportal.org/jspui/bitstream/123456789/29753/1/Crowdsourcing%20Crisis%20Information%20in%20Disaster%20-%20Affected%20Haiti.pdf.

Hoggett, J., and C. Stott. "The Role of Crowd Theory in Determining the Use of Force in Public Order Policing." *Policing and Society* 20, Nr. 2 Juni 1 (2010): 223–236. doi:10.1080/10439461003668468.

Hosseini, M., A. Shahri, K. Phalp, J. Taylor, and R. Ali. "Crowdsourcing: A Taxonomy and Systematic Mapping Study." *Computer Science Review* 17 (2015): 43–69. doi:10.1016/j.cosrev.2015.05.001.

Howard, P. N., and M. M. Hussain. *Democracy's Fourth Wave?: Digital Media and the Arab Spring*. Oxford: Oxford University Press, 2013.

Hribar, G., I. Podbregar, and I. Teodora. "OSINT: A "Grey Zone"?" *International Journal of Intelligence and CounterIntelligence* 27, Nr. 3 September 1 (2014): 529–549. doi:10.1080/08850607.2014.900295.

Jervis, R. "Intelligence and International Politics." In *The Oxford Handbook of International Security*, edited by Alexandra Gheciu and William C. Wohlforth, 516–530. Oxford: Oxford University Press, 2018. http://www.oxfordhandbooks.com/view/10.1093/oxfordhb/9780198777854.001.0001/oxfordhb-9780198777854-e-34

Juris, J. S. "Reflections on #Occupy Everywhere: Social Media, Public Space, and Emerging Logics of Aggregation." *American Ethnologist* 39, Nr. 2 Mai 1 (2012): 259–279. doi:10.1111/j.1548-1425.2012.01362.x.

Kelty, C. "Preface: Crowds and Clouds. " *Limn*, Nr. 2 (2012). https://limn.it/articles/preface-crowds-and-clouds/

Khondker, H. H. "Role of the New Media in the Arab Spring." *Globalizations* 8, Nr. 5 Oktober 1 (2011): 675–679. doi:10.1080/14747731.2011.621287.

Le Bon, G. *The Crowd: A Study of the Popular Mind*. London: T.F. Unwin, 1896.

Lim, M. "Clicks, Cabs, and Coffee Houses: Social Media and Oppositional Movements in Egypt, 2004-2011." *Journal of Communication* 62, Nr. 2 (2012): 231–248. doi:10.1111/j.1460-2466.2012.01628.x.

Lowenthal, M. M. *Intelligence: From Secrets to Policy*. Los Angeles: CQ Press, 2006.

Mackay, C. *Extraordinary Popular Delusions*. London: Richard Bentley, 1841.

McPhail, C. *The Myth of the Madding Crowd*. New York: Aldine de Gruyter, 1991.

Mellers, B., E. Stone, P. Atanasov, N. Rohrbaugh, S. Emlen Metz, L. Ungar, M. M. Bishop, M. Horowitz, E. Merkle, and P. Tetlock. "The Psychology of Intelligence Analysis: Drivers of Prediction Accuracy in World Politics." *Journal of Experimental Psychology: Applied* 21, Nr. 1 (2015): 1.

Mellers, B., E. Stone, T. Murray, A. Minster, N. Rohrbaugh, M. Bishop, E. Chen, J. Baker, Y. Hou, and M. Horowitz. "Identifying and Cultivating Superforecasters as a Method of Improving Probabilistic Predictions." *Perspectives on Psychological Science* 10, Nr. 3 (2015): 267–281. doi:10.1177/1745691615577794.

Munro, R. "Crowdsourced Translation for Emergency Response in Haiti: The Global Collaboration of Local Knowledge." 2010. http://nlp.stanford.edu/pubs/munro2010translation.pdf.

Nhan, J., L. Huey, and R. Broll. "Digilantism: An Analysis of Crowdsourcing and the Boston Marathon Bombings." *The British Journal of Criminology* 57, Nr. 2 März 1 (2017): 341–361. doi:10.1093/bjc/azv118.

Omand, S. D., J. Bartlett, and C. Miller. "Introducing Social Media Intelligence (SOCMINT)." *Intelligence and National Security* 27, Nr. 6 Dezember 1 (2012): 801–823. doi:10.1080/02684527.2012.716965.

Panagiotopoulos, P., A. Z. Bigdeli, and S. Sams. "Citizen–Government Collaboration on Social Media: The Case of Twitter in the 2011 Riots in England." *Government Information Quarterly* 31, Nr. 3 Juli 1 (2014): 349–357. doi:10.1016/j.giq.2013.10.014.

Park, R. E. *The Crowd and the Public and Other Essays.* Chicago: University of Chicago Press, 1972.

Rapoport, A. *General System Theory: Essential Concepts & Applications.* Cambridge: Abacus Press, 1986.

Reeves, J. "If You See Something, Say Something: Lateral Surveillance and the Uses of Responsibility." *Surveillance & Society; Kingston* 10, Nr. 3/4 (2012): 235–248. doi:10.24908/ss.v10i3/4.4209.

Reicher, S. "The Psychology of Crowd Dynamics." In *Blackwell Handbook of Social Psychology: Group Processes*, edited by Michael A. Hogg and Scott Tindale, 182–209. Oxford: John Wiley & Sons, 2001.

Reicher, S. D. "Crowd Behaviour as Social Action." In *Rediscovering the Social Group: A Self-Categorization Theory*, edited by John C. Turner, 171–202. Cambridge: Basil Blackwell, 1987.

Shklovski, I., L. Palen, and J. Sutton. "Finding Community through Information and Communication Technology in Disaster Response." In *Proceedings of the 2008 ACM Conference on Computer Supported Cooperative Work*, 127–136. CSCW '08. New York, NY: ACM, 2008. doi:10.1145/1460563.1460584.

Smelser, N. J. *Theory of Collective Behavior.* New York: The Free Press, 1962.

Smith, J. "Globalizing Resistance: The Battle of Seattle and the Future of Social Movements." *Mobilization: An International Quarterly* 6, Nr. 1 März 1 (2001): 1–19. doi:10.17813/maiq.6.1.y63133434t8vq608.

Starbird, K. ",Voluntweeters': Self-Organizing by Digital Volunteers in Times of Crisis." In *Proceedings of the SIGCHI Conference on Human Factors in Computing Systems*, 1071–1080. CHI '11. New York, NY: ACM, 2011. doi:10.1145/1978942.1979102.

Starbird, K., and L. Palen. "(How) Will the Revolution Be Retweeted?: Information Diffusion and the 2011 Egyptian Uprising." In *Proceedings of the Acm 2012 Conference on Computer Supported Cooperative Work*, 7–16. ACM, 2012. http://dl.acm.org/citation.cfm?id=2145212

Surowiecki, J. *The Wisdom of Crowds: Why the Many are Smarter than the Few and How Collective Wisdom Shapes Business, Economies, Societies, and Nations.* 1st ed. New York: Doubleday, 2004.

Tajfel, H. *Differentiation between Social Groups: Studies in the Social Psychology of Intergroup Relations.* Oxford, England: Academic Press, 1978.

Tapia, A. H., J. L. Nicolas, and H.-W. Kim. "Run amok: Group crowd participation in identifying the bomb and bomber from the Boston marathon bombing.", 2014.

Tetlock, P. E., and D. Gardner. *Superforecasting: The Art and Science of Prediction.* New York: Random House, 2016.

Tetlock, P. E., B. A. Mellers, N. Rohrbaugh, and E. Chen. "Forecasting Tournaments: Tools for Increasing Transparency and Improving the Quality of Debate." *Current Directions in Psychological Science* 23, Nr. 4 (2014): 290–295. doi:10.1177/0963721414534257.

Tilly, C., and L. J. Wood. *Social Movements 1768-2012.* Abingdon: Routledge, 2013.

Tufekci, Z., and C. Wilson. "Social Media and the Decision to Participate in Political Protest: Observations from Tahrir Square." *Journal of Communication* 62, Nr. 2 April 1 (2012): 363–379. doi:10.1111/j.1460-2466.2012.01629.x.

Wang, X., S. G. Matthew, and D. E. Brown. "Automatic Crime Prediction Using Events Extracted from Twitter Posts." In *Social Computing, Behavioral - Cultural Modeling and Prediction*, edited by Sun-Ki Chai, John J. Salerno, and Patricia L. Mabry, 231–238. Lecture Notes in Computer Science. Berlin, Heidelberg: Springer, 2012. doi:10.1007/978-3-642-29047-3_28.

Warner, M. "Reflections on Technology and Intelligence Systems." *Intelligence and National Security* 27, Nr. 1 Februar 1 (2012): 133–153. doi:10.1080/02684527.2012.621604.

Winner, L. "Do Artifacts Have Politics?." *Daedalus* 109, Nr. 1 (1980): 121–136.

# The civilian's visual security paradox: how open source intelligence practices create insecurity for civilians in warzones

Rune Saugmann

**ABSTRACT**

Images taken by civilians and shared online have become an important source of conflict intelligence. This article explores issues around how states and non-state actors appropriate civilians' images to produce intelligence about conflict, critically scrutinizing a practice often called open source or social media intelligence. It argues that image appropriation for open-source intelligence production creates a new kind of visual security paradox in which civilians can be endangered by their everyday visual practices because their digital images can be appropriated by outside actors as conflict intelligence. The transformation of everyday images into conflict evidence relies on what Barthes termed the photographic paradox, the paradox that while a photograph is clearly not the reality it depicts, the photograph is casually interpreted as a copy of that reality. When images are appropriated as conflict intelligence this photographic paradox translates into a security paradox. A visual security argument can be made without the intention or knowledge of the image producer, who then comes to perform the role on an intelligence agent. Yet civilians in warzones can hardly refrain from producing any images when they need to call attention to their plight, and to stay in contact with friends and relatives. The paradox, then, is that such vital visual signs of life can rapidly become sources of danger for the civilian. This civilian visual security paradox, it is argued, demands that intelligence actors respect the protected status of civilians in their online collection practices. So far, however, there is little sign of such respect.

## Introduction: the use of amateur images as conflict intelligence

This article explores issues around how states and non-state actors appropriate amateur images to produce intelligence about conflict, scrutinizing a practice that in intelligence parlance is often called open source or social media intelligence. The omnipresence of civilian photography, it is important to point out as a point of departure, is a feature of our times where the integration of digital media into everyday sociality has led scholars to conceptualize everyday life as 'media life'.[1] Producing images, thus, is not a leisurely practice that civilians can switch on and off without major repercussions for their lives, even if it is of course possible at least for some time. Many of these images are freely available online, creating a vast publicly accessible visual archive of civilians' everyday lives in contemporary conflict zones. Some of these images may be taken for purposes of representing or influencing the conflict, but many – probably the vast majority – are simply the digital detritus from the media lives of civilians trying to live as normally as possible, including discussing what goes on around them and staying in contact with loved ones who may have been scattered or difficult to visit due to the ongoing conflict. This accidental and non-partisan quality is an essential part of what makes such images attractive for intelligence actors to appropriate. A vast online archive of such images presents oppor-tunities for intelligence actors seeking to gain an advantage over an adversary, and civilians' images are – via such use – increasingly part of the logics of conflict itself, just like they have for a decade been held to be of prime importance in the representation of conflict.[2]

I argue in this article that exploitation of civilians' images for purposes related to a conflict – be that as intelligence or as war documentation – turns civilians' images into active actants in the conflict, with or without the civilian's knowledge and consent. Pointing to the implication of some images, as well as stories of how images have endangered their creators, I argue that image appropriation – or open-source intelligence as the appropriators prefer to term it – creates a new kind of visual insecurity paradox in which civilians can be endangered by their everyday visual practices because the digital traces of these everyday visual practices produce conflict actants when appropriated by other actors. Such appropriation also questions the ontological status of the digitally mediated civilian or non-combatant, pointing to how online conflict practices seem – at the moment at least – to not respect the protected status conferred upon those unfortunate enough to be in close proximity to warzones. The paper provides examples of the use of open-source intelligence in contemporary conflicts, highlighting how such practices often do not rely on an anonymous sea of images but rather – as, for example, in crucial aspects of the investigation of the downing of MH17 over eastern Ukraine – on a few images only. This confers a security gravity onto images and their producers, as they effectively act as intelligence agents. While some actors seem oblivious to the dilemmas this creates for civilian image producers, the Dutch Safety Board recently acknowledged the civilian's visual security paradox in their use of civilian imagery in its investigation of the MH17 disaster.

## Image agency and everyday images from conflict zones

While most academic attention devoted to the use of 'open source' image harvesting for doc-umenting conflict has focused on the use of civilian images in news media reporting, the harvest-ing of images for intelligence purposes is a rapidly developing practice involving both government agencies, established political actors such as think thanks, and private persons with an interest in a developing conflict. Press reports have begun to pay attention to this work with a focus on its efficiency and the new possibilities it brings for holding states and other actors in conflict responsible.[3] Little attention has, however, been paid to how the methods employed in such open source repurposing of amateur images expose civilians by using their everyday images to substitute the work of conventional intelligence agents.

When actors employing 'open source' intelligence transform an everyday image into conflict evidence and make the image play a part in a war crimes or conflict investigation, it means that the image will have different agency vis-à-vis its creator and the entity sharing it. When single images or videos become key actants evidencing the production of a war crime, those producing and publishing these images become important actors to the parties in the conflict, revered by some conflict parties and reviled by others. My claim here is that image producers are likely to become further exposed to insecurity as a consequence of their images being repurposed for conflict intelligence purposes. Such exposure is not easy to document, as those facing increased insecurity because of the images they have produced are not likely to publicly announce this, as doing so would further expose them. But there are investigative journalistic treatments of life in warzones that manage to catch some of these stories. In the following, I illustrate the danger felt by image producers by introducing three journalistic investigations of, respectively, the presence of Russian soldiers,[4] of Russian involvement in the downing of MH17,[5] and in citizens reactions to the images used by Bellingcat.[6]

A German investigative journalism initiative, CORRECT!V, is one of the few public sources to have considered the ethical dilemmas of repurposing civilians images for conflict intelligence production. They investigated the story of how MH17 was brought down, interviewing locals, visiting likely launch sites and following the same image tracks as the Bellingcat investigation that I will introduce later in this article. Through their reportage, it becomes clear that information about these occurrences is sensitive and that locals think such information can bring the civilians possessing them in danger from all conflict sides:

> The villagers will not be named in this story. The people in eastern Ukraine need to be protected from possible consequences. The inhabitants of the separatists' territory are afraid – of the pro-Russian separatists and of the Ukrainian army. They don't want to say anything wrong.[7]

Perhaps the most crucial of the images transformed into evidence is the single civilian video showing the smoke trail pointing towards a launch site for the missile that brought down MH17, and thus indicating from where, and from whose territory, the war crime was committed. According to Bellingcat, 'The original video was quickly deleted from YouTube for unknown reasons'.[8] We can only guess by whom and for what reasons, but it is at least possible that the image producer/poster was not comfortable or safe being the single most important witness at the centre of a war crimes controversy. The sensitivity of information concerning the missile launch site is evidenced in Bensmann and Crawford's reporting on finding the site. The following story describes the particularly tense scene that meets the journalist when he confronts the neighbours to the likely launch site, enquiring about the firing of a missile on 17 July:

> a villager opens his front door. 'Are you a spy?' is his first question after a quick introduction. The man fled town in August because of the fighting. But on 17 July 2014 he was here. Any question about this day scares him.
>
> 'I remember, but you know I will not tell you everything. That could end badly for me.'[9]

The transformation of an image of large military vehicles into an image of the perpetrators of a war crime presents the image creator with different threats and opportunities than any other everyday image of large vehicles. Yet the only problems that register with 'open source intelligence' actors are operational, as I will show later. While the Atlantic Council is worried about protecting intelligence methods, Bellingcat's worry is about securing video footage before the civilians involved, or others, can take it down. After noting that the smoke trail video was taken down, Higgins – the author of the Bellingcat investigation – goes on to state that 'one lesson to learn earlier on with any video of interest is to immediately download it'.[10]

As Bellingcat functions as a blog where anyone can comment on the findings published, the site itself can spawn a public[11] through its reporting acting as a matter of concern and the site providing a forum for the discussion of the ethics of appropriating images and rendering them as evidence of war crimes. One commentator focuses on the position the investigation puts the image producer in:

> Hamish – July 22nd, 2014
>
> Gotta hope the person who took the video has skipped town and got the heck out of there. They'll be looking through houses immediately around the area where this was filmed, god help anyone who lives there. Pretty ballsy to have first posted it, hats off to whoever they are. Brave, bold and right.[12]

Such a comment rightly points out the agency of the image and the interest it may provoke among those who may have preferred to keep the location and operation of the Buk missile launcher secret. Yet the comment assumes that the image producers would have been aware of the potential of the conflict agency of their images when sharing the image. It thus doesn't take into account that such agency only occurs *after* the image is produced and circulated, as the image is drafted to form part of somebody else's evidence pointing towards Russian involvement in the tragedy. The – in my opinion wrongful – assumption that the image producers were aware of the agency their image could have when appropriated and deployed as an actant in the conflict leads the commenter to characterize the act by what it would have been if it was a deliberate documentation of war crimes undertaken at personal risk – 'right', 'ballsy', 'brave' and 'bold'.

**Figure 1.** Screenshot of Vice re-enacting everyday soldier photography (Ostrovsky, pt. 14:46).

To get an idea of the kind of interest images can provoke when they are repurposed as conflict intelligence, it is instructive to turn to a short Vice News documentary that tracks down the soldier whose everyday photography was appropriated by the Atlantic Council and used as evidence that professional Russian soldiers were active in the battles around Debaltseve early in 2015 in Eastern Ukraine.

The film tracks down the soldier's route into the warzone, re-enacting his social media photographs, including one that shows him in a uniform without insignia, standing on what appears to be a captured Ukrainian position located near Debaltseve (Figure 1). As with other reportage from the battlefield, locals shown in the film are clearly wary of being filmed speaking about the foreign troops.[13] The Vice journalist contacts the soldier, Bato Dambayev, and presents him with the re-enactments of his photographs. When the journalist tells the soldier that the photographs reveal his role fighting in Ukraine, the soldier reacts tensely, insisting to the journalist that there must be a mistake, that he didn't upload the pictures, that he is not in the photos and that he didn't leave the country.[14] The reaction of the soldier and the subsequent experience of the journalist give a concrete glimpse of the dangers being activated when images are enacted as evidence of covert invasion:

> He denied everything. I think he'd actually been prepared, as all soldiers are, that they're supposed to take off their insignia before they go into Ukraine. They're supposed to not take cellphones with them. He'd broken that rule, so he knew that he was in trouble.

> I know that he reported me having contacted him immediately after I spoke with him on the phone. And this isn't in the film, but a few hours after I put the phone down, the security services came and paid me a visit in my hotel and I was essentially hounded by them out of Russia thereafter.[15]

A foreign reporter can be 'hounded out' and has a network to react to worse sanctions, luxuries that civilians in conflict zones rarely enjoy.

The wariness of local civilians speaking to CORRECT!V and Vice News and the immediate reaction to the latter's reporting point to the dangers 'open source intelligence' presents for those who – when their images are appropriated and deployed as conflict intelligence – are rendered 'open source intelligence agents' by the actions of third parties.

The following section takes a closer look at what makes such appropriation possible epistemically – at what it is about or in images that enables third parties to appropriate them and deploy them as intelligence or knowledge of a situation they were not necessarily produced as part of.

## The surveillant image

The civilian's visual security paradox rests on the ability of third parties to appropriate civilians' images and use them as evidence related to a conflict. This ability depends, to a large degree at least, on the epistemic authority of the image when it is used as evidence, the trust society puts in its transparency and veracity. This trust is what enables the images to perform as a surveillance image that faithfully depicts reality, even if we as spectators have no idea about how, why and by whom it was produced. This trust relies on stabilizing an understanding of images as factual, transparent copies of the social world. Such an understanding is one of many, and it sits uneasily with what visual scholarship has learned about the production, distribution and interpretation of images.[16] Yet, visual surveillance relies on us forgetting the alternatives.

The configuration of images as evidence can be said to rest on three semiotic requirements. First, that the images are seen as being a reliable index of a situation that really was, that is that they are indexical in vocabulary of Peirce.[17] Second, it rests on reading images as transparent – that what is depicted resembles that which it tries to depict in a naturalistic way – in the way Magritte's painting of a pipe resembles a pipe, not in the way in which Picasso's *Guernica* embodies aerial bombing. Third, in order to be evidence, images have to be shown somewhere.[18] The 'reality effect' is not specifically visual. Rather, in order to produce the effect of reality or transparent evidence of reality, the mediated experience has to mimic everyday sensorial input of the sense(s) that a given medium can store and transmit.[19]

Once this understanding is achieved, any naturalistic image can become part of a *post-hoc* surveillance apparatus, irrespective of any intention that may be behind its production. This is especially the case when images are digital and thus open to digital networked appropriation in which any copy is identical to its original, rather than a copy or reproduction that is defined in part by lacking something which the original image has.[20] The implication is that if, for example, you happened to upload a video from a political street protest that turned violent or was otherwise suspicious to capable organizations, or shared a picture from the Boston Marathon a few minutes before a bomb went off there,[21] your video would be likely to end up as part of the *post-hoc* surveillance of the event. Far from hypothetical, such 'accidental surveillance' is widespread enough that for years, NGO's with concerned about privacy and the right to assembly have produced guidelines instructing civilians in how to practice safe filming when in politically charged crowd situations,[22] and technology providers have experimented with face blurring tools to minimize the surveillance potential of images.

Images are mobilized in two different modalities of surveillance, distinguished by the different temporalities at play in the surveillant logic they build. Two quite different logics are at play in the use of images in surveillance following from whether this surveillance is aimed at providing visual foresight or visual hindsight. One the one hand, we have surveillance systems the rationale of which is to provide foresight, to anticipate and render the future known and governable. Amoore has characterized the use of images in anticipatory surveillance as the development of a 'vigilant visuality' in which 'the act of seeing becomes an act of foreseeing'.[23] Here, image data streams are often coupled with other data streams to produce risk profiles or other forecasts that can be used to do social sorting of a population.[24] The use of foresight surveillance at borders has led Bigo to argue that the combination of security and surveillance produces a 'ban-opticon' where surveillant foresight underpins the denial of entry and rights in the name of security.[25] Interestingly, Amoore argues that the paradigm of vigilance extends from the use of images in forecasting to foresight or vigilance in everyday seeing, leading to a surveillant sociality in which the fellow civilian is also 'the vigilant onlooker'.[26]

On the other hand, we find visual surveillance practices that follow a rationale of providing hindsight, a forensic desire to make the past known and transparent through making it visible. Here the desire driving the implementation is one of rendering the past stable, transparent and governable through the establishment of visible facts. The attribution of responsibility is also often a vital part of such visual surveillance, producing a forensic visuality of witnessing that 'intervenes in the world through the generation of testimonial claims'.[27] This places the spectator (usually an institution with some kind of authority in relation to global politics) in a judicial position, judging on the basis of forensic images. This spectator position has been found to occasionally extend to ordinary civilians both in relation to war surveillance images that have entered the public[28] as well as political upheavals and natural disasters.[29] Yet there have also been cases in which the authority of ordinary seeing has been dismissed in favour of incomprehensible official alternatives, the Rodney King trial and Chelsea Manning's leaked video from the war in Iraq[30] prominent among them. Faced with the latter video, then US Secretary of Defense Robert Gates found it necessary to render the images opaque,[31] telling the public that they couldn't trust what they could clearly see.[32] I have elsewhere called this the deployment of a 'semiotic fog of war' as it draws on the metaphor of the fog of war to counter the claim to veracity otherwise mobilized in surveillance images.[33]

Common to both foresight and hindsight types of visual surveillance, and irrespective of whether the images used are produced for surveillance purposes or sourced from civilians, mobilizing images in surveillant assemblages relies on viewing images as transparent rather than opaque[34]; as clear and objective imprints of the world rather than partial, subjective and possibly misleading statements dependant on interpretation to tell anything about the world. Barthes describes this as 'a new space-time category: spatial immediacy and temporal anteriority [...] an illogical conjunction between the *here-now* and the *there-then*'.[35] Even the use of images in forecasting is dependent on the view that they neutrally record the world of the past to make it available to forecasting. The entrenchment of such a view is thus the key political move in making images into surveillance images. The use of images in surveillance relies on a particular configuration of the image as not distorting or co-constructing but recording reality, configuring sight as what Amoore[36] has termed a sovereign sense on which state security decisions and risk calculations can be unproblematically grounded.

### Civilians as image producers in conflict zones: from citizen journalists to civilian spies?

Among the first to notice and exploit how new digital visual media encouraged the emergence of civilian image-producers whose images from dangerous conflict zones were freely accessible to the global public and could be rendered as evidence of conflict, were established media organizations. The availability of conflict images to anyone online, including to media institutions located far from the conflict zones, presented opportunities to bypass censorship and other forms of media control, and to access zones that were deemed too dangerous and too expensive to insure western reporters in. As sources would rarely upload images in their own full name and would thus be difficult to contact to get permissions and pay copyright fees, such reporting also saved resources. However, news media were not the only actors to adapt to the developing media landscape, and soon other actors with an interest in conflicts began to seize on the troves of freely available civilian-produced images.

To understand these new ways of leveraging the everyday image production of civilians in conflict zones, I focus on three levels of appropriation of civilian images – by state actors, by other institutional political actors and by fellow citizens. For each of these levels, I discuss a few examples, drawing mainly from the conflict in eastern Ukraine and Crimea but also discussing cases from other contemporary conflicts.

First, citizen-driven initiatives without explicit political affiliation or institutional anchoring were among the first to engage in the harvesting and repurposing of civilians' images. The initiative often credited with using civilian conflict images for doing intelligence work is the non-governmental initiative Bellingcat, which started as a blog called *Brown Moses*, run by a single individual who looked at images from the war in Syria. Today Bellingcat is using civilian imagery to conduct what it calls 'open source evidence' investigation into contemporary conflicts, and its expertise is so sought after in intelligence circles that the organization – which is financed in part by conducting how-to workshops – has been considering banning intelligence actors from its training seminars.[37] Among many other cases, the organization has investigated the downing of the Malaysia Airlines airplane MH17 over eastern Ukraine on 17 July 2014. Researchers at Goldsmiths' *Forensic Architecture* project have also been using similar techniques to leverage civilian media production to reconstruct and document instances of violence and its cover-up from the Israeli occupation of Palestine, as well as other events in contemporary conflict.[38]

Second, institutional political actors other than states – major NGOs often with an explicit political stance – make use of the abundance of civilian-produced and freely available images to produce a long range of 'facts' about ongoing conflicts. The think tank Atlantic Council is one such actor which, by employing soldiers' amateur images as 'evidence' of Russian aggression in Ukraine, blur the lines between advocacy and intelligence and, by using images from civilians and off-duty soldiers to do so, blur the lines between civilian 'media life',[39] military service and intelligence production.[40] Other organizations, such as Amnesty International, have reacted to the availability of civilian images, both not only by using such images to document war crimes but also by warning civilians that they need to be careful about what they film and share online when they are in the proximity of political conflict.[41]

Third, states increasingly make use of civilian images to legitimize and produce foreign policy. This is evident in recent episodes around the use of chemical weapons in the war in Syria – where the United States published thousands of videos to substantiate claims of the 2013 Eastern Ghouta attack.[42] Another major example of states' appropriation of citizen images, analysed here, was when the Ukrainian state used civilians' images to make the case that the 'little green men' among separatist fighters in Eastern Ukraine and Crimea were really Russian soldiers.

## Assembled intelligence: The Ukrainian Dossier and civilian authorship rights as a war casualty

'Little green men' – uniformed, disciplined and well-equipped soldiers without any distinctions marking their nationality or belonging – became a hallmark of the early stage of war among separatists in eastern Ukraine. The Ukrainian authorities, faced with the dilemma of visually attributing undistinguished forces in Eastern Ukraine after similar forces, were involved in the swift takeover of the Crimean peninsula,[43] did not turn away from visibility as a strategy for attributing responsibility, rather they leveraged civilian photography to further embrace it. On 20 April 2014, the US Department of State endorsed a dossier, provided by Ukraine to the OSCE, to substantiate that the soldiers were indeed Russian military units, and provided its contents to the *New York Times*.[44] Stating that '[t]he Delegation of Ukraine has shared the photo-materials with other [OSCE] delegations',[45] the dossier compared civilian images from the Eastern Ukraine conflict to earlier images of Russian soldiers – e.g. from the invasion of Georgia in 2008 – making the case that some of the individuals appearing in non-marked uniforms in eastern Ukraine in 2014 were pictured wearing Russian special forces uniforms in earlier conflicts.

More conventional intelligence, such as intercepted radio communications, was also presented by the Ukrainian security services,[46] but at least in western media, it was clearly the photographs that got the most attention and exposure. This was the case even if the images were not authenticated or attributed to their creators but either left unattributed or labelled as images that 'the Ukrainian government provided'.[47] The initial uncritical publication of the photographs as facts led news spectators to complain about 'alleged identifications of individuals in pairs of photographs where the faces were so fuzzy there was no way to see anything more than a vague and perhaps entirely coincidental resemblance (not to mention that the authenticity of the photographs themselves wasn't established in any way)'.[48] To the *New York Times* public editor, this produced 'a kind of "morning after" feeling', which however only led – in the paper's own words – to 'a more sober, less prominently displayed follow-up story, to deal with objections while not clarifying much of anything'.[49]

The practice was problematized when a professional photographer, Maxim Dondyuk, who had taken one of the repurposed photographs and posted it on his Instagram account, disputed both the proclaimed location of a photograph included in the dossier and the practice of appropriating photographs from image-sharing sites. The photographer, who was working for Russian news-magazine *Russian Reporter*, claimed his photograph to be taken in Slovyansk in Ukraine, not in Russia, and pointed out that '[n]obody asked my permission to use this photograph'.[50] Contrary to everyday civilians in eastern Ukraine, who have scarce access to speak up in international media, the media professional could complain that the inclusion of his work for a Russian outlet in a Ukrainian intelligence dossier caused an uncomfortable situation for him, highlighting how using unknown images in intelligence changes the images and the degree to which they can be seen to have agency in relation to a violent conflict.

When states use Instagram and other image-sharing sites as repositories of 'open source' visual intelligence, it is thus done at the expense of often silenced image producers, exposing the creators to possible hostility from those the images are used as intelligence against.

## NGO repurposing of soldier photography: hiding and exposing covert invasion

The Atlantic Council of the United States is a US think tank, founded in 1961, working on NATO-related matters, and with a history of being close to top US decision makers. Its report *Hiding in Plain Sight*[51] repurposes images from social media profiles of Russian soldiers and civilians in eastern Ukraine to make the case that Russian soldiers and equipment have been integral to the conflict in eastern Ukraine, especially the occupation of Debaltseve on 18 February 2015, just 3 days after the signing of the second Minsk ceasefire.

The report introduces its method of inquiry to track Russian equipment and soldiers in Ukraine, which it terms 'geolocation' of images to produce 'digital forensics', as a means to subvert state subversion: 'While the Kremlin continues to deny the role of regular Russian forces in Ukraine, Russian soldiers fighting in Ukraine and Ukrainian and Russian civilians on both sides of the war are posting photographs and videos of convoys, equipment, and themselves on the Internet'.[52] To buttress the credibility of its image harvesting and appropriation, the Atlantic Council report cites respected NGOs such as Human Rights Watch and Amnesty International as also using geolocation techniques on civilians' images.

To the report's authors, such videos and photographs are not primarily private documents that should be handled with care for and respect of the civilians that produced them. The images are taken as direct evidence, rather than – as in most research on war photography – ambiguous statements filled with meanings that may be obscure.[53] The Atlantic Council report views civilian images and satellite images in the same way – as valuable resources in the fight against covert Russian intervention: 'These pieces of evidence create an undeniable – and publicly accessible – record of Russian involvement in Ukraine'.[54] As described in the report, geolocation – the assigning of a geographical position to an unknown image, to mark the location of the artefacts depicted in that image – 'is a powerful and effective tool for tracking individuals and the images they produce'.[55] The report finds the procedure most useful in relation to tracking the movement of Russian military equipment 'with hundreds of videos and photographs uploaded *by ordinary Russians and Ukrainians*'.[56] As an example of the method, consider the following:

'a video was uploaded to YouTube showing the movement of a military convoy in Rostov-on-Don, Russia, heading west. The coordinates were verified through geolocation, using satellite and ground imagery available through a Russian online map service. Later in September 2014, an Al-Jazeera news crew filmed the movement of Msta-S system through Novoazovsk in Ukraine, again heading west. In both these videos, a particular unit can be seen with a number of distinctive features: the same overall camouflage pattern, white paint blotch on the turret, discoloration in the same spots, and a unique, hand-painted rail cargo marking. Taken together, these features strongly suggest that the same unit is present in both videos, and that the unit would have been transferred across the border'.[57]

Apart from using unknown civilian footage paired with satellite images to track equipment, the Atlantic Council report uses the personal everyday images of Russian soldiers to track soldiers' movement across the border, documenting how some of them perish in eastern Ukraine and others go home to Russia. To do this, the report appropriates pictures from individual soldiers' VKontakte profiles. Detailing the journeys of two young men who died in eastern Ukraine, the report uses titles like 'Life before the War', 'Training for Combat', 'Deployment and Death in Snezhnoe', 'Mysterious Funerals' and 'Cover-Up', titles that are hard to imagine as endorsed by the soldiers or those inheriting their belongings, including their image authorship rights.[58] The report also profiles one soldier whom it calls Bato Dambayev, who during his deployment was photographed standing on what according to the Atlantic Council report is a captured Ukrainian position in eastern Ukraine.[59] This soldier is also the subject of the Vice News documentary film that was introduced earlier to show the consequences of image appropriation. While using intimate photographs from the lives of these individuals and those close to them, the report declines to reflect on the appropriateness on doing so, commenting only on its efficiency.

Based on the usefulness it sees in harvesting intelligence from civilian images, the report recommends using 'new digital forensic methods and geolocation analysis to collect intelligence that is *releasable to the public* to complement covert and technical intelligence collection' and to 'make public, to the maximum extent possible, information documenting Putin's aggressive designs, the presence of Russian troops and equipment in Ukraine, and Russian officials directing the fighting in Ukraine, *while protecting intelligence methods* as needed'.[60] Underlying these recommendations is a view that while intelligence methods need to be protected and may not produce intelligence that is 'releasable' to the public, there is – to the Atlantic Council – nothing standing in the way of using civilians and soldiers' images for intelligence and publication purposes.

## Civilian-to-civilian image exploitation: Bellingcat's work on MH17

Everyday civilian-produced images harvested online are also at the heart of the work of several citizen initiatives that work to establish facts and civilian-produced reporting in conflict hotspots such as Ukraine, Syria and Palestine. Among these, the UK-based Bellingcat, an organization that has evolved from the ground-breaking Black Moses blog run by British citizen Elliot Higgins, stands out. Higgins used civilian images from Syria to document the presence of weapons sold by Croatia in the Syrian civil war.[61] With the Bellingcat team, Higgins, apart from being a co-author of the Atlantic Council report and a major inspiration for its method,[62] has been active in relation to the war in Eastern Ukraine by using civilian footage to investigate the downing of Malaysia Airlines MH17 on 17 July 2014.

Perhaps the most impressive assembly of civilians' images is Bellingcat's tracking of a convoy of BUK surface-to-air missile launchers, radars and support vehicles; the identification of one of these launchers via its visible damage and markings; the placing of this launcher next to a likely launch site pinpointed from smoke trails seen in a single civilian's twitter image; and the tracking of that vehicle's return to Russia with one of its four missiles missing.[63]

Using videos and photographs found online and presumably uploaded by civilians in Russia and Ukraine, Bellingcat points to an exact missile launcher as being likely responsible for the shooting down of MH17.[64] At the core of this tracing are the unique marks of wear and tear on the vehicle, as well as its partly obscured insignia. This innovative and extremely detail-focused use of civilian images

**Figure 2.** Identifying the missile launcher via multiple images Source: Higgins, 'MH17 – The Open Source Evidence,' 9.

as evidence is best exemplified in the identification of 'fingerprints', unique markers on the particular vehicle. One of these is the partially erased number on the side of the launcher, as seen in Figure 2.

Through everyday images, the vehicle is located in Russia, its movements through separatist controlled parts of Ukraine on the day of the attack and back to Russia on the day after the downing of MH17 are detailed.[65] Key moments of the story, such as the missile launcher's unloading from a low-loader truck that carried it under transport and movement on its own,[66] and the smoke trail pointing towards a launch area,[67] are documented by single or at the most two independent photographs or videos, making these images of crucial importance to the attribution of responsibility for the downing of the civilian plane.

While these images have possibly been no more than everyday snapshots of a large military vehicle when taken and shared, their use to document a probable major war crime killing hundreds of civilians invests the images with a completely different weight and agency vis-à-vis the conflict. That this changed agency is not of visible concern to Bellingcat is illustrated by their inclusion of a screenshot, shown in Figure 3, of the twitter post including one of the crucial videos. Introducing

**Figure 3.** Smoke trail, possibly from the missile that shot down MH17 (Higgins, "MH17 – The Open Source Evidence," 5).

the post with a sentence highlighting the good intelligence work done by the poster, Bellingcat's report states that '[t]he next sighting of the Buk was reported from the town of Zuhres, east of Donetsk, in a social media post that included a video of the Buk being transported by a low-loader matching the low-loader photographed by Paris Match in Donetsk. The post also stated the time it was reportedly recorded and the coordinates of the Buk' (Figure 4).

The publication of not only the video itself – necessary in order to document the movement of the missile launcher – but of a screenshot including the twitter handle of the image poster as well as of someone mentioned in the tweet shows that, at least on this occasion, the possible repercussions for the image producer were not of Bellingcat's concerns.

## Image actants and the visual security paradox

Scholarship in media studies and its intersection with international relations has, since the advent of major online image-sharing platforms around 2005, analysed the impact of civilians' images in relation mainly to news media representation of conflict. This includes analyses of the image use practices connected to the war on terror,[68] to crises in Burma in 2007,[69] in Iran in 2009[70] and in the later Arab Spring.[71] In this literature, civilians are often rendered discursively as something else than civilians – e.g. citizen journalists or amateur photographers – in ways that in one or other respect serves to legitimize the appropriation of their pictures – even if the terms are developed for different purposes. 'Amateur images', a widely used phrase that opposes civilians to professional photographers, is undoubtedly meant to convey the non-professional character of the image producer and different aesthetic of the images produced.[72] But the designation can also make it easier to appropriate images without concern for copyright. Likewise, the term citizen journalism[73] – adapted to civilian media production but developed with regard to concerted efforts to provide an alternative form of journalism – implies journalistic motivations where they may not be present, something that can again have the discursive effect of legitimizing further spread of images thought of in terms of citizen journalism.

In contrast, at least some work in security theory has highlighted the dilemmas presented to civilians when these become part of conflict and security practices. Articulations of threat and danger have been the key to new security theories, especially securitization theory. Drawing on securitization theory, we may say that what happens when actors appropriate an utterance (such as an image or a video) and use it as an argument concerning an active war is that the articulation is being made into a security articulation, i.e. an argument active in defining security politics.[74]

@d███████s location 48.016970, 38.301823
youtube.com/watch?v=6OJs1d... 17.07.14
11:40

🌐 View translation

↩ Reply  ↻ Retweet  ★ Favorite  ••• More

▶ YouTube

IMG 0647

View on web

**Figure 4.** Bellingcat publishing of tweet with video and identifying information [blacked out by researcher] (Higgins, "MH17 – The Open Source Evidence," 2).

In a creative appropriation of the idea of a security dilemma – originally conceived to describe how states or other actors in potential conflict produce mutual insecurity by seeking to bolster their own security militarily[75] – has been used to point to how individuals can paradoxically endanger themselves by seeking to articulate their security problems.[76] The dilemma describes 'a situation where the potential subject of security has no, or limited, possibility of speaking its security problem [since] an attempt to securitize one's situation would in these cases, paradoxically, activate another threat being faced'.[77] This 'silence' dilemma is thus one in which subjects with little political power are prevented from articulating the threats facing them, since doing so would pose these same subjects as threats to more powerful political forces, making silence the only appropriate answer to grave insecurity. When images are taken as evidence, a similar problem can arise when a third party appropriates civilians' images as evidence to point to a threat that then activates threats against the original, civilian, image producers. The repurposing of the image in a security argument thus changes the agency it possesses as an articulation, from an everyday visual utterance which, speaking in terms of security articulation, is without security 'gravity'[78] and thus similar to but of course not synonymous with silence. When this visual utterance is appropriated, everyday images can easily transform into statements engaged in (de)legitimizing extraordinary, violent politics – that is into security arguments that do possess gravity, perhaps even what securitization theory terms securitizing moves, i.e. statements that *do* security.[79] In this situation, the danger of making a security argument persists, but in a different form that the one argued by Hansen. Crucially, the image-producing civilian has little control over the role her everyday social media images are later mobilized to play, and over whether they become part of security arguments, advertising or memes. Unlike the agency in trying to voice one's security problem (or not doing so), image agency is a networked undertaking that only gains meaning as it exists in a network. Thus, the agency of an image is not fully determined in the moment of the production of the visual utterance but is co-determined by the network in which the utterance participates when it is (maybe) transformed into a conflict actant.[80] When images are used as intelligence about an ongoing conflict – or even about war crimes such as the crime of international aggression or the possible war crime of shooting down a civilian airliner – everyday images are made into high-powered conflict evidence, they become actants in the conflict they (perhaps inadvertently) depict.

This possibility for transformation is inherent in the photographic technology and culture – i.e. in the way we produce and interpret photographs. To Roland Barthes, the 'photographic paradox' is that while the photograph is certainly not that which it depicts, western visual culture tends to interpret it as a perfect copy of the section of reality that it depicts at the moment of depiction, even if the photograph of course changes almost all properties of that reality (excluding most of the view as well as all non-visual aspects)[81] and even if secondary messages – such as security intention – are read into the image by its spectator.

The everyday image can become a conflict actant exactly due to this paradox, that the photograph is interpreted as a copy of the reality of that moment when it was produced. This copy, then, can be mobilized to play a role in intelligence work. In this process, civilian image creators are made to – typically unwittingly and without consent – perform work traditionally done by intelligence assets and are likely to face individual security threats typically associated with intelligence work. The photographic paradox of a message without a code then translates into the security paradox of a security argument without intention, i.e. that third parties can assert a security argument in an utterance made without security intention or gravity.

The trouble identified in the 'little mermaid' security dilemma was how to understand silence as a meaningful individual security strategy, and thus understand that a securitization theory that sees only security articulation will remain blind to security problems of the weak. In a civilians' visual security paradox, the trouble becomes how to understand the agency and meaning of visual utterances as produced partly independently of the utterance, yet still with consequences for the actor seen as uttering.

## Civilian images and intelligence: do civilians exist online?

The situation effected when third-party actors appropriate civilians' images from conflict zones and use them as intelligence is a danger for civilians caught up in contemporary conflict, as both states, NGOs and civilian initiatives appropriate images to publicly document conflict. For states and other politically motivated actors, this has the advantage not only of being cheap and risk free but also that the resulting evidence can be made public without compromising valued intelligence assets, as these assets are unwitting intelligence participants in the first place, and the activities they undertake are not undertaken for intelligence purposes. The lack of value and consideration for these new intelligence assets who, despite being found online, are every bit as human as previous assets, is clear from the recommendation in a research paper on open-source intelligence from the Danish Defence Academy, which advises the different branches of the Danish military, that 'we want to encourage all intelligence analyst and collectors to use OSINT [open source intelligence] and social media actively regardless of specialty or function'.[82] The report de-humanises the human intelligence providers – the civilians posting images and text online – by rendering them 'avatars' and contains no reflection on which kind of position civilians are placed in when intelligence actors aim to 'fully exploit social media for intelligence purposes', instead arguing that '[f]or the intelligence services, social media is an element that cannot be ignored. It holds immense amount of information, and the potential to extract useful intelligence'.[83] Such exploitation, and the little consideration given to the civilians being repurposed as intelligence assets, is in many ways a continuation not only of intelligence practices and the antagonistic relations built around them (see other contribution in this volume) but also of the above-mentioned media exploitation of unknown civilians as 'amateur photographers' and 'citizen journalists'. These widespread practices raise fundamental questions about the translation of civilian-ness to the online sphere – whether the norms protecting certain categories of people, developed during centuries of conflict, are being translated to encompass civilians and non-combatants online, or whether such translation is unsuccessful.

Today's prominence of images in articulating security and conflict changes the security-as-silence problematique, as images can perform as free-standing evidence. This gives the possibility that the individual 'speaker' can be empowered by the possibility to voice an argument about a security problem without having to be identified as the author of the argument.[84] However, it also makes possible that actors beyond the control of an amateur image producer turn an everyday visual articulation (a digital photograph or a video) into a powerful security argument (e.g. accusing a state of committing a war crime) by presenting it as evidence, without having to bother with obtaining the consent of the author of the image. The argument may then 'activate another threat' towards the image producer just like in the security-as-silence dilemma, but the speaker does not have the possibility of controlling whether to be silent or to risk voicing the argument, as this is assembled by a third actor.

Appropriation of civilians' images as parts of a conflict – whether as intelligence, propaganda or both – not only may activate threats towards individual image producers but also deprives these of the right to look and to constitute the world through producing and sharing images.[85] This is evident if we look at contemporary conflict in western societies: Citing evidence that terrorist organizations were using civilian-produced open source evidence (images and/or verbal statements) to plan and surveil attacks and avoid capture, French and Belgian police forces have recently requested civilians not to tweet or film antiterror operations,[86] showing how civilians' imaging practices or 'media lives'[87] are affected when civilian-produced images are leveraged in violent conflicts as 'open source intelligence'.

## Notes

1. Deuze, "Media Life."
2. Pantti and Andén-Papadopoulos, "Transparency and Trustworthiness."
3. Gjerding, "Borgere Har Indtaget Rollen Som Demokratiets Vagthunde."
4. Ostrovsky, "Selfie Soldiers."
5. Bensmann and Crawford, "Flight MH17 Searching for the Truth."
6. Higgins, "MH17 – The Open Source Evidence."
7. See Endnote 5.
8. Higgins, "Geolocating the Missile Launcher Linked to the Downing of MH17."
9. See Endnote 5 .
10. See Endnote 8.
11. In the sense of Marres and Lezaun, "Materials and Devices of the Public."
12. Comment to Higgins, "Geolocating the Missile Launcher Linked to the Downing of MH17."
13. Ostrovsky, "Selfie Soldiers," pt. 13:03.

14. Ostrovsky, pt. 19:40.
15. N. P. R. Staff, "Snapshot Sleuthing Confirms Russian Military Presence In Ukraine."
16. Rose, *Visual Methodologies*.
17. Peirce, *Peirce on Signs*, cf. Barthes, "Rhetoric of Image".
18. cf. Grusin, "Premediation."
19. Kittler, *Gramophone, Film, Typewriter*, 110.
20. Benjamin, "The Work of Art in the Age of Its Mechanical Reproduction."
21. Leonard, "Why Facial Recognition Failed."
22. Nunez, "Tips for Activists Using the YouTube Face Blur Tool."
23. Amoore, "Vigilant Visualities," 221.
24. Lyon, *The Electronic Eye*.
25. Bigo, "Security, Exeption, Ban and Surveillance."
26. Amoore, "Vigilant Visualities," 220.
27. Chouliaraki, *The Ironic Spectator*, 5.
28. Shapiro, "Strategic Discourse/Discursive Strategy"; Allan and Andén-Papadopoulos, "Come on, Let Us Shoot!"; and Andersen, *Remediating Security*.
29. Chouliaraki, "RE-Mediation, Inter-Mediation, Trans-Mediation."
30. Allan and Andén-Papadopoulos, "'Come on, Let Us Shoot!'"; and US DoD and WikiLeaks, "Collateral Murder – Wikileaks (Un-Edited Version)."
31. In the sense of Bolter and Grusin, *Remediation*.
32. US DoD and WikiLeaks, "Collateral Murder – Wikileaks (Un-Edited Version)."
33. Andersen, *Remediating Security*, 217.
34. Bolter and Grusin, *Remediation*.
35. Barthes, "Rhetoric of the Image," 44.
36. Amoore, "Vigilant Visualities," 223.
37. Beauman, "How to Conduct an Open-Source Investigation."
38. Weizman, *Forensic Architecture*, 72.
39. See Endnote 1.
40. Czuperski and Atlantic Council of the United States, *Hiding in Plain Sight*.
41. Amnesty International, "Surveillance and Activism."
42. Andersen, *Remediating Security*, 9 ff.
43. MacAskill, "Does US Evidence Prove Russian Special Forces Are in Eastern Ukraine?"; and Weir, "Russia Debuts New, Sleek Force in Crimea, Rattling NATO."
44. Damon, Pearson, and Payne, "Ukraine: Photos Show Undercover Russian Troops"; Gordon and Kramer, "Scrutiny Over Photos Said to Tie Russia Units to Ukraine"; Higgins, Gordon, and Kramer, "Photos Link Masked Men in East Ukraine to Russia"; and MacAskill, "Does US Evidence Prove Russian Special Forces Are in Eastern Ukraine?"
45. Delegation of Ukraine, Statement by the Delegation of Ukraine at the 55-th joing FSC-PC plenary meeting.
46. Delegation of Ukraine; Higgins, Gordon, and Kramer, "Photos Link Masked Men in East Ukraine to Russia."
47. Higgins, Gordon, and Kramer, "Photos Link Masked Men in East Ukraine to Russia."
48. As cited in Sullivan, "Aftermath of Ukraine Photo Story Shows Need for More Caution."
49. Ibid.
50. As reported in Gordon and Kramer, "Scrutiny Over Photos Said to Tie Russia Units to Ukraine."
51. See Endnote 41.
52. Czuperski and Atlantic Council of the United States, *Hiding in Plain Sight*, 8.
53. Andersen and Möller, "Engaging the Limits of Visibility."
54. See Endnote 53.
55. Ibid.
56. Czuperski and Atlantic Council of the United States, *Hiding in Plain Sight*, 8, my emphasis.
57. See Endnote 53.
58. Czuperski and Atlantic Council of the United States, *Hiding in Plain Sight*, 25–28.
59. Ibid., 16.
60. Czuperski and Atlantic Council of the United States, *Hiding in Plain Sight*, 20, my italics.
61. Weaver, "How Brown Moses Exposed Syrian Arms Trafficking from His Front Room"; and Brown Moses Blog, "More Background On Croatian Weapons In Syria."
62. Czuperski and Atlantic Council of the United States, *Hiding in Plain Sight*, 1.
63. See Endnote 6.
64. Higgins 2015.
65. All of the movements are visualized in an interactive map at https://www.mapbox.com/labs/bellingcat/index.html.

66. https://www.bellingcat.com/resources/case-studies/2014/07/17/geolocating-the-missile-launcher-linked-to-the-downing-of-mh17/.
67. http://twitter.com/wowihay/status/489807649509478400 Higgins, "MH17 – The Open Source Evidence," 4.
68. Hoskins and O'Loughlin, "Remediating Jihad for Western News Audiences"; and O'Loughlin, "Images as Weapons of War."
69. Andersen, "Meta-Mediation, Visual Agency and Documentarist Reflexivity in Conflict Film."
70. Mortensen, "When Citizen Photojournalism Sets the News Agenda"; Andersen, 'Remediating #IranElection"; and Semati and Brookey, "Not 'For Neda.'"
71. See Endnote 30.
72. Pantti and Andén-Papadopoulos, "Transparency and Trustworthiness"; and Kristensen and Mortensen, "Amateur Sources Breaking the News."
73. Andersen, "Remediating #IranElection." adopts the term citizen micro-journalism to highlight that while civilians do journalism-like work, they do not follow journalistic norms and are likely to have different concerns.
74. Buzan, Wæver, and Wilde, *Security: A New Framework for Analysis*; McDonald, "Securitization and the Construction of Security"; Huysmans, "What's in an Act?"; and Saugmann Andersen, "Video, Algorithms, and Security."
75. Herz, "Idealist Internationalism and the Security Dilemma."
76. Hansen, "The Little Mermaid's Silent Security Dilemma."
77. Ibid., 294.
78. Huysmans, "What's in an Act?"
79. Buzan, Wæver, and Wilde, *Security: A New Framework for Analysis*.
80. Saugmann Andersen, "Video, Algorithms, and Security."
81. Barthes, "The Photographic Message," 17.
82. Juhlin, "Project Avatar," 27.
83. Ibid., 2.
84. See Endnote 82.
85. Mirzoeff, *The Right to Look*.
86. Cronin, "Brussels Police Tweet Calls For Social Media Blackout."
87. See Endnote 1.

## Disclosure statement

No potential conflict of interest was reported by the author.

## ORCID

Rune Saugmann  (iD)  http://orcid.org/0000-0002-6936-8845

## Bibliography

Allan, S., and K. Andén-Papadopoulos. "'Come On, Let Us Shoot!': WikiLeaks and the Cultures of Militarization." *Topia: Canadian Journal of Cultural Studies* 2010, no. 23–24 (2010): 244–253.
Amnesty International. 2018. "Surveillance and Activism: Keeping Your Data Safe." *amnesty.org*, August 1. https://www.amnesty.org/en/latest/research/2018/08/eng-comic-1/
Amoore, L. "Vigilant Visualities: The Watchful Politics of the War on Terror." *Security Dialogue* 38, no. 2 (2007): 215–232. doi:10.1177/0967010607078526.
Andersen, R. S. "Remediating #Iranelection: Journalistic Strategies for Positioning Citizen-Made Snapshots and Text Bites from the 2009 Iranian Post-Election Conflict." *Journalism Practice* 6, no. 3 (2012): 317–336. doi:10.1080/17512786.2012.663593.

Andersen, R. S. "Meta-Mediation, Visual Agency and Documentarist Reflexivity in Conflict Film: Burma VJ Meets Burke + Norfolk." In *Documenting World Politics*, edited by C. Sylvest and R. van Munster. Popular Culture and World Politics, 150–166. Abingdon: Routledge, 2015.

Andersen, R. S. *Remediating Security. A Semiotic Framework for Analyzing How Video Speaks Security*. Copenhagen: University of Copenhagen, Department of Political Science, 2015.

Andersen, R. S., and F. Möller. "Engaging the Limits of Visibility." *Security Dialogue* 44, no. 3 (2013): 203–221. doi:10.1177/0967010613484955.

Barthes, R. "Rhetoric of the Image." In *Image Music Text*, Translated by Stephen Heath, 32–52. London: Fontana Press, 1977.

Barthes, R. "The Photographic Message." In *Image Music Text*. London: Fontana Press, 1977.

Beauman, N. 2018. "How to Conduct an Open-Source Investigation, According to the Founder of Bellingcat." *The New Yorker*, August 30. https://www.newyorker.com/culture/culture-desk/how-to-conduct-an-open-source-investigation-according-to-the-founder-of-bellingcat

Benjamin, W. "The Work of Art in the Age of Its Mechanical Reproduction." In *Illuminations*. New York: Fontana, 1936. http://www.marxists.org/reference/subject/philosophy/works/ge/benjamin.htm

Bensmann, M., and D. Crawford. 2015. "Flight MH17 Searching for the Truth." *CORRECT!V, Spiegel, Algemeen Dagblad*, September 1. https://mh17.correctiv.org/english/#toggle-id-1

Bigo, D. "Security, Exeption, Ban and Surveillance." In *Theorizing Surveillance: The Panopticon and Beyond*, edited by David Lyon, 46–68. Devon, UK: Willian Publishing, 2006.

Bolter, J., and R. A. Grusin. *Remediation : Understanding New Media*. edited by 1st MIT press pbk. Cambridge, MA: MIT Press, 2000.

Brown Moses Blog. 2013. "More Background On Croatian Weapons In Syria." February 26. http://brown-moses.blogspot.fi/2013/02/more-background-on-croatian-weapons-in.html

Buzan, B., O. Wæver, and J. de Wilde. *Security: A New Framework for Analysis*. Boulder, CO: Lynne Rienner, 1998.

Chouliaraki, L. "Re-Mediation, Inter-Mediation, Trans-Mediation. The Cosmopolitan Trajectories of Convergent Journalism." *Journalism Studies* 14, no. 2 (April, 2013): 267–283. doi:10.1080/1461670X.2012.718559.

Chouliaraki, L. *The Ironic Spectator: Solidarity in the Age of Post-Humanitarianism*. Cambridge, MA: Polity, 2013.

Cronin, M. 2015. "Brussels Police Tweet Calls for Social Media Blackout during Search for Paris Attack Suspect." November 22. http://gawker.com/brussels-police-tweet-calls-for-social-media-blackout-d-1744082522

Czuperski, M., and Atlantic Council of the United States, eds. *Hiding in Plain Sight: Putin's War in Ukraine*. Washington, DC: The Atlantic Council of the United States, 2015.

Damon, A., M. Pearson, and E. Payne. 2014. "Ukraine: Photos Show Undercover Russian Troops." *CNN.com*. CNN, April 22. http://edition.cnn.com/2014/04/21/world/europe/ukraine-crisis/

Delegation of Ukraine. "Statement by the Delegation of Ukraine at the 55-Th Joing FSC-PC Plenary Meeting." In *Pub. L. No. FSC-PC.DEL/15/14, § OSCE 55-th joint FSC-PC plenary meeting*. 4 vols. 2014. http://www.osce.org/fsc/118277

Deuze, M. "Media Life." *Media, Culture & Society* 33, no. 1 (2011): 137–148. January 1. doi:10.1177/0163443710386518.

Gjerding, S. 2015. "Borgere Har Indtaget Rollen Som Demokratiets Vagthunde." *Information*, October 23. http://www.information.dk/549505

Gordon, M. R., and A. E. Kramer. 2014. "Scrutiny over Photos Said to Tie Russia Units to Ukraine." *The New York Times*, April 22. http://www.nytimes.com/2014/04/23/world/europe/scrutiny-over-photos-said-to-tie-russia-units-to-ukraine.html

Grusin, R. A. "Premediation." *Criticism* 46, no. 1 (2004): 17–39. doi:10.1353/crt.2004.0030.

Hansen, L. "The Little Mermaid's Silent Security Dilemma and the Absence of Gender in the Copenhagen School." *Millennium* 29, no. 2 (2000): 285–306. doi:10.1177/03058298000290020501.

Herz, J. H. "Idealist Internationalism and the Security Dilemma." *World Politics* 2, no. 2 (1950): 157–180. doi:10.2307/2009187.

Higgins, A., M. R. Gordon, and A. E. Kramer. 2014. "Photos Link Masked Men in East Ukraine to Russia." *The New York Times*, April 20. http://www.nytimes.com/2014/04/21/world/europe/photos-link-masked-men-in-east-ukraine-to-russia.html

Higgins, E. 2014. "Geolocating the Missile Launcher Linked to the Downing of MH17." *bellingcat*, July 17. https://www.bellingcat.com/resources/case-studies/2014/07/17/geolocating-the-missile-launcher-linked-to-the-downing-of-mh17/

Higgins, E. 2015. "MH17 – The Open Source Evidence." *bellingcat.com*, October 8. https://www.bellingcat.com/news/uk-and-europe/2015/10/08/mh17-the-open-source-evidence/

Hoskins, A., and B. O'Loughlin. "Remediating Jihad for Western News Audiences: The Renewal of Gatekeeping?" *Journalism* 12, no. 2 March 9 (2011): 199–216. doi:10.1177/1464884910388592.

Huysmans, J. "What's in an Act? On Security Speech Acts and Little Security Nothings." *Security Dialogue* 42, no. 4–5 (2011): 371–383. October 21. doi:10.1177/0967010611418713.

Juhlin, J. A. 2016. "Project Avatar: Intelligence Exploration of Social Media and Open Sources." *Research Paper - Cyber*. Copenhagen: Royal Danish Defence College. http://www.fak.dk/publikationer/Pages/ProjectAvatar.aspx

Kittler, F. *Gramophone, Film, Typewriter*. Translated by Dorothea von Mücke and Philippe Similon. *October* 41 (summer 1987). doi:10.2307/778332.

Kristensen, N. N., and M. Mortensen. "Amateur Sources Breaking the News, Metasources Authorizing the News of Gaddafi's Death: New Patterns of Journalistic Information Gathering and Dissemination in the Digital Age." *Digital Journalism* 1, no. 3 (October, 2013): 352–367. doi:10.1080/21670811.2013.790610.

Leonard, A. 2013. "Why Facial Recognition Failed." April 22. http://www.salon.com/2013/04/22/why_facial_recogni tion_failed/

Lyon, D. *The Electronic Eye: The Rise of Surveillance Society*. Minneapolis: University of Minnesota Press, 1994.

MacAskill, E. 2014. "Does US Evidence Prove Russian Special Forces are in Eastern Ukraine?" *The Guardian*, April 22. http://www.theguardian.com/world/2014/apr/22/-sp-does-us-evidence-prove-russian-special-forces-are-in-eastern-ukraine

Marres, N., and J. Lezaun. "Materials and Devices of the Public: An Introduction." *Economy and Society* 40, no. 4, November (2011): 489–509. doi:10.1080/03085147.2011.602293.

McDonald, M. "Securitization and the Construction of Security." *European Journal of International Relations* 14, no. 4 (2008): 563–587. doi:10.1177/1354066108097553.

Mirzoeff, N. *The Right to Look : A Counterhistory of Visuality*. Durham, NC: Duke University Press, 2011.

Mortensen, M. "When Citizen Photojournalism Sets the News Agenda: Neda Agha Soltan as a Web 2.0 Icon of Post-Election Unrest in Iran." *Global Media and Communication* 7, April 21 (2011): 4–16. doi:10.1177/1742766510397936.

Nunez, B. 2012. "Tips for Activists Using the YouTube Face Blur Tool." WITNESS. *WITNESS* (blog). http://blog.witness.org/2012/08/tips-for-activists-using-the-youtube-face-blur-tool/

O'Loughlin, B. "Images as Weapons of War: Representation, Mediation and Interpretation." *Review of International Studies* 37, no. 1 (January, 2011): 71–91. doi:10.1017/S0260210510000811.

Ostrovsky, S. 2015. "Selfie Soldiers: Russia Checks in to Ukraine." Documentary. *Vice News*. https://news.vice.com/video/selfie-soldiers-russia-checks-in-to-ukraine

Pantti, M., and K. Andén-Papadopoulos. "Transparency and Trustworthiness: Strategies for Incorporating Amateur Photography into News Discourse." In *Amateur Images and Global News*, edited by K. Andén-Papadopoulos and M. Pantti, 97–112. Bristol, Chicago: Intellect, 2011.

Peirce, C. S. *Peirce on Signs: Writings on Semiotic*. Chapel Hill: University of North Carolina Press, 1991.

Rose, G. *Visual Methodologies. An Introduction to the Interpretation of Visual Materials*. 2nd ed. London: SAGE, 2001.

Saugmann Andersen, R. "Video, Algorithms, and Security. How Digital Video Platforms Produce Post-Sovereign Security Articulations." *Security Dialogue* 48, no. 4 (2017): 354–372. doi:10.1177/09607101601671770099875.

Semati, M., and R. A. Brookey. "Not 'For Neda': Digital Media, (Citizen) Journalism and the Invention of a Postfeminist Martyr." *Communication, Culture & Critique* 7, no. 2 (2014): 137–153. doi:10.1111/cccr.12042.

Shapiro, M. J. "Strategic Discourse/Discursive Strategy: The Representation of 'Security Policy' in the Video Age." *International Studies Quarterly* 34, no. 3 (1990): 327–340. doi:10.2307/2600573.

Sullivan, M. "Aftermath of Ukraine Photo Story Shows Need for More Caution." *Public Editor's Journal*, April 24 (2014). http://publiceditor.blogs.nytimes.com/2014/04/24/aftermath-of-ukraine-photo-story-shows-need-for-more-caution/

US DoD, and WikiLeaks. 2010. "Collateral Murder - Wikileaks (Un-Edited Version)." *Wikileaks*. http://www.youtube.com/watch?feature=player_embedded&v=5rXPrfnU3G0

Weaver, M. 2013. "How Brown Moses Exposed Syrian Arms Trafficking from His Front Room." March 21. http://www.theguardian.com/world/2013/mar/21/frontroom-blogger-analyses-weapons-syria-frontline

Weir, F. 2014. "Russia Debuts New, Sleek Force in Crimea, Rattling NATO." *csmonitor.com*, April 3. http://www.csmonitor.com/World/Europe/2014/0403/Russia-debuts-new-sleek-force-in-Crimea-rattling-NATO

Weizman, E. *Forensic Architecture: Violence at the Threshold of Detectability*. Brooklyn, NY: Zone Books, 2017.

# Is social media intelligence private? Privacy in public and the nature of social media intelligence

Kira Vrist Rønn and Sille Obelitz Søe

**ABSTRACT**

SOCMINT (SOCial Media INTelligence) is increasingly considered relevant and cost efficient information, and the exploitation of social media information in the name of security and public safety is generally regarded as unproblematic. We will critically scrutinize this claim and argue that the exploitation of such information by Intelligence and Security Services raises new ethical concerns. Drawing on recent moral discussions about privacy, we will argue that individuals have an interest in privacy in public spaces, including online spaces. We will discuss the role of such public privacy interests and argue that the systematic surveillance of social media platforms by security authorities potentially entail a negative chilling effect.

## 1. Introduction

'The opportunities that the explosion of social media use offers are remarkable. SOCMINT must become a full member of the intelligence and law enforcement family.'[1]

This is one of the concluding remarks by Sir David Omand, Jamie Bartlett, and Carl Miller in a paper from 2012 on the use of social media intelligence (SOCMINT). The paper depicts a 'rapid growth of interest by law enforcement in intelligence derived from social media' and calls for a methodological and ethical framework for its use.[2] The need for such a framework seems more pressing than ever. Recently, social media data has been used for case management within the Danish tax system as well as by insurance companies in order to uncover fraud,[3] and the potential for intelligence and security services has been deemed massive and cost efficient.[4] For decades, the promise of big data analytics has been alluring as well as severely criticized. The recent scandal concerning Cambridge Analytica's exploitation of Facebook user data and the public outcry that followed show some of the potential for gathering information on social media platforms as well as the expectations of the average platform user. Presumably, what Cambridge Analytica did was to affect the 2016 US presidential election by targeting Facebook users with customized political ads based on personal information harvested through tests and quizzes on Facebook (at least that is what they say they did). Cambridge Analytica exploited Facebook's business model and they exploited the consent given by users when taking the test or quiz. The legal problem in the Cambridge Analytica case was not that they gathered information from and targeted the users who had taken the tests and quizzes. It was that they also gathered information on and targeted the users' friends, who had not consented to the use of their data by Cambridge Analytica. Morally speaking, there may be problems with both types of information gathering. Further, the public outcry shows that people in general do not feel comfortable with systemic gathering of their personal data and information.

In this case, they felt strongly that their privacy had been invaded and that their personal information had been used against them.

Intelligence and security agencies have always tried to intercept public (as well as private) life in order to gather intelligence about possible events and actions.[5] When public life moves into the realm of social media and digital platforms it is no surprise that intelligence services and practices follow suit. The question remains the same: should we have privacy in public spaces?

The nature of public and private spaces has changed in the 'digital age', and it has become even more unclear where the distinction between private and public spaces should be drawn when it comes to online spaces, which are non-physical and mediated by a digital device.[6] Consequently, a clear-cut notion of when and why online privacy should be respected is likewise difficult to capture. For instance, all activities on social media such as Facebook and Twitter are meticulously tracked and stored all the time – as far as we know for good.

Social media have a kind of dual nature: they are public but often feel private, and information from social media is therefore situated in a 'grey zone' between public and private.[7] Although the information can easily be accessed, the pressing question is whether and under which circumstances it is morally permissible for government authorities to gain access to personal social media accounts and exploit the information for safety and security issues.[8] Actual practice shows that, for the moment, we cannot expect any kind of privacy on social media, but that does not mean that we do not have an interest in such privacy both now and in the future.

In this paper, we will look at the ethical perspectives and implications of SOCMINT.[9] We will ask whether SOCMINT presents any moral challenges as regards privacy. We will not look into the legal perspectives of SOCMINT and privacy. The collection and use of SOCMINT might often be legally unproblematic, since the information is publicly available and accessed in what could be called a public space. However, there may still be some ethical problems and challenges that need consideration. In section 2, we will present and briefly discuss the concept of privacy. We will focus on *informational privacy* as the concept most closely linked to SOCMINT.[10] In section 3, we look at the use and exploitation of SOCMINT in a security setting. We will look into various cases where SOCMINT has had an actual effect on the outcome of the case. Section 4 is dedicated to discussions of the moral permissibility of SOCMINT. Based on the premise that social media platforms are public spaces (despite often feeling like private settings), we will argue that government security agencies in some cases – those characterized by *indiscriminate access* – should refrain from accessing information contained in social media profiles. The main reason for this is the potential chilling effects on the ways in which citizens act and communicate on social media platforms. We further argue that social media should be regarded as a value of democratic society which should not be indiscriminately exploited by officials. In section 5, we offer some brief concluding remarks.

## 2. Privacy

'The term "privacy" is used frequently in ordinary language as well as in philosophical, political and legal discussions, yet there is no single definition or analysis or meaning of the term.'[11]

However, '[s]ince the latter half of the twentieth century, privacy has increasingly come to be associated with concerns about protecting one's personal information, which is now easily collected and stored electronically and easily exchanged between electronic databases.'[12] Rapid technological developments and the emergence of social media are two of the reasons for the strong association between privacy and personal information – that is, *informational privacy*. Informational privacy is often described as the ability to control or restrict access to one's personal information. Hence, in informational privacy it is personal information (or personal data) which people have a right to or an interest in having protected. According to the philosopher Herman Tavani, informational privacy is just one of four distinct kinds of privacy, the others being physical/accessibility privacy, decisional privacy and psychological/mental privacy.[13] Physical privacy concerns the right to bodily security and the sanctuary status of the home. Thus, physical privacy denotes the right to non-intrusion of one's physical space. Decisional privacy can be described as a non-interference in people's choices, plans and decisions, whereas psychological or mental privacy is a non-intrusion or non-interference in people's thoughts and personal identities.[14] Psychological or mental privacy 'is essential either (a) for a person's awareness to think and be conscious of one's self or (b) for the protection of the integrity of one's personality.'[15] The four different kinds of privacy co-exist and overlap. Thus, a violation of physical privacy can at the same time be a violation of informational privacy, for instance when the intrusion into someone's home gives the intruder access to otherwise restricted personal information. Likewise, the violation of informational privacy can at the same time be a violation of decisional privacy if, for instance, the lack of control over one's personal information affects and interferes with one's possibilities for making choices and decisions.

Most accounts of privacy deal with the concept as either *a unitary, a derivative*, or *a cluster concept*. In defining privacy as a unitary concept, the task – and challenge – is to distinguish privacy from other related concepts (such as secrecy and confidentiality) in order to clarify the notion. Derivative approaches to privacy are linked to the idea of privacy as a right and therefore define privacy as derivations from other basic rights such as the right to property and bodily security.[16] Finally, approaching privacy as a cluster concept entails that our intuitions about privacy are of such varied nature that no single concept can capture them all. Our various privacy interests are best seen as a cluster of related concepts – related in ways similar to the Wittgensteinian idea of family resemblance.[17] Privacy is most often seen as a value we ought to protect. However, the philosopher Judith DeCew argues that:

> Discussion of the concept [of privacy] is complicated by the fact that privacy appears to be something we value to provide a sphere within which we can be free from interference by others, and yet it also appears to function negatively, as the cloak under which one can hide domination, degradation, or physical harm to women and others.[18]

This is the constant dilemma of privacy as well as many kinds of intelligence activities – i.e., that it is necessary to violate individuals' privacy in order to uncover shady activities – and the reason why the intelligence literature often points to a conception of intelligence ethics as an *oxymoron*.[19] Debates about privacy also deal with questions concerning *why* we value privacy. According to Solove, debates about why privacy is valuable turn on the question of whether privacy has intrinsic or instrumental value, and further of whether privacy is about 'a moral duty to respect each individual's dignity and autonomy' (Kantian deontology) or is valued 'in terms of its practical consequences' balanced 'against opposing interests' (Solove's own pragmatic and consequentialist account).[20] The political philosopher Annabelle Lever proposes a different account of why privacy is valuable and important:

> For example, the point of protecting privacy, from a democratic perspective, is not that privacy is some preeminent individual good because of its connection to human dignity, intimate and familial relationships or to property ownership – as it would be from liberal perspectives. Privacy may or may not be justified on these grounds. The point, rather, is that protection for anonymity, confidentiality, seclusion, and intimacy – to name a few characteristics of privacy – helps to foster the freedom and equality necessary for democratic politics by structuring and limiting competition for power in ways that enable people to see and treat each other as equal despite incompatible beliefs, interests and identities.[21]

Thus, for Lever, privacy is one of the core components of a well-functioning democracy. Without privacy protection and privacy rights people will not be capable of taking part in democratic politics. Without the possibility of freely opposing the majority view, deliberative democracy cannot function (we will return to Lever's claim in section 4).

## 2.1. Informational privacy

As mentioned, informational privacy concerns the protection of personal information. Thus, personal information is the core notion of informational privacy. However, it is not always clear what personal information actually is. According to the European Commission's Data Protection Working Party, personal information is information about, or relating to, identified or identifiable individuals.[22] In online spaces, personal information is most often depicted as, or tacitly understood to be, *digital footprints* – that is, digital traces of people and their actions with a 1:1 correspondence to their personalities.[23] The underlying assumption is that this personal information is truthful, conducive to truth, or correct in some sense. However, this is not necessarily the case, since people do all sorts of things online for various reasons – what they do will not necessarily reflect their own preferences or someone else's preferences at all. In fact, they may do deliberately misleading things in order to protect their privacy.[24] The sociologists Haggerty and Ericson propose that online profiles should be referred to as *data doubles*, a term that emphasizes that these are not accurate depictions of real-life people. Instead they are Deleuzian assemblages created by online actions, networks and relations.[25] Thus, we oppose the concept of *digital footprints* by questioning the idea of data and information as equivalent to fact.[26] However, through the gathering of enormous amounts of personal information, the platforms become capable of deriving patterns and inferring new personal information (whether correct or incorrect, non-misleading or misleading, or simply just messy). Thus, informational privacy in platform settings is a question of protecting against illegitimate access to and use of personal information. Further, protection of informational privacy is often defined as the restriction of access to personal information or control of the flow of personal information. This restriction of access or control is exercised through the use of *informed consent* – that is, we have to consent to others gaining access to our personal information.[27] Informed consent is a central concept when addressing the question of informational privacy on social media platforms. Users give the specific platform their consent to allow the companies to access and use their personal information which is available on the specific platform. However, if it is possible for the platforms to infer new personal information, as argued above, it becomes difficult if not impossible to restrict access to and control over the flow of such information.[28]

Another dimension of information aggregation, data mining, and profiling (the techniques used to derive and produce new personal information) is the concept of *participatory surveillance*. According to Fernanda Bruno: 'Participation has been understood as the defining principle of digital culture, having consolidated itself as one of the most important models for action, sociability, communication, and content production and distribution, especially on the internet.'[29] The idea is that, by participating on social media platforms, ordinary people enable the surveillance of themselves and others, and partake in the actual surveillance themselves. The various surveillance procedures designed for ordinary users to monitor family and friends all 'appear to have one thing in common: the assumption that this information has some degree of authenticity or power as evidence that encourages and excites not only police and corporate inspection, but also curiosity, voyeurism, distrust and watchfulness in affective and personal relationships.'[30] This participatory surveillance by family and friends adds yet another layer to the impossibility of restriction of access and control over the flow of personal information. Platforms and digital tools are designed to exploit our curiosity and our desire be part of groups and social structures.

The possibility of inferring, deriving, generating or producing new personal information – whether by platform providers, ordinary co-users or authorities – is the reason why Solove criticizes what he calls the *reasonable-expectation-of-privacy* approach to addressing and identifying privacy interests. In this approach, people's actual actions as well as what society deems reasonable to expect are used to identify privacy interests. However, as Solove argues 'Without a normative component to establish what society should recognize as private, the reasonable-expectations approach provides only a status report on existing privacy norms rather than guides us toward shaping privacy law and policy in the future.'[31] This is due to the problem of *information asymmetries*, which arises

> when people lack adequate knowledge of how their personal information will be used, and bounded rationality, when people have difficulty applying what they know to complex situations. [...] People often surrender personal data to companies because they perceive they do not have much choice. They might also do so because they lack knowledge about the potential future uses of the information. Part of the privacy problem in these cases involves people's limited bargaining power respecting privacy and inability to assess the privacy risks. Thus looking at people's behavior might present a skewed picture of societal expectations of privacy.[32]

It is exactly the problem of information asymmetries which is at play on social media platforms. It is not necessarily clear to the user what they consent to when using the platform and it is certainly not clear what their information can be used for in the future – which partly depends on future technological developments (cf. section 4.2 for a critique of informed consent). However, it is not only potential future uses of personal information that might pose a privacy problem. For instance, a recent study shows that, '[c]ompared with the accuracy of various human judges [...] computer models need 10, 70, 150, and 300 Likes, respectively, to outperform an average work colleague, cohabitant or friend, family member, and spouse.'[33] Thus, the accumulation of innocent Likes on Facebook can presumably tell more about a person, when run through a computer, than that person's closest friends and family. The computer-based analysis of Likes might actually be able to tell more about a person than the person knows herself. Such prospects are only just beginning to surface in the awareness of the average user of social media platforms. Further, it is worth mentioning that although these prospects are based on a definition of personal information as *digital footprints* – a concept we oppose – it does not mean they are unproblematic. Quite the contrary. Even if the profiles that are generated are misleading, they can still intrude on people's privacy – especially if one acknowledges that putting someone in a *false light* is a privacy tort.[34]

## 2.2. *Online privacy interests*

We suggest that social media platforms have a dual nature. That is, while they feel private to users, they are in fact public spaces. George argues that people in general have an intuition of privacy when they act online, since they act online 'in the privacy of their homes or offices' and they neglect the fact that the 'transaction does not take place in the physical space they delimit as private'.[35] This dual and conflicting nature renders social media platforms gray zones when it comes to accessing and exploiting personal information. The question is who you are actually protecting your privacy against. On Facebook, the privacy settings only enable users to block other users – strangers, friends and family members – and only for certain types of information. The most basic information, such as your name and profile picture, is open to everybody. And all content is freely available to Facebook. Given this dual nature of social media platforms, a pressing question is to what extent people's privacy interests should be protected in such 'quasi-public spaces'.[36] According to Lever:

> People have privacy interests in public [...] which we can provisionally define as interests in anonymity, seclusion, confidentiality, and solitude. These are morally and politically important, even though it is unreasonable to demand the same degree of protection for our privacy in public places, to which all have access, as in areas where we are entitled to exclude others. Privacy in public places, such as parks, streets, museums, cinemas, and pubs matters because many of us live in such crowded conditions that public space provides some of our best chances for peace and quiet, for a heart-to-heart with friends, or for relaxation and fun.'[37]

Thus, Lever argues convincingly for the protection of privacy interests in physical public spaces. The question is then whether this argument should apply to quasi-public digital spaces. To return to the dual nature of social media platforms and the information available on these platforms, Tavani points out that '[t]he practice of collecting and using personal information is hardly new.'[38]

The question is whether current practices have 'introduced new kinds of privacy worries that are qualitatively different from traditional concerns.'[39] In some sense, we ask the same question in relation to social media intelligence: does the access to personal information on social media platforms introduce new privacy worries? Tavani argues that:

> the effect that computer/information technology has had for personal privacy can be analyzed in terms of four factors: (1) the amount of personal information that can be collected, (2) the speed at which personal information can be exchanged, (3) the duration of time that the information can be retained, and (4) the kind of information that can be acquired. Whereas (1)-(3) are examples of privacy concerns that differ quantitatively from traditional worries, (4) introduces a qualitatively different kind of information about persons to merit our concern.[40]

The new *qualitatively different* kind of information that can be acquired through the new technologies is the kind of information that is particularly relevant when discussing the protection of online privacy, and the factor Solove additionally points to when he speaks of information asymmetries.[41] That is, new information derived and inferred from big data pools through big data analytics. It is information which is different in kind because it is based on patterns emerging from vast amounts of personal information from billions of people, and thus a kind of information which these people can neither foresee themselves nor have deliberately fed into the platform or system. When companies and governments have the ability to acquire personal information without the awareness of the affected individuals, it becomes increasingly difficult (if not impossible) to control the information flow, restrict access to the information, and predict what it will be used for. This is what gives rise to the fourth privacy concern, the qualitatively different kind of personal information described in Tavani's analysis. It is also in relation to this privacy concern that the dual nature of social media platforms is especially problematic.

## 3. The emergence of social media intelligence

The value and importance placed on information from open sources in intelligence analysis is old news. There is a saying in the intelligence community that about 80 per cent of available and relevant intelligence is derived from open sources.[42] Social media platforms such as Facebook, Google+, Twitter and Instagram are increasingly essential elements of our social lives, and unsurprisingly they are considered significant sources of information in the context of security and public safety.[43]

The public's intense use of social media in all areas of their lives creates new possibilities for police authorities. Security and safety authorities use social media information in various ways. For instance, social media information can help the police obtain a timely and detailed impression of a particular event before arriving at the specific location – for example, a riot or a crime scene in a public place. Additionally, social media platforms are important sources of information gathered to detect specific committed crimes, and thus serve as important sources for reactive crime detection.[44] Anderson emphasizes the importance of information derived from social media profiles in the prosecution of terrorist offences in the United Kingdom:

> The significance of messaging and social media in terrorism prosecutions is immense. The CPS [the Crown Prosecution Service] reviewed a snapshot of recent prosecutions for terrorist offences and concluded that in 26 recent cases, of which 17 have concluded with a conviction, 23 could not have been pursued without communications data and in 11 cases the conviction depended on that data.[45]

Finally, social media platforms serve as important intelligence-gathering tools for police and security purposes in general, for instance in identifying potential acts of terror. As an example, the police in Seattle was able to prevent the shooting of soldiers and civilians due to information provided by citizens on social media platforms, according to the Seattle Police Department.[46] Additionally, information from social media can be used to identify potential radicalized persons or networks with the purpose of general crime prevention and early warnings.[47]

Hence, SOCMINT can potentially serve many purposes for security and safety authorities, and the value of social media information in police and intelligence work seems indisputable. The question we pose is whether the use of information from social media for the purpose of public safety or national security should be restricted for privacy reasons.

In line with George, Omand, Bartlett and Miller see social media as similar to a 'public space'. From this perspective, the status of SOCMINT could be regarded as more or less equivalent to open-source intelligence (OSINT), which is broadly speaking information derived from publicly available sources.[48] Steele defines OSINT as information which is '[not] classified at its origin; is [not] subject to proprietary constrains (other than copyright); is [not] the product of sensitive contacts with U.S. or foreign persons; or is [not] acquired through clandestine or covert means.'[49] Hence, following this definition of OSINT, most information from social media seems to equal OSINT – since it is publicly available – and it could therefore be argued that the use of SOCMINT is morally unproblematic. These ideas echo a specific line of thought in privacy studies, according to which no privacy intrusions take place as long as the personal information accessed is part of the public record – that is, is documented and publicly available – not even in future use of that information.[50]

However, even if we agree that social media platforms are public spaces (at least to some degree), the gaining of access by government authorities to information available on these platforms would equal surveillance of public spaces – especially if the access is gained systematically. Thus, the moral permissibility of systematically exploiting such information becomes more questionable, since surveillance of public spaces often entails intrusion on the privacy of the affected individuals, as argued above. We will return to this claim in the section below.

Other types of social media intelligence would obviously not be OSINT, for instance if access to social media information is acquired by clandestine means (e.g., fake profiles or hacking technologies). Omand, Bartlett, and Miller specify the distinct differences between the levels of intrusion entailed in various types of SOCMINT: 'To gather and analyze a suspect's open tweets looks similar to the surveillance of someone in public, whilst to gather and analyze someone's Facebook messages seems closer to reading their private correspondence.'[51]

Consequently, Omand, Bartlett and Miller distinguish between 'open-source, non-intrusive SOCMINT and closed-source, intrusive SOCMINT.'[52] Hence, in the following section we will further investigate the moral permissibility of accessing specific types of SOCMINT. We will start with Omand, Bartlett and Miller's claim that access to open-source information is per se non-intrusive. We will revisit and extend our claim that access to pieces of publicly available information can in fact entail intrusion of the privacy of the affected individuals and that the endeavour can also be problematic for other reasons than privacy.

## 4. The moral permissibility of accessing social media information

To shed light on the question of the permissibility of governmental authorities accessing social media profiles, we will consider two cases from Denmark below.

### 4.1. Access to personal social media profiles by authorities and other bodies

In 2011, the Danish Tax Agency used the Facebook profile of an employee to gain access to personal information about a Danish citizen (whom we shall call S), in order to check whether she had informed the Tax Agency correctly about her financial situation. When S realized this, she complained to the Danish Ombudsman, arguing that her right to privacy had been violated. The Ombudsman's conclusion was that S's privacy was not invaded in a problematic way and that the method used by the Tax Agency was not legally problematic – either according to the Danish Act on Processing of Personal Data or according to Facebook's guidelines. In the conclusion, the Ombudsman emphasized that S's Facebook profile was open to all Facebook users (i.e., public) and referred to Facebook's 'Statement of Rights and Responsibilities' from 2011, which states that:

> When you publish content or information using the Public setting, it means that you are allowing everyone, including people off of Facebook, to access and use that information, and to associate it with you (i.e., your name and profile picture).[53]

The additional fact that the Danish Tax Agency did not use a fake Facebook profile to gain access led to the conclusion that the authority could not be criticized for applying this method.[54]

A similar case recently occurred in the Danish media, when an insurance company used publicly available information from a running app and a Facebook profile in order to contest a client's claim of compensation for a neck injury.[55] The case created a lot of attention and debate about the permissibility of accessing social media profiles. However, the conclusion in this case, as in the tax case, was that the insurance company did nothing illegal since the information was publicly available and accessible. In the wake of this case, the Danish Consumer Council stated that more public awareness on the nature of social media information is needed, since posting on social media is apparently similar to publishing the information in a public newspaper.[56]

These cases do not specifically concern security and safety issues, and they may therefore involve different kinds of moral intuitions than if they concerned the uncovering of organized crime or conspiracy of terrorism, for instance. However, the cases are useful for identifying certain categories of exploitation of social media information. Both cases suggest that there is nothing legally problematic about acquiring personal information from open Facebook profiles (at least in the Danish legal context). In this sense, the cases illustrate Omand, Bartlett and Miller's distinction between open-source non-intrusive and closed-source intrusive exploitation of social media information. This conclusion, however, does not necessarily mean that the governmental use of personal information obtained from social media platforms is also morally unproblematic. Recall the concept of *participatory surveillance* emerging from the social media logic of participation as sharing of personal information and being part of a community.[57] *Participatory surveillance* suggests that the social costs of not participating and sharing personal information might be higher (or deemed higher) than worries about privacy and intrusion by authorities. Thus, people might actually feel forced to share more than they would otherwise – forced by a desire to belong and curiosity.[58] Omand, Bartlett and Miller furthermore state that: 'Just because it can be done does not mean that it should be done', and that 'there are a number of key challenges that need to be addressed before SOCMINT can be fully exploited in the interest of national security and public safety'.[59] According to these authors, such challenges include ensuring: *public acceptance* of the exploitation of such information in the name of security and public safety; that the means are *efficient*; that the information *brings value* to decision-makers; and that the use of social media information is *proportionate*.[60] According to Omand, Bartlett and Miller the exploitation of social media information is a balancing act between competing and opposing interests; a view that is similar to Solove's arguments for a pragmatic account of privacy and its value.[61]

It is beyond the scope of this paper to address all the criteria suggested by Omand, Bartlett and Miller. Therefore, below we will primarily address their suggestion concerning *public acceptance* and discuss the feasibility of this criterion in the context of social media.

### 4.2. Exploiting ignorance and the flaws of informed consent on social media

The complaint by the targeted individual in the Danish tax case illustrates to some extent that people do not necessarily feel comfortable with the fact that governmental authorities can gain access and use information from personal Facebook accounts in order to prove a case against them. This resistance towards official use of social media information could suggest that some social media users do not expect such exploitation of their social media profiles and that they have not accepted these types of actions. The question is whether this lack of public acceptance should play a role when determining the permissibility of accessing social media information.

First, the complexity of the privacy settings on Facebook suggests that public acceptance of exploitation of social media information is a tricky area. Many Facebook users are most likely not aware of the public nature of their Facebook profiles; hence many will reasonably assume that their status updates and other activities on their profiles are more or less private (at least delimited to the Facebook 'friends'). To some extent, the ignorance of social media users when it comes to the public nature of social media information is understandable. Many users of social media platforms will be acting in good faith when they assume that their privacy settings on social media platforms will prevent governmental access and other unwanted prying eyes, and one could argue that the users have a reasonable expectation of privacy.[62] Second, according to Solove's critique of 'reasonable-expectation' approaches to privacy regulation, even if privacy settings are not tricky, reasonable expectation and public acceptance still are. Solove's claim is that what people actually have reason to expect does not tell us what should be expectable and acceptable, that is, it does not provide us with normative guidelines, only a status quo. Solove's critique hinges on the problem of information asymmetries, which is exactly what is at stake when it comes to the complexity of privacy settings and personal information on Facebook (as well as on other social media platforms). To return to a previous quote by Solove:

> People often surrender personal data to companies because they perceive they do not have much choice. They might also do so because they lack knowledge about the potential future uses of the information. Part of the privacy problem in these cases involves people's limited bargaining power respecting privacy and inability to assess the privacy risks. Thus looking at people's behavior might present a skewed picture of societal expectations of privacy.[63]

We believe that the same argument and critique applies to the idea of public acceptance. This claim leads us back to the informed consent policies of social media platforms, which are somewhat problematic (to say the least). The reason for this claim is that, not only is the scope of these policies unmanageable, there is also what could be called a mismatch between the nature of social media platforms and the core idea behind consenting. Giving your informed consent to something naturally (and in very broad terms) means that you know and understand what you are consenting to. As privacy scholar Helen Nissenbaum writes:

> almost all privacy policies are long, abstruse, and legalistic [which] adds to the unrealistic burden of checking the respective policies of the websites we visit, the services we consider and use, and the content we absorb. Compounding the burden is an entity's right to change its policy at will, giving due notice of such change, ironically, within the policy itself and therefore requiring interested individuals to read it not once but repeatedly.[64]

Moreover, such policies ideally aim at respecting the autonomy and the control of personal information by the user/client, etc. The fact that Facebook users can share other users' personal information with any other of the 845 million Facebook users seems to suggest that the notions of acceptance, informed consent and privacy are in need of revision when it comes to social media. In this connection Nissenbaum makes the further claim that, 'While it may seem that individuals freely choose to pay the informational price, the price of not engaging socially, commercially, and financially may in fact be exacting enough to call into question how freely these choices are made.'[65] The free choice is for Nissenbaum based on deliberation, that is, the backbone of our democracy. Thus, Nissenbaum's critique is in line with Lever's arguments that privacy, even in public, is paramount to a democratic society. Further, Nissenbaum's critique is implicitly a critique of the exact mechanism that makes *participatory surveillance* work.

Hence, the fact that social media users have actively consented to the privacy policies of the platform does not entail that they have in fact also consented to the access and exploitation of their personal information by government authorities. The concept of consent seems to be a pseudo-concept when it is transferred to the context of social media, whereby it creates a 'transparency paradox.'[66] That is, the paradox that full transparency of the information-handling practices would be far to difficult, technical and legalistic to understand, whereas 'an abbreviated, plain-language policy' would be easy to read but also leave out all the important details which make all the difference.[67] Thus, the security and public safety authorities in many cases seem (probably unwillingly) to exploit an understandable ignorance of many social media users (or to exploit the participatory surveillance trap that these users find themselves in). The existing consent policies result in situations where the users have legally accepted the public nature of their (personal) information without necessarily understanding and endorsing this acceptance. Even though accessing information on social media is unproblematic in a legal sense, the question of permissibility appears to be more blurry from a moral perspective.

## 4.3. Privacy in public spaces

In the following section, let us revisit Omand, Bartlett and Miller's claims that social media platforms constitute public spaces, and furthermore that accessing open-source information is a non-intrusive activity, whereas only access to personal information via closed sources would be intrusive. Following their argument, if social media platforms are public spaces, then the surveillance of such platforms should be regarded as inherently non-intrusive. Above, we have contested this claim by arguing for the dual nature of social media platforms and for the informational asymmetry (and resulting challenges) of informed consent surrounding the use of social media. George calls for 'informed public discussions' on the possible harms resulting from the blurriness of the public/private nature of social media information and the commercial and official exploitation of digital personal information.[68]

We will leave this discussion on acceptance, consent and information asymmetry for now. In the following, we will follow another type of argument against the claim that access to open-source information by government authorities does not intrude on the privacy of the affected individuals. Annabelle Lever has recently written thoughtfully on people's privacy interests in public spaces.[69] She argues that, naturally, we should not expect the same kind of privacy in public spaces as we expect in our homes. However, because many of us live large parts of our lives in public spaces (e. g., in parks, streets, museums, cinemas and pubs) and because these spaces give us opportunities for 'peace and quiet, for a heart-to-heart with friends, or for relaxation and fun,' Lever argues that we do indeed have 'interests in anonymity, seclusion, confidentiality and solitude' (i.e., privacy) in public spaces.[70] Lever further argues that 'the cost to privacy of surveillance' in public spaces varies depending on the nature of the specific space (calling to mind Solove's pragmatic account of privacy). She provides an example from the British context where government authorities suggested installing CCTV cameras in every pub to reduce aggression and violence. In large pubs full of people, it is easier for the customers to hide from the cameras and blend in with the crowd, whereas in small pubs it is not as easy. Therefore, customers in large pubs (where aggression and violence are most common) would be less affected by the surveillance than customers in the small pubs (which often function as second homes). Thus, despite the fact that both types of pubs are considered public spaces, the costs to privacy of the cameras would vary significantly, meaning that privacy in public spaces is dependent on the context.[71] Lever argues that a similar dynamic is present when it comes to our online lives. Naturally, the appearance of police authorities cannot and should not be exempted from public online spaces:

> However, just as our privacy interests in parks, cinemas, streets, and pubs are more complex and diverse than is often assumed, so our privacy interests in public communications, including on the Internet, cannot be simply divided into a public area – where police scrutiny or social research is assumed to pose no problems – and a private area, where complex legal safeguards are supposed to be required before we are subject to such scrutiny. If we would be troubled by the routine presence of unidentified police officers in health clinics or public libraries, we should be uncomfortable with the suggestion that no special justification or supervision is required for police scrutiny of, and participation in, debates on public websites.[72]

Lever suggests that despite the fact that people's actions in public spaces could be subjected to systematic surveillance; the costs of doing so suggest that they shouldn't be. For instance, it might have an effect on the way we act and behave in certain public settings – a *chilling effect*. Lever further argues that:

> A uniformed police presence, for example, might inhibit us from picking up the information pamphlets on sexually transmitted diseases discreetly available in the health clinic or seeking information about cancer or drug addiction in the library. But official surveillance that we do not know about leaves us vulnerable to misinterpretation of our thoughts and actions as well as to the misuse of state power.[73]

It seems clear that citizens do indeed also have legitimate interests in privacy in online public spaces, and that accessing and collecting personal information in public spaces (both physical and digital ones) can be intrusive on the privacy of the affected individuals. The possibility of mis-interpretation of people's actions online poses a particularly serious privacy problem, and might add considerably to the *chilling effect*. People do all sorts of things online for reasons that the social media platforms do not accurately reflect. Thus, the accessed information might turn out to be misleading (i.e., misinformation or disinformation) and result in a misuse of state power.[74] The awareness that ordinary non-covert actions might be misinterpreted by authorities and others might cause users to refrain from specific actions that could be beneficial for them or others. An example could be a user not seeking advice about depression due to the fear of being mis-categorized as mentally ill, even if the advice is for a relative or friend.

When officials gain access to social media profiles in the name of public safety and security, the privacy costs will differ depending on the specific space, exactly as was the case in the example of differences in privacy costs between CCTV cameras in large and small pubs. Whereas customers in the large pubs in general would not expect a space for intimate conversations but would expect more or less to blend in with the crowd, customers in small local pubs would in general expect the opposite. The same can be said about the users of various types of social media. Users of some types of social media platforms – for example, Snapchat and Facebook's Messenger App – would expect a greater degree of privacy than the users of Twitter, which is more or less a tool for public communication. The costs and degree of privacy-intrusion, of official surveillance, will then vary depending on the specific situation.

Following Lever's analysis, we suggest that surveillance of public spaces is not inherently unproblematic, even though it might be legally unproblematic. This conclusion seems to suggest a further nuancing of the division made by Omand, Bartlett and Miller between 'open-source, non-intrusive SOCMINT and closed-source, intrusive SOCMINT',[75] since social media intelligence can in fact be both *open-source and intrusive*.

As mentioned above, the cost of surveilling public spaces will in example be a *chilling effect* whereby people will refrain from doing what they would usually do. In the worst case, such refraining can 'affect the quality of our social relations and our subjective sense of ourselves [...] as well as our objective capacities to shape our own lives [...].'[76] Hence, a relevant (yet broader) question to ask is whether free (and un-surveilled) communication on social media platforms in general and elsewhere online constitutes a societal value in need of protection – for example, in order to avoid the chilling effect that Lever argues is the outcome of systematic surveillance of such public spaces. Solove would suggest that privacy does constitute a societal value. According to him, part of the problem is that privacy is framed in individualistic terms: 'Often, privacy receives inadequate protection in the form of damages to compensate individual emotional or reputational harm; the effects of the loss of privacy on freedom, culture, creativity, innovation, and public life are not factored into the valuation.'-[77] Instead, Solove proposes a pragmatic approach whereby '[t]he value of privacy should be assessed on the basis of its contributions to society. Protecting individual privacy need not be at society's expense – in fact, the value of safeguarding people's privacy should be justified by its social benefits.'[78] Thus, Solove would agree with Lever's suggestion that we should not accept that there are no requirements of 'special justification or supervision' when officials (e.g., police) gain access to 'debates on public websites.'[79] This would lead to a call for more nuances in the way *availability* is often equated with *permissibility* in the current debates on open-source information. Perhaps stricter requirements are needed when it comes to accessing publicly available and open information. Let us look more closely at this claim in the section below.

### 4.4 Permissible SOCMINT? Random scans and targeted surveillance

The case concerning the Danish Tax Agency is useful once again when attempting to identify when accessing social media profiles and thus intruding on the privacy of the affected individuals by officials can be viewed as morally permissible or impermissible. Despite the fact that S argued that her privacy had been violated, it seems intuitively easier to justify this specific intrusion of S's privacy than if S had done nothing to attract the attention of the authority. Hence, we would argue that there is a distinct difference between surveilling individuals who have done nothing to become a target of official surveillance, and surveilling individuals who have acted in such a way that the authorities have a reasonable suspicion regarding that specific individual. Whereas Lever's examples all concern situations in which the surveilled individuals have done nothing to warrant becoming targets of the official surveillance in public spaces, S did in fact attract the attention of the authorities for a reason, and this makes a difference when it comes to judging the moral permissibility of privacy intrusions. Naturally, the question of when there is enough evidence for the authorities to gain access to, for example, social media profiles will further raise questions concerning roles and powers when legitimizing such actions.[80] Our claim here, however, is that official surveillance of social media platforms when there is no evidence or reasonable suspicion regarding the specific individuals, is indeed difficult (if not impossible) to justify. In line with this argument, Omand, Bartlett and Miller compare the use of broad and systematic scans of social media profiles to mass surveillance.[81] The post-Snowden surveillance debates suggest that mass surveillance is indeed (morally) problematic, for instance because of its indiscriminate nature.[82] Hence, if official surveillance of social media profiles equates to mass surveillance, the same kind of critique could be directed at the kind of SOCMINT characterized by no evidence of suspicion.[83] In this way, the debates on official exploitation of information on social media profiles lack nuances in regard to differentiating between the potential costs to privacy when initiating surveillance of social media profiles. The debates also suggest the need to specify the situations where such surveillance methods could be regarded as legitimate and morally permissible. Hence, we would argue that the legitimacy of accessing specific social media profiles depends on *the liability* of the affected individuals – meaning the extent to which the affected individual is implicated in the problem, which is (partly) solved by initiating the surveillance.[84] Hence, in the case of systematic scans of random social media profiles, the privacy costs and the chilling effect of such official online surveillance would be disproportionate and morally problematic, just as mass surveillance in general is morally problematic due to its indiscriminate nature.

With this said, it is beyond the scope of this paper to dive deeper into the question concerning the moral permissibility of official surveillance of social media profiles and the questions concerning liability.[85] The main aim of this paper is to broaden and elaborate the discussion concerning the privacy interests of social media users and to emphasize that core democratic values might be at stake if government authorities systematically enter social media without any specific warrant. The broader democratic effects of exploiting social media information in the name of public safety and security have not been addressed in previous scholarly debates on the possibilities of SOCMINT, and the cost-efficient approach to SOCMINT has gone somewhat unchallenged. In this paper, we have attempted to challenge the notion of SOCMINT by arguing that access to publicly available information on social media platforms can indeed be intrusive on the privacy of the affected individuals and thereby affect society at large, if we agree that privacy is 'justified by its social benefits.'[86] The intrusion would be akin to official surveillance in the waiting room of a public health clinic – it would be uncomfortable and implicate a refrainment from acting in ways we would otherwise have done; acts which are not necessarily covert or criminal in nature but would reveal personal information which we might consider private or embarrassing (e.g., information about certain diseases, substance use, etc.).

## 5. Concluding remarks

Omand, Bartlett and Miller call for an ethical framework for SOCMINT due to the growing interest on the part of public authorities in information on social media platforms. Their suggested framework echoes the principles of just wars. It includes requirements for 'sufficient sustainable cause', 'integrity of motive', 'proportionality and necessity', 'authority', 'last resort' and 'informed consent.'[87] These principles are somewhat ambiguous; hence, they could potentially be useful when discussing the ethics of SOCMINT. However, as we have argued in this paper, the specific dual nature of social media platforms and the difficulties surrounding the concept of 'informed consent' – a concept which most privacy scholars agree does not work in the online realm, leaving social media users with literally no control over the flow of their personal information – seem to suggest that we should start elsewhere.

As Lever suggests, we do indeed have privacy interests in public spaces, and the fact that information can be accessed legally from social media platforms does not mean that official surveillance of social media platforms should be regarded as morally permissible, non-intrusive and without restrictions. Official surveillance of social media profiles may have negative effects on the ways we interact with each other and use social media. In the end, it is society as a whole and democracy specifically that pays the price. We have argued that it makes a difference whether the official surveillance is conducted with or without evidence or reasonable suspicion – that is, whether the surveillance is targeted or not. Moreover, we have argued that whereas it might be morally permissible to access social media profiles in cases where the officials have a reasonable suspicion of criminal behaviour, it is much more morally problematic if the surveillance is conducted on random citizens.

In the wake of the insurance case presented earlier, the Danish Consumer Council called for greater awareness of the non-private nature of social media information and compared information on social media profiles to newspaper articles. Hence, it called for awareness on the part of social media users, which certainly seems relevant in the current approach to and use of social media. We, however, also call for greater awareness on the part of the authorities conducting surveillance activities. Social media platforms give people the opportunity to communicate in a free and open way, and this benefit may be negatively affected if stories of systematic bulk surveillance of social media platforms appear. The public outcry following the Cambridge Analytica scandal shows some of the possible consequences of accessing and using massive amounts of information. People become frightened and change the ways they interact with one another online.

## Notes

1. Omand et al., "Social Media Intelligence," 822.
2. Ibid., 802.
3. E.g., Folketingets Ombudsmand.
4. E.g., Juhlin, *Project AVATAR*.
5. Darnton, *Poetics and the Police*; and Skouvig, "Records and rumors."
6. George, "Privacy, Public, Personal," 114.
7. Rønn, "Ethics of intelligence analysis."
8. Omand, Bartlett and Miller emphasize that when it comes to SOCMINT, the term 'gaining access' should be used instead of 'collecting' or 'gathering' intelligence. In this way they underline a difference between addressing non-digital information by using traditional collection methods and digital information by using new collection means (Omand et al., "Social Media Intelligence," 808).
9. We consider SOCMINT a form of so-called OSINT. OSINT covers all types of information that can be collected via open sources and previously mainly meant newspapers, books, etc. SOCMINT is thus a specific type of OSINT; however, not all types of SOCMINT are openly available and it therefore needs its own INT category.
10. We are not discussing the differences between public and private institutions, companies, or corporations. Some of the other contributions to this special issue apply other distinctions between public and private, and

they discuss for instance the interplay between public and private institutions, companies, and corporations in the context of intelligence and security.

11. DeCew, "Privacy," intro.
12. Tavani, "Informational Privacy," 135.
13. Ibid.
14. Ibid.
15. Ibid., 138.
16. Tavani, "Informational Privacy."
17. Solove, *Understanding Privacy*.
18. See note 11 above.
19. Rønn, "Intelligence Ethics," 762.
20. Solove, *Understanding Privacy*, 84–7.
21. Lever, "Democracy, Privacy and Security," 135.
22. Data Protection Working Party, *Opinion 4/2007*.
23. Youyou et al., "Computer-based personality judgments."
24. Bucher, "The algorithmic imaginary."
25. Haggerty and Ericson, "The surveillant assemblage."
26. Søe, "Misleadingness, algorithm society"; and Søe, "Misinformation and disinformation."
27. Tavani, "Informational Privacy"; DeCew, *Privacy*; and Solove, *Understanding Privacy*.
28. Nissenbaum, "Privacy Online"; and Solove, *Understanding Privacy*.
29. Bruno, "Surveillance and participation," 343.
30. Ibid., 346.
31. Solove, *Understanding Privacy*, 73.
32. ibid.
33. Youyou et al., "Computer-based personality judgments," 1037.
34. See Le Morvan, "Information, Privacy, False Light."
35. George, "Privacy, Public, Personal," 115.
36. Ibid., 114.
37. Lever, "Democracy, Privacy and Security," 137–8.
38. Tavani, "Informational Privacy," 139.
39. Ibid.
40. Ibid., 139–140.
41. See above 17.
42. Hulnick, *OSINT: Is it really Intelligence?*; Mercado, *Sailing the Sea of OSINT*.
43. Omand et al., "Social Media Intelligence," 803.
44. The role of social media in policing is widely discussed. It involves numerous aspects; therefore the provided examples are not exhaustive. The use of social media platforms by police authorities is also regarded as 'trust-building' and as a 'tool for public engagement' in police matters (Allen (2017)). However, it is beyond the scope of this paper to examine this claim in detail.
45. Anderson, *A Question of Trust*, 169.
46. Hanson, "Social Media is Changing Law Enforcement."
47. Omand et al., "Social Media Intelligence."
48. See note 43 above.
49. Steele in Trottier, "Open source intelligence," 531.
50. DeCew, *Privacy*.
51. See note 1 above..
52. Ibid., 820.
53. Folketingets Ombudsmand, 5.
54. Folketingets Ombudsmand, *Myndigheder åbne Facebook-profiler*.
55. Maach, "Svært at bebrejde forsikringsselskaber."
56. Ibid.
57. Bruno, "Surveillance and participation."
58. For more about the sharing of personal information as linked to desire see Harcourt, *Exposed*.
59. Omand et al., *Social Media Intelligence*, 821; and Ibid., 806.
60. Ibid., 816 .
61. See note 17 above.
62. Solove, *Understanding Privacy*, 73. Observe that Solove's critique of the reasonable-expectation approach only concerns whether it is a suitable approach for privacy regulation. Solove's claim is that what people actually have reason to expect does not tell us what should be expectable, i.e. it does not provide normative guidelines, only a status quo.
63. Solove, *Understanding Privacy*, 73.

64. Nissenbaum, "Privacy Online," 35.
65. Ibid..
66. Nissenbaum, "Privacy Online," 36.
67. Ibid..
68. See note 35 above.
69. Lever, "Democracy, Privacy and Security."
70. Ibid., 137–8 .
71. See also George, Privacy, Public, Personal and Solove's pragmatic account of privacy in Understanding Privacy.
72. Lever, "Democracy, Privacy and Security," 138–9.
73. Ibid., 139 .
74. Søe, Misinformation and Disinformation.
75. Omand et al., "Social Media Intelligence," 820.
76. Lever, "Democracy, Privacy and Security," 139.
77. Solove, Understanding Privacy, 89.
78. Ibid., 91.
79. Lever, "Democracy, Privacy and Security," 139.
80. Nathan, "Deception and Manipulation."
81. Omand et al., "Social Media Intelligence," 816.
82. Stahl, "Indiscriminate mass surveillance."
83. Omand and his colleagues stress that emphasis should be placed on information provided voluntarily by the citizens to safety and security authorities (termed 'crowdsourcing' (822)). Naturally, this raises another question concerning the inclusion of the public in public safety issues (see, e.g. Petersen & Tjalve).
84. Here we draw on Jeff McMahan's definition of liability, presented in Killing in Wars.
85. See note 80 above.
86. Solove, Understanding Privacy, 91.
87. See note 47 above.

## Acknowledgements

We are very thankful for valuable comments on a previous version of the paper from the participants at the seminar at Centre for Advanced Security Theory (CAST), UCPH on 25 April 2018. Especially good comments from Kristoffer K. Christensen, Tobias Liebetrau, Karen Lund Petersen and Rune Saugman. Furthermore, we are grateful for comments from the members of the research group 'Surveillance, Information Ethics and Privacy' at the University of Copenhagen – especially from Jens-Erik Mai, Laura Skouvig, Gry Hasselbalch and Karen Søilen.

## Disclosure statement

No potential conflict of interest was reported by the authors.

## Funding

This article is conducted as a part of Kira Vrist Rønn's research project "Out of Proportions?" Just Intelligence and the Proportionality of Information Gathering" funded by the independent Research Fund Denmark [4180-00030B FKK].

## ORCID

Sille Obelitz Søe  http://orcid.org/0000-0002-5055-3397

## Bibliography

Anderson, D. *A Question Of Trust. Report Of The Investigatory Powers Review*, 2015. https://terrorismlegislationreviewer. independent.gov.uk/wp-content/uploads/2015/06/IPR-Report-Print-Version.pdf

Bruno, F. "Surveillance and Participation on Web 2.0." In *Routledge Handbook of Surveillance Studies*, edited by K. Ball, K. Haggerty, and D. Lyon, 343–351. London & New York: Routledge, 2012.

Bucher, T. "The Algorithmic Imaginary: Exploring the Ordinary Affects of Facebook Algorithms." *Information, Communication & Society* 20, no. 1 (2017): 30–44. doi:10.1080/1369118X.2016.1154086.

Darnton, R. *Poetry and the Police. Communication Networks in Eighteenth-Century Paris*. London, UK: The Belknap Press of Harvard University Press, Cambridge, Massachusetts, 2010.

Data Protection Working Party. "Opinion 4/2007 on the Concept of Personal Data." *Article 29*, WP 136. Brussels: European Commission.

DeCew, J. "Privacy." *Stanford Encyclopedia of Philosophy*. Spring 2005 Edition, 2002. https://plato.stanford.edu/archives/spr2015/entries/privacy/

George, R. "Privacy, Public Space and Personal Information." In *Core Concepts and Contemporary Issues in Privacy, AMINTAPHIL: The Philosophical Foundations of Law and Justice 8*, edited by A. E. Cudd and M. C. Navin, 107–120. Cham: Springer International Publishing, 2018. doi:10.1007/978-3-319-74639-5_8.

Haggerty, K. D., and R. V. Ericson. "The Surveillant Assemblage." *The British Journal of Sociology* 51, no. 4 (2000): 605–622.

Hanson, W. E. "How Social Media Is Changing Law Enforcement Social Media Raises Positive and Negative Issues for Police" *Government Technology*, December 2011. http://www.govtech.com/public-safety/How-Social-Media-Is-Changing-Law-Enforcement.html

Harcourt, B. E. *Exposed. Desire and Disobedience in the Digital Age*. London, UK: Harvard University Press Cambridge, 2015.

Hulnick, A. "The Dilemma of Open Sources Intelligence: Is OSINT Really Intelligence?" In *The Oxford Handbook of National Security Intelligence*, edited by L. K. Johnson, 230–241. Oxford: Oxford University Pres, 2010. doi:10.1093/oxfordhb/9780195375886.003.0014.

Juhlin, J. Alastair *Project Avatar: Intelligence Exploration of Social Media and Open Sources*, Research Paper, Royal Danish Defence Academy, 2016. Available at: http://www.fak.dk/publikationer/Documents/Project%20Avatar.pdf

Le Morvan, P. "Information, Privacy, and False Light." In *Core Concepts and Contemporary Issues in Privacy, AMINTAPHIL: The Philosophical Foundations of Law and Justice 8*, edited by A. E. Cudd and M. C. Navin, 79–90. Cham: Springer International Publishing, 2018. doi:10.1007/978-3-319-74639-5_8.

Lever, A. "Democracy, Privacy and Security." In *Privacy, Security and Accountability: Ethics, Law and Policy*, edited by A. D. Moore, 105–124. London: Rowman & Littlefield International, Ltd, 2016.

Maach, M. L. "Svært at bebrejde forsikringsselskaber, at de følger med i, hvad der foregår" Danish Radio News, 13. marts, 2018. https://www.dr.dk/nyheder/penge/svaert-bebrejde-forsikringsselskaber-de-foelger-med-i-hvad-der-foregaar

McMahan, J. *Killing in Wars*. Oxford: Oxford University Press, 2009.

Mercado, S. C. "Sailing the Sea of OSINT in the Information Age: Venerable Source in a New Era." *Studies in Intelligence* 48, no. 3 (2004). https://www.cia.gov/library/center-for-the-study-of-intelligence/csi-publications/csi-studies/studies/vol48no3/article05.html.

Nathan, C. "Liability to Deception and Manipulation: The Ethics of Undercover Policing." *Journal of Applied Philosophy* 34, no. 3 (2017): 370–388. doi:10.1111/japp.12243.

Nissenbaum, H. "A Contextual Approach to Privacy Online." *Daedalus* 140, no. 4 (2011): 32–48. doi:10.1162/DAED_a_00113.

Omand, S. D., J. Bartlett, and C. Miller. "Introducing Social Media Intelligence (SOCMINT)." *Intelligence and National Security* 27, no. 6 (2012): 801–823. doi:10.1080/02684527.2012.716965.

Ombudsmand, F. *Myndigheder må bruge oplysninger fra åbne Facebook-profiler* [Authorities are allowed to use information from open Facebook profiles] Jan. 2011 http://www.ombudsmanden.dk/find/udtalelser/beretningssager/alle_bsager/2011-15-1/

Petersen, K. L., and V. S. Tjalve. "En offentlig hemmelighed: Når sikkerhedspolitik går fra statsmandskunst til allemandseje." *Politik* 3 (2015): 13–23.

Rønn, K. V. "Intelligence Ethics: A Critical Review and Future Perspectives." *International Journal of Intelligence and CounterIntelligence* 29, no. 4 (2016): 760–784. doi:10.1080/08850607.2016.1177399.

Skouvig, L. "Records and Rumors: Surveillance and Information in Late Absolutist Denmark (1770–1849)." *Surveillance & Society* 15, no. 2 (2017): 314–325. doi:10.24908/ss.v15i2.5999.

Søe, S. O. "Misleadingness in the Algorithm Society: Misinformation and Disinformation" *Medium*, March 6, 2017. https://medium.com/big-data-small-meaning-and-global-discourses/misleadingness-in-the-algorithm-society-misinformation-and-disinformation-28f78f14e78f

Søe, S. O. "Algorithmic Detection of Misinformation and Disinformation: Gricean Perspectives." *Journal of Documentation* 74, no. 2 (2018): 309–332. doi:10.1108/JD-05-2017-0075.

Solove, D. J. *Understanding Privacy*. London, UK: Harvard University Press, 2008.

Stahl, T. "Indiscriminate Mass Surveillance and the Public Sphere." *Ethics of Information Technology* 18 (2016): 33–39. doi:10.1007/s10676-016-9392-2.

Tavani, H. T. "Informational Privacy: Concepts, Theories, and Controversies." In *The Handbook of Information and Computer Ethics*, edited by K. E. Himma and H. T. Tavani, 131–164. Haboken: John Wiley & Sons, Incorporated, 2008.

Trottier, D. "Coming to Terms with Social Media Monitoring: Uptake and Early Assessment." *Crime Media Culture* 11, no. 3 (2015): 317–333. doi:10.1177/1741659015593390.

Trottier, D. "Open Source Intelligence, Social Media and Law Enforcement: Visions, Constraints and Critiques." *European Journal of Cultural Studies* 18, no. 4–5 (2015): 530–547. doi:10.1177/1367549415577396.

Youyou, W., M. Kosinski, and D. Stillwell. "Computer-Based Personality Judgments are More Accurate than Those Made by Humans." *PNAS* 112, no. 4 (2015): 1036–1040. doi:10.1073/pnas.1418680112.

# Shared secrecy in a digital age and a transnational world

Didier Bigo

**ABSTRACT**

This article examines the notion of shared secrets and the procedures by which secrecy is not the opposite of exchange of information, but the restriction of it to a certain 'circle' of people and the maintenance of others in ignorance. It creates corridors depending on the objectives of secret information, the persons having access, and the knowledge of this access by other people. Shared secrecy has been considered as an exception to common practice, but it has changed in scale with digitization and transnationalization of information, especially when suspicion is becoming used in statistical terms for prevention purposes.

## Sharing secret information about suspects left in ignorance: mechanisms of transnational logics of intelligence in a digital world

I begin this article by investigating the relations between secret information, national security and the common understanding of secret intelligence as an exclusive product delivered by the intelligence community regarding the politicians who decide what policy to follow regarding threats, risks and vulnerabilities. I cross-examine the strong relation of exclusivity of secrecy between the national intelligence agencies and their reluctance to share information with foreign countries. From the Snowden disclosures of the National Security Agency (NSA) practices as the leader of an alliance composed of different SIGINT-internet intelligence services (the so-called Five Eyes), we have evidence of the fact that information which has been intercepted in the digital space concerning localization of individuals and things, identification of these individuals by interconnections of different data pertaining to various bureaucracies and private companies, as well as information on social networks, is shared between different foreign countries and sometimes for very different purposes. I propose the notion of *shared secret information*, even if it looks like a paradox, to understand what is at stake today in a world where the argument of a global insecurity pushes the different services to transfer some information to their 'counterparts' in allied countries, and the impact of this transnationalization of 'national' security when the digital world destabilize the state boundaries. I analyze here the notion of shared secrecy in the field of exchange of information through the procedures by which a specific product of a logic of doubt regarding marginal behaviours (as if they were a sign of guiltiness), produces a list of suspects, which have no right to know why and how they became suspects. In that case, secrecy is not the strict opposite of exchange of information, but the result of the collaboration of bureaucracies allowing the restriction to a certain 'circle' of people with authority to maintain the others in ignorance of the criteria of this suspicion and their modalities of evaluation as well as the techniques they use. This creates a problem regarding rule of Law and democratic principles, and supposes new discussions about the boundaries between secrecy, security, publicity and scrutiny.

As we will see, shared secrecy is therefore not a new phenomenon opposed to exclusive secrecy, but a long practice of communicating and exchanging information between different secret services organized into more or less informal alliances that simultaneously collaborate on certain topics while competing in others, or even on the same ones. This so-called *coopetition* was regulated when intelligence was centrally about spying and counter-spying around military state secrets. However, the scale of sharing secret information has been radically transformed when they have addressed individuals at the world scale and when the digitization of the world has simultaneously allowed them to follow the traces left by mobile or chatting individuals in the digital realm. In addition, nowadays the de-monopolization of intelligence practices correlated with the easiness to put others under surveillance has challenged the boundaries of the professionals of secrets. Private companies and individuals have used for their own purpose everyday forms of digital surveillance. Shared secrecy has therefore reconfigured the field of practices of secret services far beyond their official denominations and has included more and more traditional bureaucracies working at the borders, on finance, on insurance, as well as many private companies, including those who are not internet providers, but simply taken into the unbound securitization of everyday life. If many scholars accept this increase of the scale of exchange of secret information between an impressive range of actors, they still disagree on the reasons of such an increase. For some, this is the result of the rise of insecurities beginning with transnational terrorist activities, organized crime and infiltration of people on the move by these dangerous actors. Without denying that statistically it may exist, most researchers consider that it is ultra-marginal, and that the dynamics of institutions in their competitions and alliances are not reducible to a functionalist answer from external threats. They insist on the existence of a field of security professionals which exist as such, and not only as the addition of national fields. This field is organized around services who have the same kind of techniques, methods and ethos. They are indigenously called 'natural counterparts'. This is in our view one key element to understand the development of these different channels, 'corridors' of segmented information that nevertheless travel globally as secret information shared by many, even if it is in an asymmetric way.

So, if secret intelligence is not any longer an exclusive property of a national community of intelligence, who is now communicating with whom and on what type of secret intelligence information? How and for what purposes? We are clearly beyond small numbers in circulation, we have a mass production of 'shared secrets'. The argument of national security has obscured this phenomenon for a while. As long as this practice of exchanging secret information between different services pertaining to different countries was restricted to a world of spying and counter-spying, i.e. a small world of professionals that supposedly knew each other, it was possible to maintain the belief of a national exclusivity. But the targets of these exchanges of intercepted communication regarding individuals or behaviours of non-identified persons has become so intense, and so many observers have spoken of mass surveillance to characterize this large-scale intrusive practice of building intelligence data on list of suspects, that it cannot be sustained anymore.

In a second part, I detail the change of configuration of the field of the professionals of secretive information which is correlated with the change of scale of shared information and the transformation of the boundaries of this field under the effects coming from its digitization, its privatization and its transnationalization. I indicate that the current game of intelligence gathering is not led only by the games of spying but by its penetration to the intimacy of so many individuals that are objects of suspicion by correlations of profiles which are sometimes not associated with a reasonable cause and generate arbitrariness.[1] But, in my view, if the extension of the field of shared secrecy and intelligence is so advanced, it is not at the same moment a homogeneous phenomenon leading towards a trend of a global society of surveillance. The analysis of intelligence service actors, their social use of technologies, their own beliefs, show that old and new actors, heirs and pretenders, compete between themselves, and disagree on the limits, the boundaries of legitimate actions of an economy of doubt expanding to millions of people put under suspicion beyond fact finding, on the basis of correlations structured by algorithms based themselves on the flow of data considered as shared secret information. In democratic societies, it implies a public debate about these limits. Publicity, scrutiny and secrecy have to be held simultaneously, and strategies of communication are now crucial for secret services. They have to explain their policies, not in detail, but on the principles by which they conduct them. Karen Lund Petersen suggests a change in the mode of communication by intelligence services with their audiences. They may be considered as earmarked only for the government and completed only for those who are elaborating national security decisions. In this vision sharing information is limited and needs to be constructed on an ad hoc base. The idea of public scrutiny is considered as antithetic with the role of secret services, and numerous publications of intelligence services insist on the fact that their purpose is to exist outside of the realm of the rule of Law, to do what is expressly forbidden by law but necessary for the country. Public scrutiny has therefore no place, control has to be done internally and by those who have given orders in case of malpractices. Nevertheless, at least two new paradigms emerge where the public plays a role. In the post-war on terror, it has been considered necessary to increase both the number of players and scrutiny. Information sharing within the sphere of the different agencies collecting information for the common struggle against terrorism, especially jihadism, has decompartmentalised the search for national interest and promoted more automated forms of data sharing with a large number of partners beyond traditional alliances, and encouraged a policy explaining to the public what secret services are doing for their protection and why they are cooperating between them. Beyond this more 'pedagogical' approach, a third model even suggests that the citizen collaborate and co-produce information in an encompassing view of protection against catastrophic events and organisation of resilience. This co-production may lead in that case to more scrutiny and oversight[2]

## Secrecy today: reformulating the question

Against a certain common sense, secrets are not a way to mask information to everyone and a form of solipsism, they are always shared and almost always partially disclosed to create an attraction around their importance. A secret forgotten by everyone is not any more a secret. Procedures to restrict access are central as they mask part of the content but advertise the existence of a secret. Procedures therefore organise asymmetrical relations and provide for a group a certain amount of symbolic power by distributing the information along a continuum going from who is completely ignorant to who is less ignorant, instead of creating an impassable border between ignorance and knowledge. Everybody knows a bit of secrecy but not everything.

This creates an internal hierarchy and differentiates the insiders and the outsiders on the basis of the subtraction of a document or just a couple of relevant lines to the list of available documents. The social relation of secrecy is therefore functioning as a hierarchy inside those who share the knowledge that a secret exists, and this hierarchy is certainly more important for the everyday of the actors than the barrier opposing all of them to the people who ignore completely the existence of a relevant secret.

Secrecy is therefore like a pole in a magnetic field attracting people of different origins, and different services. It creates a form of 'complicity' between them and is a marker of objective relations into a field of practices. In the words of David Omand: 'If all knowledge is power, secret knowledge is turbo-charged power. It is in the nature of secret intelligence that it can be used to ensure access to policy-makers and build influence and prestige for the collecting agency. The risks in terms of over-promising to buy favour and then under-delivering, as seems to have been the case with Iraq WMD intelligence, become all the greater if secrecy is being used to reinforce personal relationships and ensure face-time with the leader'.[3] In his narrative the national committee (here the Joint Intelligence Committee) is a crucial mediator for the exchange, but while that may exist in the UK, our research shows that in other countries the mediation is almost inefficient or even non-existent despite the discourse of collaboration or the existence of formal fusion centres that replicate old data analysis instead of contributing to the production of timely intelligence. In other countries like the US, France, Germany, Spain, Italy, it seems that the different agencies exchange more with their foreign counterparts than with the national agencies doing data interception by other means, and who have limited trust in the other methods. The level of competition between national intelligence services seems higher and the collaboration weaker.

In addition, this type of sharing of secret information works only if the participants of all the continuum are eager to know, if they believe in the value of secrecy. If they do not, if they consider the secret superfluous, the information not valuable for their own purposes, the power based on the differential of (lack of) knowledge disappears.

So, if secrecy, as we proposed is not a technical element, but a politics, then secrecy is used and considered as a form of symbolic power having strong effects on the positions of the actors, vis a vis each other. The resource is not concentrated on a specific case or document giving access to certain knowledge, it is the authority emerging from the right to know which is important, and which is sometimes different from the bureaucratic structure itself. To say that differently, it is not because the absence of knowledge reveals an unknown which, once known, will give an additional reality, a key to understand the world, that secrecy is powerful. The discovery of a secret is rarely changing a situation in itself. What count in fact, are the transformations by which the procedures of secrecy are operating or not by selecting who is entitled to claim that he knows 'things' that the others don't know, and that he cannot reveal these elements for their own good, as it may endanger them. Trust in him, in his role of protector by those who know less is therefore necessary (and even more inside the services).

Secrecy is therefore not the object of the different intelligence services but the architecture, the exoskeleton which built internal hierarchies as a result of the performative claims and rituals around the right of access and the proclamation that a specific element has to be classified. This is what constructs the chains of dependence between the actors of the field and these hierarchies are also what destroy the so-called sense of a 'community of intelligence' where equality inter pares (experts) would be the rule. Part of the life of secret services is organised along this discrimination which also directs the sense of allegiance, which may differ from the official flow-chart.

## Shared secrets in transnational alliance: yes to exchange of information but not everything is for your eyes

It would be an illusion to think that national security acquired by national means only has been the rule until recently. National security has almost always been acquired through transnational types of collaboration. But a nationalist take on this topic which overvalues the coherence of the government and the national state as 'one' actor has led to this illusion (in the Bourdieusian sense) of a national sovereignty on the data regime of intelligence, which in fact does not exist in practice, but is repeated again and again as a form of justification of the intrusive practices, especially regarding the fact that they are and were addressed centrally towards foreigners. This justification by the national means only of capture of data exists as a categorical imperative for a narrative valorising the legitimation of national security over the rule of law as it existentializes some events and masks others. In practice, sharing information between different national services of different countries has been a very common practice. Different governments had to exchange different bits of information to make sense of the overall picture. The first books on the raison d'Etat in the 16th century explain immediately the advantages of sharing information, but the IR narrative of the mid 1960s has invisibilized these sources and insisted that 'intelligence services' don't share information abroad, that they capitalise them and enter into collaboration only at the national level and rarely, selectively, with foreign allies. But it is obvious that the two phenomena are not opposed. Secrecy works very well with exchange, and not only with a monopoly of one person or group. National exclusivity on the means and construction of intelligence data is a doxa from the World War II and the cold war, but has never been a practice. Sharing began as soon as technologies of communication and surveillance at distance existed. Galileo's spyglass, for example, provided one of the first ways to anticipate fights to come, and the advent of the telegraph changed the scale of combat, integrating transnational activities for local fights.[4] The US army during the World War I was certainly among the first to develop a strategy of intelligence sharing with certain protocols organising levels of differential access.[5] It became even more important during the Second World War and from that time, transnational alliances have existed with high level of exchanges while keeping levels of secrets into a small group of 'specialists' of management of sensitive information.[6] Nevertheless, the process of extension of meaning of intelligence information, the globalisation of the risk narrative and digitization, have extended the phenomenon beyond the capacity of controls, and with internet developments it was almost impossible not to have disclosures of the practices of interception.

As Warner develops; 'finally intelligence took on a multiplicity of meanings, some of them only barely overlapping. It remained a synonym for espionage, of course, but it also came to mean any sort of information that decision makers might need to select a course of action. It also came to mean the overall system that manages the state's espionage (and counterespionage) function, its collection of secrets and non-secrets for ministers and commanders, its interaction with friendly intelligence services, and the work product of these functions. In short, those secret activities had become systematized as intelligence'.[7]

This implies a reversal of causality. Intelligence has been the end results of many different practices, heterogeneous and on the move in terms of purposes and technologies. It has not been an organisational principle regulating nationally state survival and interests. The government of one country has never been in practice in a monopolistic position. The state is a field of action, not an actor. And some transnational fields have intersected strongly with the national state field, even gaining supremacy where sending secret information to a foreign agency was considered as a more important loyalty to respect than the one with the national politicians. The BND affair in Germany and its link with the NSA are one among many examples of these practices. This does not mean that in other cases the national imperative is not working against foreign collaboration if sensitive matters (industrial secrets for example) are at stake. In the Five Eyes messages, the NSA has flagged messages with the label NOFORN to restrict access to the knowledge of another country selectively. Typically, the CIA has posted advice for US government operatives infiltrating Shengen explaining how to avoid controls to conduct action on allied territories without their knowledge. It was under NOFORN (WikiLeaks release 21 December 2014). But, beyond the anecdotes of commercial influences and the fact that some countries are not under a no-spy agreement, even those with such an agreement have been subjected to spying through collaboration between the agencies working on the same domain but simultaneously with the ignorance of the other national agencies, and even of the government. Allegations have been made that if the suspicion of terrorism regarding a foreigner may compromise US interests, they may not inform the targeted country, even if it is an ally. In addition to these complex situations, where important information is not delivered, we may add also cases where the allied agencies are aware but do not communicate with their own political authorities. Paradoxically, it could be said these cases are rare, but are often among the most important to know for the national security of the country at the governmental level. When they are kept inside a specific channel, the game is therefore more highly complex than the image on national-foreign exchange may suggest. It pluralises the 'corridors' of information, depending on the bilateral relations between the agencies, independently of national government's disagreement.[8]

The consequences of this de-monopolisation are sometimes not fully considered. The national state game is only one of the many games for intelligence data. Despite the break through, Michael Warner for example continues to believe in the supremacy of states and in a Westphalian world where Max Weber's definition of the state continues to be pre-eminent, where private is obeying public through delegation, where internet companies are subordinate to government, where digital is just an expression of the 'real' (off line). We suggest the need to de-essentialize the state even more. It is important to take into consideration the changes to the fields of power at the transnational level and how they affect politics. Reasoning in terms of national security is no longer a coherent way to understand how shared secrecy is connected and circulates, how public and private actors are now so intertwined that we have to speak of hybrid security and not of a public-private partnership, and in addition to explain the multiplication of the effective practices of secret services which pass through the publication of nominal lists of suspects (individual and organisations) and call for the collaboration of the public in the identification and localisation of these suspects. This shift is what I have called the emergence of a digital reason of state on a transnational scale

## Towards the emergence of a field of digital reason of state populated by transnational guilds of extraction of secret information

If it is crucial to do a sociogenesis of the secret intelligence field to avoid the illusion that it is completely new, it is also important to observe the transformations connected with the eruption of the digital age and the ease of surveillance which facilitate both the sharing of information and the explosion of secrets and uncovering of them via internet technologies and the role of private companies. I insist here that the scale and scope of surveillance and the transnationalization of intelligence services we have witnessed over the last few years require a renewed investigation of contemporary world security practices on the one hand, but also a careful mapping of our very own categories of analysis on the other.

Sovereignty, secrecy, security communities, territory, border control, technology, intelligence and rule of law have inevitably ended up meaning different things for different people. What is under question is not one of these categories over another, but how all these categories have simultaneously changed. I am arguing here that this boils down to an argument over the digitisation and heterogenization of *Raison d'Etat* (Reason of State) destabilising public and private, internal and foreign, shared and (national) secret distinctions.

Key to my argument about the transnational fields of shared secret information channels (or corridors), is to understand and analyse how the classic *Raison d'Etat* and its contemporary iterations, such as national security, have undergone profound mutation with the process of digitisation, the emerging 'datafication' of our societies and the extension of police and intelligence services. I do not develop here the long genealogy of these relations and causations, but I consider that the field of shared secret information is dependent in its extension and reconfiguration towards less HUMINT and more SIGINT activities on 'the emergence of a digital reason of state' based on the possibility for intelligence services of different countries extending their goals of prevention and prediction of crime to a global reach, convincing their own politicians that the future of intelligence is clear: it is to include and expand technologies collecting traces of human activities.[9] This increase in and need to gather digital communication and data, once accepted politically, has nurtured in return a wider transnational collaboration amongst national intelligence and security professionals and resulted in an extension of the category of foreign intelligence to share data that could be of national concern more specifically. This has created a spiral effect. By projecting *national security 'inside out'*, via a transnational alliance of the professionals of national security and sensitive data, *an 'outside in' effect of suspicion* for all Internet subjects has been created, destabilising the protection for national citizens if they are communicating with foreigners. It changes the categories of 'foreign' and 'domestic' by dispersing them and transforming the line that separated them into a *Möbius strip*.[10]

The division between internal and external practices of intelligence and secrecy, while maintained to ease the possibility without warrant on foreign intelligence is de facto obsolete. It does not mean that we are encountering a merging of internal and external into a global without boundaries, but we observe a logic where, intersubjectively, everything is analysed either as external or internal depending on the interests of the surveillant-actors, even if, more recently, the Courts have tried to reverse the reasoning of the services and to show that they cannot choose the legislation of foreign or domestic the way they want, but have to regulate the interception with more general principles: necessity, proportionality.[11]

This is what we will examine now. What have been the consequences for the targets of intelligence of the change of regime of intelligence data privileging transnational exchanges and digitization? Certainly, digitization at the world scale has been contemporary to the phenomenon of hybridization of the public and private logic. This has created many questions about the level of participation of many private entities into the circulation of information on one side and of their participation in channels of secret intelligence, either indirectly, as provider of information they retain but do not analyse themselves, or more directly when they are asked to contribute to develop them.

These two phenomena of hybridization and digitization have transformed the relation between intelligence, surveillance and obedience (or compliance) in everyday democracy. This has been done in western countries without much protest, and even after the disclosures of practices in such a detailed manner and with the participation of major newspapers, the general public has considered that it was a question for professionals, not for them, to decide on the boundaries between secret procedures and democratic rulings.[12] Some commentators have therefore considered that 'the people' have accepted the fate of an evolution that they like (or not) but cannot change.[13]

This is the belief of a technological determinism within surveillance that I want nevertheless to challenge because in the end this is the main argument in favour of the prolongation of secrecy procedures without proper oversight and scrutiny by public mechanisms. People do not accept surveillance, they are just unaware of the high level of circulation of shared secrets and if they knew, they would be less keen to participate to it. But, before discussing the consequences of this circulation of shared secrets, we need to emphasize how they are exchanged today in such increasing numbers.

## Channelling secret information? How and for what purposes?

As explained by Sir David Omand: 'For intelligence and law enforcement to be able to identify communications of interest and, where authorized, to access the content of relevant communications themselves is in fact a harder technical challenge than the many internal NSA PowerPoint presentations stolen by Snowden might suggest'.[14] And this is certainly true. PowerPoints are oriented towards presentations and so simplify techniques, they are not 'truth' about practices. Nevertheless, they give indications about the ways the services enter into contact, what software helps them to automatize some type of exchanges, and the correlations between the technical systems and the judicial obligations.

Obviously secret services share much data between them, but in very asymmetrical ways and through very different levels of right of access.[15] Exchange has never meant equality of situation. Here exchange is the result of the structural positions of the different services regarding each other and not just a relation of 'trust' between them. Sharing information is highly differentiated: what is on offer for a 'foreign' partner may be the data on some individuals if the foreign partner asks and already knows who they are, or key elements of the identification. It may be access to far more general and numerous data that can facilitate a search for identification criteria (for example a bank account transaction, or vaguer criteria where the period is a full month with the criteria only that money is coming from an unknown bank account but whose country deposit is known – Mali to Norway transiting via…). It may also be a series of tools interconnecting databases via interoperability platforms or search tools but limited access to data. And it may be general results of data analytics but without any names. All these modalities are different. Some like the first and the last are old practices. The second and third are more recent, connected with digital capacities to deliver large scale of data for imprecise criteria quickly. The human capacities to treat the data once filtered are therefore of crucial importance. Technical skills are insufficient if they are automatized, they need to be held by specialists.

Only the powerful services get a chance to use to their profit the sharing of data. Their number of personnel, budgets and position regarding the internet traffic are key elements that we have analysed elsewhere.[16] In addition, to add a layer of complexity, they are not, by far, the only actors involved. The access in bulk to substantial quantities of the Internet supposes the interception and storage of metadata and sometimes the data related to these metadata. To access internet cables they often work with their own private companies who have built or collaborate in the construction of cables and the latter are key actors in the interception practices of data and the secrecy about this interception.

Once the services have the saved metadata which can provide information concerning when and to whom phone calls are made or emails and texts are sent, they still have to identify the suspects, and they are often obliged, beyond their own national resources, to look at international databases through different requests, either directly in a bilateral manner if they know in what country they may be, or via what is called 'Advanced "front end" tools allowing analysts to efficiently access and run advanced queries on intercepted data, in particular, in order to discover new leads in their investigations'.[17]

Among different tools, one can quote ICREACH for exchange between US agencies and their closed counterparts, and one which has been highly popularized, Xkeyscore. Xkeyscore is a program that has been shared with other intelligence agencies including the Australian Signals Directorate (ASD), Canada's Communications Security Establishment, New Zealand's Government Communications Security Bureau, Britain's Government Communications Headquarters, but also Japan's Defense Intelligence Headquarters and the German Bundesnachrichtendienst. Xkeyscore allows searching and analysis of global Internet data, with specific selectors and a high speed answer. According to an NSA slide presentation about XKeyscore from 2013, it is a 'Digital Network Intelligence Exploitation System/Analytic Framework'. According to a good Wikipedia article, 'XKeyscore holds raw and unselected communications traffic, so analysts can perform queries using "strong selectors" like e-mail addresses, but also using "soft selectors", like keywords, against the body texts of e-mail and chat messages and digital documents and spreadsheets in English, Arabic and Chinese.'[18]

A second program, less well known, is ICREACH.[19] In a nutshell, the National Security Agency is secretly providing data to nearly two dozen U.S. government agencies with a 'Google-like' search engine built to share more than 850 billion records about phone calls, emails, cellphone locations and internet chats. ICREACH contains information on the private communications of foreigners and, it appears, millions of records on American citizens who have not been accused of any wrongdoing but have entered into some previous profiles of suspicion and have been kept there, just in case. As Ryan Gallagher explains 'ICREACH has been accessible to more than 1,000 analysts at 23 U.S. government agencies that perform intelligence work, according to a 2010 memo. A planning document from 2007 lists the DEA, FBI, Central Intelligence Agency and the Defense Intelligence Agency as core members. Information shared through ICREACH can be used to track people's movements, map out their networks of associates, help predict future actions, and potentially reveal religious affiliations or political beliefs.'[20] The search tool was designed to be the largest system for internally sharing secret surveillance records in the United States, capable of handling two to five billion new records every day, including more than 30 different kinds of metadata on emails, phone calls, faxes, internet chats, and text messages, as well as location information collected from cellphones. ICREACH does not appear to have a direct relationship to the large NSA database, previously reported by The Guardian that stores information on millions of ordinary Americans' phone calls under Section 215 of the Patriot Act. Unlike the Section 215 database, which is accessible to a small number of NSA employees and can be searched only in terrorism-related investigations, ICREACH grants access to a vast pool of data that can be mined by analysts from across the intelligence community for 'foreign intelligence'. Data available through ICREACH appears to be primarily derived from surveillance of foreigners' communications, and planning documents show that it draws on a variety of different sources of data maintained by the NSA.[21]

It seems that on specific occurrences, ICREACH was also opened to other partners of the Five Eyes plus, including Canada and Australia, but this has been denied. We cannot know if it was a two-way circulation between agencies or if it was only one-way, with Australian and Canadian data being stored into ICREACH. In that case the ASD may have fed information into the NSA's vast ICREACH search engine but not had access to it.[22]

We have certainly to learn more on the right of access and to avoid the sensationalism of some media, but we are clearly beyond small numbers. Shared secrecy is about the millions of pieces of individual information and metadata circulating between transnational data bases. They are the virtual 'haystack' mobilized when profiles of suspicion are constructed for a specific purpose. But, and it is one of the specifics of the data analytics program, they are oriented towards prevention and conceived to build predictive profiling around a specific hypothesis of doubt concerning 'abnormal behaviours' and-or trajectories and-or multiple identities. This future perfect orientation of a future already known is in itself a problem as machine learning works to confirm hypotheses, not to invalidate their basic assumptions, and the correlations uncovered by the analytics cannot be considered as proof of causality, a lesson Emile Durkheim set out in his famous book on suicide with reference to the correlation of suicide and sunspots.[23]

## The arguments of prevention and prediction: an ideology or a reasonable justification for exceptional means?

A story is constructed based on the potentiality of the system. It is said that it is now possible to trace almost all of the online activities that an Internet user undertakes during the day: what they read on the web or purchase on Amazon, what they send to colleagues and family members via email, what sort of holidays they take and whether they travel abroad, and what kind of online payment system they use. The capacity to act at distance has increased the traceability of data; the possibility of data retention; the capacity to build software that enables complex relations between databases, and to deduct from these data emerging trends, statistical categories of behaviours or individuals; and the belief that these emergent and minority trends give intelligence services an advantage in conducting their various activities such as espionage, economic intelligence, and the struggle against terrorism and crime.

The overall argument of a permanent war on terror and its claimed necessity to connect always more of the lacking dots to the large network of people under electronic surveillance, succeeds, it seems, to move the people living in liberal states to consider that they need Total Information Awareness against erratic violence led by revenge and widespread diffusion. Authorities need to have a grip to anticipate the future, to suspect rightly the people who act abnormally, because they are preparing the worst. The argument of a pre-crime society has replaced that of a society liberated from communist collectivism.

This is the new utopia of a society conducted by anticipative knowledge built through data analytics where profiling is more and more subtle and self-correcting, while data collected are bigger and bigger and, once retained, filtered, and selected on specific requests. They allow for better detection of the white noises, the black swans, the abnormal behaviours, everything that does not fit with the 'normal' order. A different political imagination has radicalized the fear of global terrorism and the necessity of a maximum and global security regime to counter terrorism on the one side, and on the other has also produced a fear of an Orwellian world in the making, in which citizens are systematically spied upon in their everyday practices.[24] But most secret intelligence professionals fight against this ideological stance and resist the argument of a scientific prediction. They accept the idea of forecasting on precise consequences, but do not see themselves as astrologers. Nevertheless, some are tempted to play that role to please politicians in charge and the industry building these systems.

This 'knowledge' of predictive analytics is said to be the answer to the dissemination of violence into inter-individual relations, a technological fix that reconstructs the political in liberal democracies far from the eruption of political violence. Politics will no longer be a question of ideological judgments, but a question of anticipation of the hidden enemy, of its stealth moves. Politics will be the art of war supplied by the technology of traceability and the use of a Maxwell's Demon activated in some computers to know the positions and trajectories of all human beings suspected of distorting the norms and of being at the margins. Joining the dream of expertise with astrology, connecting hard science and religious sacrificial rituals, destroying the political as a relation to focus on the margins, mixing the image of the future with an old past of superstition, this reasoning is in addition the one that favours protection of society over the rights of the individual and destroys the very idea of privacy and freedom of thought. But, to the despair of many activists, people on the web do not react in mass against these practices.

## De-monopolization of the field of secrecy: spying and counter spying, secret defence, national security, industrial secrets, everyday surveillance

If answers about the activities and group of people in charge of the extraction of secret, sensitive and personal information was easy during the period of the Second World War and then the Cold War, with its rituals around spying and counter spying, monopolised by the most powerful states to monitor the activities of the other system of alliance in terms of armaments and technological progress, this is not the case anymore. We have developed in detail the conditions under which the specialised group or more exactly the guilds of secret, sensitive and personal information have evolved with the digitization of the reason of state.[25] Consider the example of the specific politics of hostility against lawyers by the Bush administration to create the idea that technological progress needs to be used at its full scale and without restriction because of the context of secret war. In that context without even the need to know, any opportunity to know cannot be neglected to anticipate the future. Every data that can help to build profiles of suspects is therefore considered as a legitimate source by the intelligence services. This vision is one that is at war with the rule of Law and public-judicial scrutiny but the neo-conservatives nevertheless succeeded in modifying the economy of the field of secret intelligence by justifying large-scale collection of data captured almost directly from internet cables and without proper warrants.[26] Polls have not shown strong resistance. As a result, it has allowed a course to harvest data, a form of digital encomienda authorizing the people involved into the interception of data, and the enrolment (by coercion or strong suggestion) of the biggest US companies in the field of Internet data and social networks to consider individual data as their 'property'.[27] More structurally, if this has been possible to pursue beyond the official end of the war on terror, it is also because intercepting data which are confidential can be done very cheaply and with considerably less effort than before, the ratio of surveillant-surveillees moving from 4/1 to 1/hundreds.[28] Even more generally, as very well explained by Warner in *The Rise and Fall of Intelligence*: 'Today, many states (beyond the cold war alliances) can do so once again; and what is more, private entities and even individuals (some with criminal motivations) can gather secrets and manipulate events around the globe. The skills needed to "do" intelligence have diffused around the world and across societies; they can literally be purchased online. The problems caused by this spread of intelligence, moreover, now reach beyond the security services to corporate offices and private homes. In short, intelligence has traded uniqueness for ubiquity'.[29]

Secrecy of little secrets coming from intimate life has invaded the world of intelligence while secrets, even of some importance, are shared by more and more people who have not been trained by their education and profession to respect the rituals around them. To sum up, for decades, the field was delimited along crystallized lines. The actors were public bodies called secret services and they were arguing that secrecy was a necessity for protecting the national security of each state, but now with the digitization of information and the globalization of the exchange of information as well as the riskification of the world where distant catastrophes may have an impact in every local place, the boundaries are no longer 'waterproof' between the 'secret' services and other public or private bodies.

The legitimacy of the 'public secret services' claiming to be the sole experts in providing analysis for national security is now destabilized. Private organizations collecting data, managing them with more efficient tools, challenge their monopoly and invade their territory of secrecy obliging them to have collusive transactions enlarging the sphere of shared secrets.[30] International exchange of information and the belief that 'big' data analytics are based more on big numbers than on small and smart data, are also challenging the national character of the collection-interception of data and privilege large groupings of services who have the same know-how but different nationalities and interests. The fact that specialists are sceptical about these capacities of artificial 'unintelligence' has not yet changed popular and journalistic beliefs.

## The notion of shared secrets in a transnational world: the five eyes plus practices revealed

The disclosures in 2013 by Edward Snowden of the secret US-NSA programme, PRISM, and of more than a thousand types of intrusive software with genuinely hush-hush codenames have raised serious concerns about the scope and scale, the qualitative and quantitative dimensions, of surveillance of everyday internet users for intelligence purposes. What has been done by the NSA and the Five Eyes network during the previous 10 years, in secret? Is it possible in democracies to act in such a way, which is certainly less directly violent than the CIA's physical networks, but nevertheless problematic for democratic forms of states?

Quite clearly, Snowden's disclosures of NSA practices have sparked significant public and political concerns. Some concerns about security to start with – security for whom? – were identical to the critique of the war on terror, but they were followed by questions about technological progress and a sense of the ineluctability of the deprivation of confidentiality and privacy in our modes of communication, wrapped around an overall argument about the inherently violent, unsecured and dangerous state of the world.

The extension via the digitization of information of the number of people inside a procedure of restriction of access, as well as the generalization of large transatlantic channels of exchange of information exacerbates the tensions between the actors participating to the production of secrecy. And this is what we will analyze now. Are the secret services losing the control of secrecy for (national) security? Are they obliged to compose with other actors who manage more secret procedures of secrecy than themselves inside the general management of information? Who has the authority to control sensitive information and to frame it under secrecy? It seems that the destabilization of the initial conditions of secret services regarding spying and counter spying where the rules for national security secrets (including exchanging individuals) were set up is so strong that the barriers distinguishing who the secret services are have exploded, with the de-monopolisation of the practices of spying and counter spying, with the privatization of surveillance, with the commercialization of the Internet and its willingness to make money from personal data, with the desire to anticipate the future of human beings. The de-assembling and re-assembling of the secret services beyond the public services of a state including private contributors, and beyond the national territory with the integration of heterogeneous information beyond internal collection of data, is interrogating the very nature of the group of persons who are the professionals of extraction of (secret, sensitive and personal) information.

There certainly lies a change in the regime of justification of national security within this argument. First a justification has been expressed and presented openly, because the scandal open by the disclosure of large-scale surveillance was too strong to enable a return to opacity, to the traditional: 'no comment, no denial' policy. But, the national security argument has been connected centrally with the large-scale intrusive data interceptions the press has called mass surveillance and bulk collection, while the services and the internet providers have considered that their methods were necessary, appropriate and proportionate.

The controversy has implied on the technological side a branching out of existing rhizomatic commercial surveillance for profit and intrusive methods of interception and collection of personal information by specialized intelligence services and their contractors. It has also opened a legal conflict with the judiciary on many fronts, and the national security terminology, which was in many countries a doctrine coming from the US and the UK, has nevertheless entered legislation after the Snowden disclosures of 2013, even if for most of them – France, Germany, Spain, Italy – the notion of 'secret defense' is still more relevant in a legal context than that of national security.

## A counter move: rule of law, human rights countering technological arguments and necessity of intrusive intelligence?

National Courts and European Courts have been more and more clear in their judgements post-2010 that if it is to the government to decide the content of national security, this cannot be completely discretionary. This has been and is still the main challenge theoretically for the term national security and the encapsulated practices of human and technological intelligence. National security (and the secrecy around it) cannot be transformed into a blanket for executive arbitrariness that other powers and citizens cannot check. Even when citizens believe that, in general, agents of secret services are also good citizens, they want nevertheless to have the capacity to differentiate inside the group, to punish those who have acted against inviolable rights, like the prohibition against torture, and to know who has given these orders. From the 2010s, in a not yet stabilised doctrine, a framing, which has been developed in Europe via the role of Courts (ECJ and ECHR), but also in national courts in the UK or Germany, has contradicted the US NSA approach of the post-war on terror era based on a more military and strategic vision justifying the president's power and its own practices. It seems that in Europe, legally, national security cannot trump the Rule of Law and democracy for political opportunist interest, the derogations have to be necessary and proportional to the threat. The threat itself cannot be the product of a flourishing imagination, it needs some evidence of an actual project of realisation. Prevention is not fiction, anticipation has to have grounds.

Nevertheless, the reactions of the highest courts, acclaimed by activists and lawyers challenging the government have not transformed the everyday practices of internet users, and push them to defend by themselves their rights of data protection, privacy and forms of freedom which are endangered by intrusive intelligence. The argument of the necessity of struggle against terrorism has been quite powerful, as well as the argument that the traces left by the use of internet and the limitations of privacy are the normal counterpart of more communication at distance, as Zuckerberg bluntly said. Nevertheless, after the Cambridge Analytica scandal involving researchers, strategic communication firms and google research for profit via the brokerage of personal data for other commercial (or political) means, and the development in Europe of General Data Protection Regulation (GDPR), the argument of the necessity of collecting data to have access to digital tools simplifying everyday life begins to be challenged, as well as the politics of the SIGINT-Internet secret services, and the logics of the capitalism of platforms which are intertwinned with the escalation of the numbers of little secrets in circulation.

## Conclusion: Is it possible to be innocent in a world of suspects? Conformity regarding the diagonal of intelligence, surveillance and compliance

The consequences of this taming of the future are affecting democratic dimensions. Do we have 'scientific' oracles to listen or is this noise about the new form of reasoning a way for an industry of surveillance to sell products and to convince us that anyone in the public is innocent, but he is the only one, all the others being for good reason, suspects? Is it in that case a way to advance compliance of consumers towards a more invisible surveillance? The conjunction of capacities to collect data easily and massively at a cheap price, reversing the relation between intelligence work and surveillance by collection of large-scale data, and facilitating the accumulation over the quality of information contained into these data, has reinforced this dream of anticipation of the future and the discourse of a pre-emptive or preventive action. It has dressed this myth with some clothes of informatics sciences that do not fit together. It has destroyed guilt and innocence for a policy of permanent suspicion. More importantly even, it has transformed the image of potential suspect into the one of an enemy criminal, of an intimate public enemy, and has rendered banal this figure of the suspect with no right, no chance to defend himself, no chance to change his mind. As soon as the suspect emerges from a list of names, he is not anymore a potential suspect, a potential terrorist, he becomes a terrorist, a murderer. Digitization operates magically with a politics of number that concretise, operationalise the figure of the invisible, of the unknown. This is why analysing the conditions of the emergence of digitization and the link with the transformation of intelligence is so important. It is not just a correlation, a chance for the Sigint Service that their field has exploded in size and importance, it goes further. The Internet is not just an accumulator of data, it is a translator of logic. We are now all virtually living as the only innocent in a world of suspects.

To sum up, to understand the effects of the connection between intelligence practices and the rise of technologies connected to the digitization of the world is complex. So too is the possibility of tracing actions with the ambition of knowing and anticipating the future. Methodologically, it is difficult to distinguish between the pretenses to know, and the effective capacities to discover trends oriented towards future human actions. This depends on the belief about preventive actions and scientific prediction coming as an outcome of large-scale collection of information (in bulk). But, I contend here against other analysts, who argue that this transformation is the inevitable product of an evolution of technologies related to the internet and the more general digitization of the world and its impact on the 'off-line' world. The path transforming the Internet into a tool of surveillance and the social networks into forms of co-watching reinforcing in-group rules as well as reframing subjectivities by reinforcing compliance, is not an historical necessity, and is not with us forever. It is the product of discretionary acts of politics at a certain moment.

The so-called inevitability of escape from a society of surveillance today is therefore not a description of the world as it is, but a form of doxa inherited from the extension of the field of extraction of information to a new set of actors, which is the product of certain dynamics of struggle between the actors managing digital information and especially data based on individual traces, be they from private actors and commercial logics or from governments and their services of interception of communication and security logics. Surveillance is therefore not inherent from communication and information gathering. It depends on a specific configuration of actors that succeed in differentiating themselves from other actors as the legitimate owners of secrecy, and the ones distinguishing suspects from innocents.

## Notes

1. The distinction between correlation and causality is here a central element. See Emile Durkheim who insists that sociology is about causality and not simply correlations. Correlations may help find causality, but they may be the product of hazards or embedded stereotypes creating false causalities.See more recently Colburn 2008: p 10. For a more optimistic view Dhar 2013: pp 64–73.
2. Petersen, Karen Lund in this issue.
3. Omand, *Securing the State*, 191.
4. Weaver and Pallitto, *Extraordinary Rendition*.
5. Information processing drove an imperative to share information across national lines with allies.
6. The UK-USA agreement to share signals intelligence was a key moment. It covered • collection of traffic • acquisition of communication documents and equipment • traffic analysis • cryptanalysis • decryption and translation • acquisition of information regarding communications organizations, practices, procedures and equipment. In short, the British and American codebreakers would share almost everything, from the raw take to their finished analytical products, nevertheless UKUSA agreement excluded sharing with 'third parties'.
7. Warner, *The Rise and Fall of Intelligence*, 1.
8. See Greenwald Glenn Foreign Officials In the Dark About Their Own Spy Agencies' Cooperation with NSA Intercept 13 March 2014. Greenwald develops different cases including cases where the ally partner of the NSA is asked to spy, for the profit of a foreign partner, on its own citizen ot its own government (as in the case of Angela Merkel phone). The French DGSE has also exchanged a lot of information with the CIA during the War

on Terror despite the official split between Jacques Chirac and George Bush on Iraq. It is still difficult to know if it was with his agreement or not.

9. Bigo et al., "Mass Surveillance of Personal Data"; and Bauman et al., "After Snowden."

10. Bigo, "Internal and External Security(Ies)"; Bigo, "Political Sociology"; and Bigo, "Sécurité intérieure, sécurité extérieure," 316.

11. Cole et al., *Surveillance, Privacy*.

12. Mueller, *Public Opinion*.

13. Harcourt, *Exposed*.

14. Omand, *Securing the State*, 11.

15. Cf the notices: for US eyes only, or not for UK eyes on some messages. For details see the excellent website: https://search.edwardsnowden.com/docs/OperationalLegalities2015-06-22_nsadocs_snowden_doc .

16. Bigo et al., "Digital Data and the Transnational Space."

17. Omand, "Understanding Digital Intelligence," 7.

18. Xkeyscore- See Wikipedia, and for more details: The Unofficial XKEYSCORE User Guide; https://search.edwards nowden.com/docs/TheUnofficialXKEYSCOREUserGuide2015-07-01_nsadocs_snowden_doc .

19. https://theintercept.com/2014/08/25/icreach-nsa-cia-secret-google-crisscross-proton/ .

20. See annex 1.

21. Excerpts of Gallagher 2014. See also https://theintercept.com/document/2014/08/25/sharing-communications-metadata-across-u-s-intelligence-community/. ICREACH is 'not a repository [and] does not store events or records in one place.' Instead, it appears to provide analysts with the ability to perform a one-stop search of information from a wide variety of separate databases. The mastermind behind ICREACH was recently retired NSA director Gen. Keith Alexander, who outlined his vision for the system in a classified 2006 letter to the then-Director of National Intelligence John Negroponte. The search tool, Alexander wrote, would "allow unprecedented volumes of communications metadata to be shared and analysed, opening up a 'vast, rich source of information' for other agencies to exploit.

22. https://www.theguardian.com/world/2014/oct/13/australias-defence-intelligence-agency-conducted-secret-programs-to-help-nsa.

23. Durkheim, *A Study in Sociology*.

24. Against this idea that intelligence services spy on their own citizens, the answer is to distinguish the different users of the Internet by the origins of the communication and the supposition of their nationality. Western intelligence services would respect their citizens and would have safeguards. This is certainly true, but it is also a justification for almost no limits on the surveillance of foreign internet users, and it comes at a huge cost for privacy and democracy that cannot be reserved to one nationality against the others. Members of transnational agreements like the 5 eyes plus, have also sometimes switched their national who are foreigners for the other services, and exchanged targets of surveillance to bypass their legislation in the two distinct ways to intercept data differently depending if the process is purely external and therefore a foreign interception of intelligence or if it is an internal one subjected to more judicial control and often specific warrants both in the US and in Europe. This has created one of the most central controversies between judicial review and justifications of intelligence services which is not yet settled, and discussion continues about retention of data, definition of meta data, circuit of foreign intelligence in regard to internal security intelligence, third party disclosure exceptions, and the validity of the UK Investigatory Powers Act.

25. Bigo, "Beyond National Security."

26. Weber et al., *The Routledge International Handbook*.

27. See note 16 above

28. Reith lectures by MI5 former head Eliza Manningham-Buller: https://www.bbc.co.uk/programmes/b0145x77 To have a list of suspects is not having them under effective surveillance- Cf also the problem in France with the number of terrorist attacks in 2015 done by individuals put on the S (surveillance) list and the later debates about the capacity of the services.

29. See note 7 above.

30. Dobry, "Le renseignement politique dans."

## Disclosure statement

No potential conflict of interest was reported by the author.

## Funding

This article is an original piece doing the synthesis on the questions of use of secrets of the research on the professionals of societal security SOURCE (FP7 Security 313288) and of the research on intelligence services UTIC (ANR-14-CE28-0024).

## ORCID

Didier Bigo 🆔 http://orcid.org/0000-0002-1908-6532

## Bibliography

Bauman, Z., D. Bigo, P. Esteves, E. Guild, V. Jabri, D. Lyon, and R. B. J. Walker. "After Snowden: Rethinking the Impact of Surveillance." *International Political Sociology* 8, no. 2 (2014): 121–144. doi:10.1111/ips.12048.

Bigo, D. "Internal and External Security(Ies): The Möbius Ribbon." In *Identities, Borders, Orders*, edited by M. Albert, D. Jacobson, and Y. Lapid, 91–116. Minneapolis: University of Minnesota Press, 2001.

Bigo, D. "Sécurité intérieure, sécurité extérieure: Séparation ou continuum ?." In *Transformations et réformes de la sécurité et du renseignement en Europe*, edited by É.-Y. Laurent and B. Warusfel, 121–144. Bordeaux: Presses Universitaires de Bordeaux, 2016.

Bigo, D. "Beyond National Security, the Emergence of a Digital Reason of State(S) Led by Transnational Guilds of Sensitive Information. The Case of the Five Eyes Plus Network." In *Kettemann and Kilian Vieth: Research Handbook on Human Rights and Digital Technology*, edited by B. Wagner and C. Matthias, 61–82. Global Politics, Law and International Relations, 2018.

Bigo, D., and L. Bonelli. "Digital Data and the Transnational Space of Intelligence." In *Data Politics, Routledge International Political Sociology*, edited by D. Bigo, E. Isin, and E. Ruppert. 2019. Forthcoming.

Bigo, D., S. Carrera, N. Hernanz, J. Jeandesboz, J. Parkin, F. Ragazzi, and A. Scherrer. "Mass Surveillance of Personal Data by EU Member States and Its Compatibility with EU Law." CEPS Liberty and Security in Europe No. 61. 2013.

Bigo, D., and R. B. J. Walker. "Political Sociology and the Problem of the International." *Millenium. Journal of International Studies* 35, no. 3 (2007): 725–739. doi:10.1177/03058298070350030401.

Colburn, A. "Correlation and Causality." *The Science Teacher* 75, no. 2 (2008). https://www.questia.com/read/1G1-182530694/correlation-and-causality.

Cole, D., F. Fabbrini, and S. Schulhofer. *Surveillance, Privacy and Trans-Atlantic Relations*. London: Bloomsbury Publishing, 2017.

Dhar, V. "Data Science and Prediction." *Communications of the ACM* 56, no. 12 (2013).

Dobry, M. "Le renseignement politique dans les démocraties occidentales. Quelques pistes pour l'identification d'un objet flou." Cahiers de la sécurité intérieure (I.H.E.S.I.), 1997. n°30, 1997.

Durkheim, E. *Suicide: A Study in Sociology*. Abingdon: Routledge, 2005.

Gallagher, R. "The Surveillance Engine: How the NSA Built Its Own Secret Google." The Intercept. 2014. https://firstlook.org/theintercept/2014/08/25/icreach-nsa-cia-secret-google-crisscross-proton.

Harcourt, B. E. *Exposed: Desire and Disobedience in the Digital Age*. Cambridge: Harvard University Press, 2015.

Mueller, J., and M. G. Stewart. *Public Opinion and Counterterrorism Policy*. Cato Institute, 2018. https://www.cato.org/publications/white-paper/public-opinion-counterterrorism-policy.

Omand, D. *Securing the State*. Oxford: Oxford University Press USA – OSO, 2014.

Omand, D. "Understanding Digital Intelligence and the Norms that Might Govern It." CIGI, Global Commission on Internet Governance, No. 8. 2015.

Petersen, K. Lund in this issue.

Warner, M. *The Rise and Fall of Intelligence: An International Security History*. Washington, DC: Georgetown University Press, 2014.

Weaver, W., and R. Pallitto. *Extraordinary Rendition*. The Oxford Handbook of National Security Intelligence, Oxford University Press, 2010. doi:10.1093/oxfordhb/9780195375886.003.0020

Weber, L., E. Fishwick, and M. Marmo, eds. *The Routledge International Handbook of Criminology and Human Rights (Hardback)*. Routledge, 2018. https://www.routledge.com/The-Routledge-International-Handbook-of-Criminology-and-Human-Rights/Weber-Fishwick-Marmo/p/book/9781138931176.

## Annex 1.  Disclosure of NSA documents by Edward Snowden- Gallagher Ryan 2014

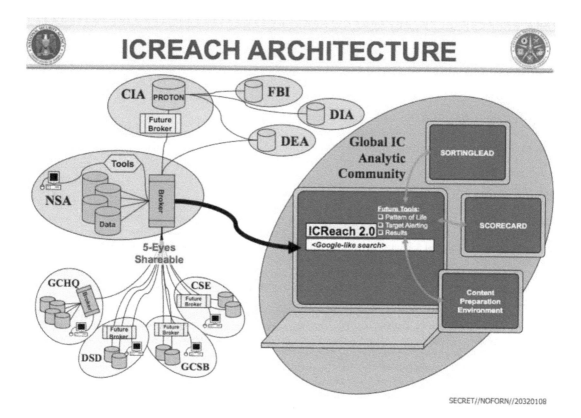

# A new role for 'the public'? Exploring cyber security controversies in the case of WannaCry

Kristoffer Kjærgaard Christensen and Tobias Liebetrau

**ABSTRACT**

As cyber-security incidents become increasingly prevalent, we are facing a major political and democratic challenge: who comprises "the public" in relation to such incidents? Based on a study of the controversies surrounding the WannaCry ransomware attack, this article unpacks issues facing the creation of publics in contemporary ICT-mediated security practices. It shows how cyber-security incidents, such as WannaCry, do not neatly align with traditional national security politics and democracy, and it demonstrates the need to attend to how security publics are created. This may paradoxically entail both political and democratic challenges and possibilities for security politics in the digital age.

## Introduction

'There is plenty of blame to go around for the WannaCry ransomware'.[1]

In May 2017, a highly virulent new strain of self-replicating ransomware known as WannaCry encrypted hundreds of thousands of computers and held users to ransom across the world. This caused great chaos. It severely affected hospitals, government offices and major companies in more than 150 countries. However, WannaCry rapidly transformed 'from an acute situation to be dealt with by security experts to a symbol of how fundamentally vital cyber security protection is and the true scale of what can happen when systems and devices lack crucial defenses'.[2] One of the reasons why WannaCry spread so quickly and viciously was because it leveraged a vulnerability in Microsoft's widely used Windows operating system. It did so in part by appropriating an exploit developed by the NSA (known as EternalBlue). This exploit had been stolen in the summer of 2016 and later (in April 2017) publicly released by the hacking group Shadow Brokers. Yet only in February 2017, several months after the theft, did the NSA notify Microsoft of the vulnerability, so that the company could release an update to patch the vulnerability in March.[3] Nevertheless, many computers and servers clearly never ran the update, leaving those organizations open to attack. Consequently, as the opening quote by Bruce Schneier[4] indicates, the disputes over responsibility surrounding WannaCry involved several actors and were many and profound.

As cyber security incidents like WannaCry become increasingly prevalent on the international security agenda, we are facing a significant political and democratic challenge: who comprises 'the public' in relation to these incidents? The WannaCry attack exemplifies that both the nature and the scope of cyber security is characterized by a fundamental uncertainty. Cyber threats and risks evade state borders and hence the conventional delineation and organization of security politics. Moreover, the case also demonstrates how a plethora of different security actors – and not necessarily state actors – plays a part in security and intelligence practices in the digital age. This makes public oversight increasingly challenging. Traditionally, national security organizations have been accountable to nationally defined publics as a way to bridge the tension between exceptional national security politics and normal democratic politics. However, as security practices, as well as their implications, disperse, they challenge and evade traditional, state-based measures of democratic control. This leaves us with the question of who is to be held accountable, for what, and, not least, *to and by whom* when a cyber security incident like WannaCry occurs.

We argue that this calls for a more contextual and pragmatic approach for how to engage with security politics and democratic accountability in relation to incidents like WannaCry. Such an enquiry should ask not only what happens to the formal procedures when security politics evades the state as the fulcrum of political authority and responsibility. Rather, we need to explore what happens to the understanding of 'the public' towards whom security actors are to be held accountable. When the public of security politics cannot be neatly defined in terms of a national political community, it becomes much more opaque who has a right to security and a legitimate say in holding those responsible to account. We need to attend to how new security publics, rather than being defined a priori, are brought into being in relation to a given security issue. The making of a public is hence by no means an innocent endeavour but a highly political practice that requires active participation of its members. In other words, a public is not automatically designated but actively partakes in its own creation – in 'sparking it into being', as Marres[5] puts it. An enquiry into the making of publics in relation to cyber security thus attunes us to the transformation of contemporary security politics. That is, it attunes us to the negotiation of the security issues at stake, political authority, responsibility and the right to security and protection in the digital age.

To develop this line of argument we, first, argue that cyber security evades the state as the natural political fulcrum of security politics and thereby challenges traditional understandings of security politics. Indeed cyber security is characterized by a fundamental uncertainty, in terms of both its nature and scope. Second, we turn to a brief discussion of the role of 'the public' in security politics. We argue that the identification of the relevant publics of security politics is increasingly difficult, especially in relation to cyber-security incidents, such as WannaCry. Whereas 'the public' and its rights and responsibilities in relation to security politics have historically been assigned by default to a national community, the relevant publics of cyber security are actively brought into being and negotiated. Third, we therefore explore how various security issues and potential publics were brought forth in the controversies that emerged in the wake of WannaCry. Fourth, we turn to the political implications of the challenges of identifying the relevant cyber-security publics – or what we with Beck call the 'subpolitics' of cyber-security publics – before we wrap up and conclude.

## Cyber security beyond the state

The understanding of security as a territorially demarcated national public good is a foundational feature of modern security politics.[6] The state has historically been considered the organizing principle of security politics – both as responsible for the provision of national security and in terms of delineating the public with a right to this provision. However, many of today's pressing security issues, including climate change, terrorism, and not least cyber threats and risks, are quite elusive, complex and often hard to delimit. They call for a wide range of different security efforts and actors across different scales and settings.[7] To be sure, the challenge to the privileged position of the state as the fulcrum of security politics is not unique to cyber security. Yet, while the transversal and uncertain nature of threats and risks may be a general trend in contemporary security politics, nowhere is the trend perhaps more apparent than in relation to cyber security and the governance of cyber threats and risks. Cyber security is in many ways the quintessence of this development.

Cyber security is characterized by a fundamental uncertainty, in terms of both its nature and scope. Central to uncertainty is the dynamic, dispersed and pervasive nature of information and communication technologies (ICT). ICT permeate nearly all spheres of life today. In addition, many of these technologies tend to be highly interconnected. This means that cyber threats and risks are not restricted to a specific physical location, as such. In principle, they may come from anywhere. 'The complex interconnection of cyber infrastructures forms a vast topological mesh where small events and disruptions can impact relations and elements near and far'.[8] Hence, cyber security evades the neat segmentation of security politics in accordance with traditional scales, such as 'global', 'national' and 'local'. Actually, cyber security threats and risks may potentially be both none and all of the above simultaneously. The fast-paced technological development and the fact that even existing technologies may be put to use in new and unforeseen ways further add to the difficulties in pinning down the security challenges related to cyber security.

Consequently, cyber security significantly challenges and transforms the conventional delineation of security politics. The attempts at governing cyber threats and risks neither plays out in a discrete political space nor is it the task of state actors alone. Already 20 years ago Deibert,[9] discussing the impact of ICT on international relations, argued that what he called 'postmodern world order',

'is, paradoxically, a world made up of plural worlds, multiple realities and irrealities…Not a single "global village", and even less a system of territorially-distinct nation-states, postmodern world order is, rather, a pastiche of multiple and overlapping authorities – a quasi-feudal, "multicentric" system'.

Similarly, the governance of cyber threats and risks like WannaCry generally involves a multitude of complex, dispersed and dynamic relations between different actors and technologies. In other words, it is, to borrow a term from James Der Derian,[10] 'heteropolar'. That is to say, it involves 'actors who are different in power and kind (state, corporate, group, individual) and connected nodally through networks rather than hierarchically through states'. As we will explore in further detail below, this is clearly exemplified in the case of WannaCry by debates over the roles of Microsoft and NSA as security actors vis-à-vis different potential security publics.

Indeed private companies are key actors in cyber-security governance. Among other things, because most of the ICT infrastructure is privately owned and operated. Moreover, companies like Microsoft develop and produce the digital devices and the software that are used throughout contemporary society. This means that corporate security decisions are potentially significant for the functioning and security of society. It is thus hardly surprising that there has been an increasing focus on the involvement of the private sector in national security concerns related to cyber security. Around the world public-private partnerships on cyber security are mushrooming.[11] As former American president Barack Obama concluded in his State of the Union Address in 2015: 'This has to be a shared mission. There's only one way to defend America from these cyber threats, and that is through government and industry working together, sharing appropriate information as true partners'.[12]

Yet, to be clear, in relation to cyber security private companies are not just security actors when mobilized by state agencies, as we will show below. They also take on cyber-security issues without the state. Corporate security politics does not necessarily revolve around the territories of nation-states. Their businesses are not defined by the borders of states, and hence nor are the security risks that they are facing. To them a particular national security context is but one political context that they have to navigate, whereas in other instances the state may be irrelevant or even the very problem, as argued by Microsoft in the case of WannaCry. The governance of cyber threats and risk is thus characterized by a fundamental uncertainty and the proliferation of security actors and practices, including multinational corporate actors, that attempt to organize and manage this uncertainty.[13] This also affects the other side of the equation of contemporary security politics, so to speak: the public to be protected and ensure democratic accountability and oversight. Therefore, we now turn to a discussion of the transformation of 'the public' in security practices in the digital age.

## The problem of cyber-security publics

Historically, the identification of the relevant public of security politics has been (relatively) simple: it was generally defined in terms of the national community of the state. Yet, the fundamental uncertainty of cyber security and the central role of corporate actors also create uncertainty in terms 'the public' of cyber-security practices. Above we argued that cyber security challenges the privileged role of the state as the fulcrum of security politics. Consequently, the public of cyber security cannot be delineated simply through reference to traditional state-centric formalized procedures but has to be scrutinized anew. Understandings of 'the public' – often pitted against 'the private' – are a key component in modern politics, not only security politics.[14] Indeed it may refer to a host of things and dynamics that organize politics, including the space of politics (e.g., the public sphere), the division of labour and responsibility (between state and market), and the political community that is the 'audience' of politics.[15] Critical (re)engagements with the concept of the public has lately attracted the attention of scholars within global governance and politics[16] and security studies.[17] Yet, critical examination of the role of the public in contemporary security politics is still nascent.

In the sense of the 'audience' of politics, the public traditionally plays an important double role in security politics. On the one hand, the public is the community of people that have a right to be protected by the security provision. In other words, it is the community for which security agents are responsible. On the other hand, the public also plays a prominent role in ensuring the democratic accountability of security politics. It is often argued that security politics is an exceptional kind of politics that evades normal political and democratic rules and procedures.[18] Still, to contain security politics and maintain its democratic legitimacy the public should ideally provide a counterbalance to, as well as democratic oversight and control of, security politics – either directly or via, for example, its elected representatives. In short, identifying the relevant public is pivotal to the delineation of both responsibility and democratic accountability in relation to security politics. It requires us to engage with the questions of *who is responsible, for what*, and *to whom*.

With the dispersal of (cyber-)security politics beyond the state and its institutions the narrow confinement of responsibility and accountability to a national community is, as argued above, severely challenged. Various scholars have suggested that the public as a political community needs to be (re)envisioned in transnational, post-national, or perhaps even global terms.[19] The state cannot provide the ultimate political foundation for a delineation of the relevant public of security politics; rather it ought to be a matter of the effects of a particular issue, the argument generally goes.[20] Following from this line of reasoning, we might say, simply put, that the relevant public of cyber security politics are those, wherever they are, who are affected by a given cyber security issue. Hence, there can be various diverse and overlapping publics depending on the issue at stake. It follows that what is needed are the proper institutions and procedures to ensure the right to protection of the public of the issue in question and/or their ability to hold those responsible to account.

This critically hinges on the possibility of identifying those affected by cyber-security incidents, such as WannaCry – and, even before that, of identifying the very issue at stake. However, as we have argued hitherto, cyber security is characterized by a fundamental uncertainty. This means that it is often unclear who is affected by any given cyber-security issue or incident, as well as what it is the issue at stake. In other words, neither the relevant public(s) nor the political stakes are given in the order of things.[21] Instead, as we demonstrate in the case of WannaCry, various different security issues and hence publics may potentially be in play. Consequently, this raises a problem for the delineation of the relevant public in terms of who is affected by a cyber-security issue. The dynamic complexity of ICT means that the people affected may lack both the knowledge and the opportunity to hold those responsible to account, to know who it is, and sometimes even the awareness that they themselves are affected.[22] In other words, even if notions of 'the public' are generally associated with visibility, i.e., 'publicity',[23] the potential publics here face conditions of opacity.

To make sense of how the uncertainty of cyber security and ICT affects the role of the public we instead draw on insights from the literature on publics in science and technology studies (STS), by especially Noortje Marres. In her work on 'material publics' Marres emphasizes how the entanglement of social actors and technologies shapes the capacities for participation in political and democratic processes. 'The deployment of things may affect the very specification of politics and democracy as public forms'.[24] That is, the dynamic relations between different actors and technologies, both near and far, enable publics. While this has certain affinities with the argument above about publics as communities of people affected by an issue, there are important differences. In line with our argument above, Marres[25] also stresses the relative opacity and uncertainty that characterize material publics and their relation to an issue. Owing to the complex and dynamic entanglement, it becomes increasingly difficult to determine the boundaries of the relevant publics. As the distinction between inside and the outside collapses and publics take on properties similar to the Möbius Ribbon,[26] actors can simultaneously be both insiders and insiders.

A public is hence not a coherent community but rather an inherently problematic and emergent accomplishment.[27] That is, rather than already existing communities, publics are continuously negotiated and mobilized in relation to a given issue. They are 'sparked into being'.[28] However, this requires active participation. Taking her cue from the work of American pragmatists John Dewey and Walter Lippmann, Marres argues that publics partake actively in their own making. Moreover, just like the positions of actors in relation to an issue may be elusive and subject to negotiation, this also goes for the political stakes of an issue. Indeed the uncertainty of cyber security affords ample space for contestation and disagreement over the security issues at stake, on the one hand, and, on the other hand, who has a right to security and a legitimate say in the matter, as well as the role of holding those in power to account. Consequently, the making of publics is far from a neutral undertaking, but a highly political practice. It is pivotal that we subject this political practice to close scrutiny and refrain from a priori delineation of both the relevant cyber-security publics and the political stakes in play in relation to any cyber security issue. Instead, as we will turn to next, we suggest that we investigate the political controversies in which cyber-security publics are shaped and negotiated.

## Exploring publics and security controversies over wannacry

Now we turn to the security controversies related to WannaCry to show how various potential publics are at play in relation to this incident. As mentioned in the introduction, WannaCry infected hundreds of thousands of computers all over the world, including hospitals, government offices, major companies and home users in more than 150 countries over a weekend in May 2017. The WannaCry malware is designed to attempt to automatically spread itself over local networks onto new computers, like most computer worms. The malware scans for other computers with the same vulnerability that can be exploited with the help of the EternalBlue, an exploit developed by the NSA. When the WannaCry malware find a vulnerable machine, it attacks it and encrypt files on it. This semi-automated process makes WannaCry highly dynamic.[29]

The dynamic and dispersed behaviour of WannaCry speaks to the fundamental uncertainty of cyber security, as argued above, and elides the conventional security political ordering of the world in accordance with conventional scales, such as the global, regional, national and local. On the one hand, WannaCry was ostensibly global in scope given the presence of infected devices in countries across the globe. Yet, on the other hand, it was extremely local if we turn to the vulnerability of the individual computer. Hence it is hard to distinguish the global from the local in the case of WannaCry. Rather than being on opposite ends of the continuum, the WannaCry incident was simultaneously both. As such, it calls into question basic assumptions underpinning the traditional thinking about how to identify those to be protected, as well as designating the responsibility for providing security.

It is no surprise that immediately after the attack victims, politicians and media all over the world raised questions: who was behind the attack? Who was to be held responsible? Due to the (mainly technical) difficulty in attributing the attack, no one knew. Still, as for who was to blame, the finger pointing began straightaway. Bruce Schneier, the internationally renowned cryptographer and computer security professional, summarized the blame game on his blog in the wake of the attack:

> 'There is plenty of blame to go around for the WannaCry ransomware that spread throughout the Internet earlier this month, disrupting work at hospitals, factories, businesses, and universities. First, there are the writers of the malicious software, which blocks victims' access to their computers until they pay a fee. Then there are the users who didn't install the Windows security patch that would have prevented an attack. A small portion of the blame falls on Microsoft, which wrote the insecure code in the first place. One could certainly condemn the Shadow Brokers, a group of hackers with links to Russia who stole and published the National Security Agency attack tools that included the exploit code used in the ransomware. But before all of this, there was the NSA, which found the vulnerability years ago and decided to exploit it rather than disclose it.'[30]

The quote illustrates that a plentitude of actors were involved in making WannaCry happen. The right to protection and the responsibility for providing it were highly debated in the aftermath of WannaCry. Therefore, we focus on the controversies over WannaCry and the related cyber-security practices and how these controversies provided sites and openings for public involvement. This allows us to explore how publics are negotiated along with the security issues at stake.

Here controversies are, in short, situations where actors disagree. They 'display the social in its most dynamic form', as Venturini[31] argues. In controversies the precariousness and contestation of the relevant security practices and publics are hence more readily visible and articulated.[32] However, the disagreements related to WannaCry cannot be reduced to a single, distinct controversy. Instead, as we demonstrate below, WannaCry is a dynamic entanglement of various controversies that despite their relation may revolve around entirely different issues or matters of concern. Consequently, the actors involved in these controversies may even disagree about what is that they disagree about. Yet, as Venturini notes, 'the task of unfolding the complexity of controversies should never be separated from the task of ordering such complexity'.[33] To structure the analysis we hence look at how these controversies involve mobilization of different potential publics and the negotiation of the distribution of responsibility for the security provision between public and private actors, in particular the NSA and Microsoft. The analysis thus proceeds in two parts. First, we examine the controversies around the NSA's practice of hunting and hoarding vulnerabilities. Second, we turn to the controversy regarding Microsoft's self-proclaimed role as 'first responder' when it comes to cyber security.

## Hunting and hoarding vulnerabilities: exploring publics caught between national security and collateral damage

From the start, the NSA took a lot of blame from the community of IT-security professionals following the WannaCry attack. It was generally argued that if guilty parties were going to be named and lessons learned from naming them, those names should include the U.S. government and the NSA, since the NSA built and then lost control of the EternalBlue exploit that was incorporated into WannaCry. Without EternalBlue WannaCry would not have been nearly as devastating. As Kevin Bankston, the director of the New America Foundation's Open Technology Institute, told Wired magazine[34]:

'As we talk about to whom to attribute the WannaCry attack, it's also important to remember to whom to attribute the source of the tools used in the attack: the NSA. By stockpiling the vulnerability information and exploit components that made WannaCry possible, and then failing to adequately shield that information from theft, the intelligence community made America and the world's information systems more vulnerable.'

According to the *Washington Post*, the development of EternalBlue did not go unnoticed within the NSA: 'Those entrusted with deploying it marvelled at both its uncommon power and the widespread havoc it could wreak if it ever got loose'.[35] Allegedly, this lead some NSA officials to debate whether the flaw was so dangerous they should reveal it to Microsoft. Nonetheless, giving up and disclosing the exploit was seen as regular disarmament within the NSA. In the words of a former NSA official, the agency thus continued 'fishing with dynamite' for five years.[36]

However, the White House sought to deflect blame away from the U.S. government and the NSA. Tom Bossert,[37] then Homeland Security adviser to President Trump, said that 'this was a vulnerability exploited as one part of a much larger tool that was put together by the culpable parties and not by the US government'. He continued,

'this was a tool developed by culpable parties, potentially criminals and foreign nation states, that have put it together in such a way as to deliver it with phishing emails, put it into embedded documents, and cause infection, encryption and locking'.

In December 2017 the U.S. government hence pinned the digital disaster on North Korea. In an opinion piece in the *Wall Street Jounal* Bossert[38] wrote, 'North Korea has acted especially badly, largely unchecked, for more than a decade, and its malicious behaviour is growing more egregious. WannaCry was indiscriminately reckless...Pyongyang will be held accountable'

Clearly, the controversy over the responsibility of the NSA and the U.S government is a significant one. It also nicely captures how these dynamics are not shaped by rival political arguments or appeals to interests alone, but also through the affordances of ICT. It demonstrates how the uncertainty and unruliness of ICT play an irreducible role in shaping controversies in the cyber-security domain. The ways in which ICT implicated the NSA in the controversy over the responsibility for WannaCry displays how ICT becomes as an ambiguous and controversial security political object. One that is not neatly bound by the conventional national-territorial political ordering of security, but rather 'consists of tangles of which it is not clear where they begin or where they end, and what exactly they are made up of'.[39]

Because of the complex and dispersed nature of ICT, Americans, users of Microsoft and other information systems across the world could all be seen as affected by WannaCry. These different potential publics all play into to the controversy regarding NSAs role and responsibility in the WannaCry affair. Yet, the communities of affected are neither exclusively nor automatically endowed with the right to protection from the state nor given the opportunity to contest its security practices. On the contrary, they have to claim these rights. The relevant public is thus always in the need of recognizing itself as such and act as one. It is, however, challenging to recognize oneself and fight for ones rights when the arena for it is (beforehand) tightly linked to the practices of foreign national intelligence agency. What we witness is the challenge of cyber-security publics to form as the arena for claiming the right to protection or contestation of security practices puzzlingly sits between traditional secretive national security political institutions and the affordances of ICT.

As such, WannaCry and the related controversy over the responsibility of the NSA indeed speaks to a long-standing debate regarding the role of intelligence services and the hunting, hoarding and stockpiling of vulnerabilities. In the digital age the intelligence community and its collection apparatus relies to a wide extent on zero-day vulnerabilities to compromise enemy systems and access information vital to ensure national security and public safety. The controversy regarding the responsibility of NSA is thus not created ex nihilo. Rather, it taps into a significant controversy regarding whether the NSA and the U.S. government – or indeed any intelligence service or government – should retain zero-day vulnerabilities or disclose and share them so they can be patched. As Microsoft's president and chief legal officer, Brad Smith, proclaimed in the wake of the WannaCry attack[40]:

> 'this attack provides yet another example of why the stockpiling of vulnerabilities by governments is such a problem. This is an emerging pattern in 2017. We have seen vulnerabilities stored by the CIA show up on WikiLeaks, and now this vulnerability stolen from the NSA has affected customers around the world…We need governments to consider the damage to civilians that comes from hoarding these vulnerabilities and the use of these exploits'

Vulnerabilities that are found in widely used software can provide some of the most valuable intelligence because they may enable access to a large number of targets. On the contrary, the discovery of a vulnerability in widely used software, such as a Windows operating system, also means that the potential harm done with it could be far-reaching. Typically, this is argued to be a balancing act between exploiting the vulnerability to keep a nationally defined public safe while at the same time not exposing that same public to the same exploit. WannaCry exemplifies this inherent 'collateral damage' dilemma build into the exploration, buying and stockpiling of vulnerabilities for intelligence purposes, since keeping these vulnerabilities undisclosed poses a risk to both American and foreign citizens, companies and public institution who are reliant on vulnerable software. Because zero-day vulnerabilities are discovered and not created, keeping a vulnerability secret means other governments or cyber offenders may steal or independently discover and use the vulnerability to the disadvantage of citizens and businesses.

Still, to return to the public of WannaCry, it can be argued that most of its potential constituents failed to qualify as participants in the affairs, in the sense of not having the opportunity, will, connections, skills or vocabularies required to address the issues of the NSAs practices of hoarding and hunting of vulnerabilities. Most of the affected were not American and they were, so to speak, both external and internal to the institutional-political security controversy regarding NSA and WannaCry. They were not outsiders, since they were severely affected by and thus entangled in the attack. But they were, at the same time, too much strangers to the attack as a to form a public (affair), as they didn't have access to the means required to deal with it.

## Companies as first responders: exploring publics between citizens and users

One of the staunchest critics of the NSA in the aftermath of WannaCry was Microsoft, which in response proclaimed that itself (and other companies), as a result, ought to take on the role as 'first responders' in relation to cyber security. It is to this puzzling claim that we now turn.

> 'The governments of the world should treat this attack as a wake-up call. They need to take a different approach and adhere in cyberspace to the same rules applied to weapons in the physical world. We need governments to consider the damage to civilians that comes from hoarding these vulnerabilities and the use of these exploits. This is one reason we called in February for a new "Digital Geneva Convention" to govern these issues, including a new requirement for governments to report vulnerabilities to vendors, rather than stockpile, sell, or exploit them. And it's why we've pledged our support for defending every customer everywhere in the face of cyberattacks, regardless of their nationality. This weekend, whether it's in London, New York, Moscow, Delhi, Sao Paulo, or Beijing, we're putting this principle into action and working with customers around the world.'[41]

This statement from Brad Smith, Microsoft's president and chief legal officer, following WannaCry, is worth quoting at length. It provides another opening for engaging with WannaCry, as it is a quite different contribution to the controversies over the responsibility for cyber security and its many potential publics. Smith directs our attention to the ways in which the cyber-security practices of big corporations like Microsoft are part of (re)configuring the organization and distribution of responsibility for cyber security and hence the potential creation of new security publics.

The quote demonstrates how Microsoft not only acts as a cyber-security actor when mobilized by a state agency in support of matters pertaining to national security. Instead,

Microsoft claims to be actively seeking to liberate its customers from the tentacles of the nation state defending them 'everywhere in the face of cyberattacks, regardless of their nationality'. Nevertheless, Microsoft, still calls for governmental protection of civilians in this new security arena: cyberspace. Paradoxically, Microsoft's services hence imply both a contestation of and a reliance on bounded state authority. In a sense, Microsoft takes on the role as the protector by contesting the authority of the states regarding the security of its customers while referring to the international community of states in doing so.

As part of the controversy over the responsibility for WannaCry Microsoft thus also links it to the controversies over determining the political ordering of cyberspace as a political space and its relation to the conventional political landscape. On the one hand, Microsoft portrays cyberspace as a political space that defies physical state territories and metric distances. Rather this political space is here characterized by the relations between Microsoft and its customers, notwithstanding their national affiliations. As a result, these individuals are no longer solely endowed with the right to protection by their states. Rather, as Microsoft claims, WannyCry 'demonstrates the degree to which cybersecurity has become a shared responsibility between tech companies and customers'.[42] On the other hand, it also refers to a conventional political space in which governments are called upon to sustain the (international) legislative model that we have known for years.

How does that then relate more specific to the formation and mobilization of publics? Microsoft mobilizes different communities of affected. With regards to the former political space, well known nationally defined communities are mobilized towards whom governments are responsible to deliver security by e.g., agreeing on a Digital Geneva Convention. This is, however, also the communities to claim their national or citizen rights and put pressure on the governments of the world to stop intelligence services from hoarding and buying vulnerabilities and instead negotiate a Digital Geneva Convention. Second, Microsoft's pledge for protecting and supporting customers despite their geographical location bring to the fore a community of user or customer. This potential publics traverse a (cyber)space in which security is enacted and distributed differently. Some have their software is often updated and secured by Microsoft, while others do not. Accordingly, there is a differentiation of rights and responsibilities. For those who pay for the newer versions of Microsoft's software cyber security is managed, while those who use older versions of Microsoft's software solutions are left with the insecure software. Thus, while our rights have traditionally been defined by our citizenship of a particular state, we are now also brought into being as potential publics through our relations to big corporations, such as Microsoft. Another quote by Brad Smith encapsulates this change:

> 'Let's face it, cyberspace is the new battlefield. The world of potential war has migrated from land to sea to air and now cyberspace. But cyberspace is a different kind of space. Not only can we not find it in the physical world, but cyberspace is us. For all of us in this room, it is us. Cyberspace is owned and operated by the private sector. It is private property, whether it's submarine cables or datacenters or servers or laptops or smartphones. It is a different kind of battlefield than the world has seen before. And that puts us in a different position. It puts you in a different position, because when it comes to these attacks in cyberspace, we not only are the plane of battle, we are the world's first responders. Instead of nation-state attacks being met by responses from other nation-states, they are being met by us'.[43]

In other words, the social contract is, to state it polemically, supplemented by our terms of service with these companies. One potential public that is brought forward is the one consisting of what Benjamin Bratton (2016) has called 'citizen-users'.

## The 'subpolitics' of cyber-security publics

That publics might be defined both in relation to big corporations and national security communities is no trivial matter. This effectively highlights how people are not endowed with the right to protection, more or less automatically; rather they have to claim this right in particular arenas and always under specific conditions. What perhaps makes the difficulties of identifying these cyber-security publics an even bigger challenge to our conventional ideals of liberal politics and democracy is that the arena for fighting for the right to (acquire or contest) security need not be the traditional political institutions. In other words, it is by no means clear or easy to see how, under these conditions, cyber-security politics and issues can acquire the public pertinence necessary for effective public action to be taken. Our current state of affairs is then perhaps better understood as a move towards what Ulrick Beck[44] aptly called 'subpolitics'. Hence what characterizes cyber security is, as we have demonstrated above, ad hoc political participation and coalitions outside and beyond traditional political institutions often at 'sites' that were previously considered 'unpolitical'. Security politics thus moves to a plethora of new sites beyond the traditional confines of the state, including technologies and boardrooms. Security has, in the words of Jef Huysmans,[45] become unbound.

This obviously carries significant consequences for security politics. Yet, paradoxically it can be both a blessing and a curse. To begin with the latter, people may understandably have hard time determining where to turn for (acquiring or contesting) security. They risk coming out short trying to navigate their many potential public identities as, for example national citizens or citizen-users, and deciding which one to mobilize and enact. Also, if we accept the centrality of private companies as providers of security, it is also a matter of who has the economic resources to retain the services of the 'right' companies. To be clear, it is hardly an option to opt out of the identity as citizen-users completely. Bruce Schneier[46] have likened our relationship to tech companies to a feudal one:

> 'We might distribute our allegiance among several of these companies, or studiously avoid a particular one we don't like. Regardless, it's becoming increasingly difficult to not pledge allegiance to at least one of them'.

In other words, we can hardly expect everyone to always have the possibility to speak up, claim their right to security and hold those responsible to account. These are indeed very real issues and challenges and we may very well end up with winners and losers with respect to the political economy of security in the digital age – a new kind of 'digital divide', so to speak.

On the other hand, this also paves the way for new forms of public participation and holding those in power to account. To quote Beck,[47] 'subpolitics sets politics free by changing the rules and boundaries of the political so that it becomes more open and susceptible to new linkages – as well as capable of being negotiated and reshaped'. That is to say, there is a possibility for actively engaging in the process of determining what cyber-security politics can and should be, determining the political issues at stake, and, not least, who have a legitimate stake in these issues and a right to security. Or, as Noortje Marres observantly puts it 'here, the composition of the public – which entities and relations it is made up of – must be understood as partly the outcome of, and as something that is at stake in, the process of issue articulation'.[48] Consequently, the uncertainty of ICT and cyber-security practices provide an opening for the bottom-up creation of new security publics.

Navigating the tension between the challenges and opportunities that cyber security faces us with in this regard is no small task. It points to the need for a new role for the public(s) of cyber security. As such, the idea that publics spark themselves into being is not merely diagnostic. It is also prescriptive in the sense that this situation calls for active participation in the political process of negotiation the political issues at stake, as well as the relevant stakeholders; that is, the relevant public(s). But, as noted above, we need to pay attention to who gets to partake in this political process. This is not just an economic issue. It also requires a certain (technical) expertise to engage with these issues. This prompts the question whether some people, such as (tech) experts, specialized interest groups and media, have a special responsibility in this regard. This can hardly just be the task of the individual average citizen-user. In other words, this is not a silver bullet. There are still a number of caveats and challenges to be faced. In any case, it is clear that defining responsibility and ensuring democratic accountability in relation to cyber security strongly calls for (new forms of) active public participation.

## Conclusion

In this article, we have shed light on the difficulties of 'the public' in view of the continuing political and democratic challenges brought about by ICT and cyber security. Based on a study of the WannaCry ransomware attack, we unpacked how controversies surrounding the NSA's practice of hunting and hoarding vulnerabilities and Microsoft's self-proclaimed role as 'first responder' made visible the significant issues facing the creation of relevant publics in contemporary ICT-mediated security practices. We showed how cyber-security incidents, such as WannaCry, do not completely align with the traditional space, community and institutions of national politics and democracy. Intelligence services and business, such as the NSA and Microsoft, are not only democratically accountable to a well-defined public in the traditional state-based sense. As demonstrated, the NSA's and Microsoft's cyber-security practices partake in mobilizing various different security issues and potential non-national publics.

This challenges the traditional role of citizens as subjects of rights and responsibilities within a (territorially) well-defined community. Our security and our democratic rights in relation to cybersecurity are hence not defined through our national citizenship alone. They are also shaped through our interactions with ICT and private companies. This development generates multiple potentially relevant publics and, as such, it raises new and challenging dilemmas of inclusion and democratic control. In short, we cannot just fall back on the liberal state, its rule of law[49] and formal institutions for democratic control in relation to cyber security. To rely solely on traditional modes of state regulation and democracy would be insufficient, and we would be hard pressed for appropriate forms of engagement with some of the most pressing security issues of our time. However, as we argued, this also entails the potential for new publics to emerge and contest security practices outside the traditional sites of security politics. In sum, coping with security politics of the digital age calls for a new and more active role for all the potential security publics.

## Notes

1. Schneier, 'WannaCry and vulnerabilities'.
2. Newman, 'Secret software bugs'.
3. Microsoft, 'Microsoft Security Bulletin and Protecting Customers and Evaluating Risk'.
4. Bruce Schneier is an internationally renowned cryptographer and computer security professional.
5. Marres, 'Issues Spark A Public into Being'.
6. Abrahamsen and Williams, *Security Beyond the State*; and Petersen, *Corporate Risk and National Security*.
7. Beck, *World Risk Society*, and Petersen and Tjalve, 'Intelligence Expertise'.
8. Simon and de Goede, 'Bureaucratic Vitalism and European Emergency'.
9. Deibert, *Parchment, Printing, and Hypermedia*.
10. Der Derian, *Military-Industrial-Media-Entertainment-Network*.
11. Carr, 'Public-Private Partnerships'; Cavelty and Suter, 'Public-Private Partnerships'; Christensen and Petersen, 'A Question of Loyalty'; Lowenthal, *Intelligence: From Secrets to Policy*; and Nussbaum, 'Communicating Cyber Intelligence'.
12. Obama, State of the Union Address, 2015.
13. Power, *Organized Uncertainty*.
14. Brighenti, *Visibility in Social Theory*; Owens, 'Public and Private Force'; and Weintraub, 'The Public/Private Distinction'.
15. Habermas, *Transformation of the Public Sphere*; Heald, 'Varieties of Transparency'; and Weintraub, 'The Public/ Private Distinction'.
16. Best and Gheciu, *The Public in Global Governance* and Abraham and Yehonatan, 'The (global) public and its problems'.
17. Monsees, Paper presented at the EISA Annual Conference 2018, Forthcoming and Walters and D'Aoust, 'Bringing Publics into Critical Security Studies'.
18. Buzan et al., *Security: a New Framework for Analysis*.
19. Beck, *World Risk Society*; Habermas, *The Post-National Constellation*; Held, 'Rethinking Democracy'; and Ruggie, 'Reconstituting the Global Public Domain'.
20. Held, Global Covenant, 2004 and Marres, *Material Participation*.
21. Liebetrau and Christensen, The Ontological Politics of Cyber Security, Forthcoming.

22. Ananny and Crawford, 'Seeing Without Knowing'.
23. See e.g., Brighenti, 'Visibility: A Category for the Social Sciences'.
24. Marres, 'Devices of Participation', 423.
25. Marres, *Material Participation*.
26. Bigo, 'The Möbius Ribbon' and 'The Field and the Ban-Opticon'.
27. See note 25 above.
28. Marres, 'Issues Spark A Public into Being'.
29. Kaspersky, 'WannaCry: Are you safe?'
30. See note 1 above.
31. Venturini, 'Diving in Magma', 261.
32. Bueger, 'Pathways to Practice'; Latour, *Reassembling the Social*; and Venturini, *Diving in Magma*.
33. Venturini, 'Building on faults', 797.
34. Greenberg, 'Accountable for WannaCry'.
35. Nakashima and Timberg, NSA Officials Worried.
36. Ibid.
37. Bossert, 'White House Press Briefing'.
38. Bossert, 'North Korea Is Behind WannaCry'.
39. Marres, *Material Participation*, 35.
40. Smith, 'Lessons from last week's cyberattack'.
41. Ibid.
42. Smith, 'The Need for a Digital Geneva Convention'.
43. See note 40 above.
44. Beck, *World Risk Society*, 1999.
45. Huysmans, *Security Unbound*.
46. Schenier, *Data and Goliath*, 69.
47. Beck, *World Risk Society*, 40.
48. Marres, 'Material Politics', 55.
49. Also, legislative developments tend to be reactive and slow and it would hence be difficult for the legislation to keep up with the technological innovation. Even if this were possible, it would hardly be ideal for the notion of rule of law if new and constantly changing laws were to be rushed through parliament. Moreover, it is often far from clear which state should be the regulating authority.

## Disclosure statement

No potential conflict of interest was reported by the authors.

## ORCID

Tobias Liebetrau 🆔 http://orcid.org/0000-0001-6996-9328

## Bibliography

Abraham, J. K., and A. Yehonatan. "A Pragmatist Vocation International Relations: The (Global) Public and Its Problems." *European Journal of International Relations* 23, no. 1 (2017): 26–48. doi:10.1177/1354066115619018.
Abrahamsen, R., and M. C. Williams. *Security beyond the State: Private Security in International Politics*. Cambridge: Cambridge University Press, 2010.

Ananny, M., and K. Crawford. "Seeing without Knowing: Limitations of the Transparency Ideal and Its Application to Algorithmic Accountability." *New Media and Society* (2016): 1–17. doi:10.1177/1461444816676645.

Beck, U. *World Risk Society*. Cambridge: Polity, 1999.

Best, J., and A. Gheciu. *The Return of the Public in Global Governance*. Cambridge: Cambridge University Press, 2014.

Bigo, D. "The Möbius Ribbon of Internal and External Security(Ies)." In *Identies, Borders, Orders: Rethinking International Relations Theory*, edited by M. Albert, D. Jacobson, and Y. Lapid, 91–116. Minneapolis: University of Minnesota Press, 2001.

Bigo, D. "Globalized (In)Security: The Field and the Ban-Opticon." In *Terror, Insecurity and Liberty: Illiberal Practices of Liberal Regimes after 9/11*, edited by D. Bigo and A. Tsoukala, 10–48. Abingdon: Routledge, 2008.

Bossert, T. "It's Official: North Korea Is behind WannaCry." *The Wall Street Journal*, (December 18 2017). https://www.wsj.com/articles/its-official-north-korea-is-behind-wannacry-1513642537.

Bossert, T. "Press Briefing on the Attribution of the WannaCry Malware Attack to North Korea." White House. Accessed December 19, 2017. https://www.whitehouse.gov/briefings-statements/press-briefing-on-the-attribution-of-the-wannacry-malware-attack-to-north-korea-121917/

Bratton, B. H. *The Stack: On Software and Sovereignty*. Cambridge: MIT Press, 2016.

Brighenti, A. "Visibility: A Category for the Social Sciences." *Current Sociology* 55, no. 3 (2007): 323–342. doi:10.1177/0011392107076079.

Brighenti, A. *Visibility in Social Theory and Social Research*. Basingstoke: Palgrave Macmillan, 2010.

Bueger, C. "Pathways to Practice: Praxiography and International Politics." *European Political Science Review* 6, no. 3 (2014): 383–406. doi:10.1017/S1755773913000167.

Buzan, B., O. Wæver, and D. W. Jaap. *Security: A New Framework for Analysis*. Boulder: Lynne Rienner, 1998.

Carr, M. "Public-Private Partnerships in National Cyber-Security Strategies." *International Affairs* 92, no. 1 (2016): 43–62. doi:10.1111/1468-2346.12504.

Cavelty, M. D., and M. Suter. "Public-Private Partnerships are No Silver Bullet: An Expanded Governance Model for Critical Infrastructure Protection." *International Journal of Critical Infrastructure Protection* 2 (2009): 179–187. doi:10.1016/j.ijcip.2009.08.006.

Christensen, K. K., and K. L. Petersen. "Public-Private Partnerships on Cyber Security: A Question of Loyalty." *International Affairs* 93, no. 6 (2017): 1435–1452. doi:10.1093/ia/iix189.

Davidson, A. I. "In Praise of Counter-Conduct." *History of Human Sciences* 24, no. 4 (2011): 24–41. doi:10.1177/0952695111411625.

Deibert, R. J. *Parchment, Printing, and Hypermedia*. New York: Columbia University Press, 1997.

Der Derian, J. *Virtuous War: Mapping the Military-Industrial-Media-Entertainment-Network*. New York: Routledge, 2009.

Greenberg, A. "Hold North Korea Accountable for WannaCry—And the NSA, Too." Wired. Accessed December 19, 2017. https://www.wired.com/story/korea-accountable-wannacry-nsa-eternal-blue/

Habermas, J. *The Structural Transformation of the Public Sphere: An Inquiry into a Category of Bourgeois Society*. Cambridge, MA: MIT Press, 1989.

Habermas, J. *The Post-National Constellation: Political Essays*. Cambridge: Polity, 2001.

Heald, D. "Varieties of Transparency." In *Transparency: The Key to Better Governance?* edited by C. Hood and D. Heald, 25–43. Oxford: Oxford University Press/British Academy, 2006.

Held, D. "The Changing Contours of Political Community: Rethinking Democracy in the Context of Globalization." In *Global Democracy: Key Debates*, edited by B. Holden, 249–261. London: Routledge, 1999.

Huysmans, J. *Security Unbound: Enacting Democratic Limits*. London: Routledge, 2014.

Kaspersky, L. "WannaCry: Are You Safe?" Kaspersky Blog. Accessed May 13, 2017. https://www.kaspersky.com/blog/wannacry-ransomware/16518/

Latour, B. *Reassembling the Social: An Introduction to Actor-Network-Theory*. Oxford: Oxford University Press, 2005.

Liebetrau, T., and K. K. Christensen. "The Ontological Politics of Cyber Security." Paper presented at the annual meeting for the Danish Political Science Association, Vejle, October, 2017

Linda, M. "Socio-Technical Controversies and the Emergence of Multiple Publics." Paper presented at the annual meeting for the European International Studies Association, Prague, September, 2018

Lowenthal, M. M. *Intelligence: From Secrets to Policy*. 6thed. Los Angeles: SAGE, 2015.

Marres, N. "Issues Spark A Public into Being: A Key but Often Forgotten Point of the Lippmann-Dewey Debate." In *Making Things Public: Atmospheres of Democracy*, edited by B. Latour and P. Weibel, 208–217. Cambridge, MA: MIT Press, 2005.

Marres, N. *Material Participation: Technology, the Environment and Everyday Politics*. Basingstoke: Palgrave Macmillan, 2012.

Marres, N. "Why Political Ontology Must Be Experimentalized: On Eco-Show Homes as Devices of Participation." *Social Studies of Science* 43, no. 3 (2013): 417–443. doi:10.1177/0306312712475255.

Microsoft. "Microsoft Security Bulletin MS17-010 - Critical." Microsoft TechNet. Accessed April 14. https://technet.microsoft.com/en-us/library/security/ms17-010.aspx.

Microsoft Security Response Center. "Protecting Customers and Evaluating Risk." Microsoft TechNet. Accessed April 14. https://blogs.technet.microsoft.com/msrc/2017/04/14/protecting-customers-and-evaluating-risk/

Nakashima, E., and C. Timberg. 2017. "NSA Officials Worried about the Day Its Potent Hacking Tool Would Get Loose. Then It Did." Washington Post. Accessed May 16. https://www.washingtonpost.com/business/technology/nsa-officials-worried-about-the-day-its-potent-hacking-tool-would-get-loose-then-it-did/2017/05/16/50670b16-3978-11e7-a058-ddbb23c75d82_story.html?noredirect=on&utm_term=.0aa0d014c820

Newman, L. H. 2017. "WNew Yorkhy Governments Won't Let Go of Secret Software Bugs." Wired. Accessed May 16. https://www.wired.com/2017/05/governments-wont-let-go-secret-software-bugs/

Nussbaum, B. H. "Communicating Cyber Intelligence to Non-Technical Customers." *International Journal of Intelligence and CounterIntelligence* 30, no. 4 (2017): 743–764. doi:10.1080/08850607.2017.1297120.

Obama, B. "The 2015 State of the Union Address." Accessed January 20. https://obamawhitehouse.archives.gov/the-press-office/2015/01/20/remarks-president-state-union-address-january-20-2015

Owens, P. "Distinctions, Distinctions: "Public" and "Private" Force?" *International Affairs* 84, no. 5 (2008): 977–990. doi:10.1111/j.1468-2346.2008.00750.x.

Petersen, K. L. *Corporate Risk and National Security Redefined*. Oxford: Oxford University Press, 2007.

Petersen, K. L., and V. S. Tjalve. "Intelligence Expertise in the Age of Information Sharing: Public–Private 'Collection' and Its Challenges to Democratic Control and Accountability." *Intelligence and National Security* 33, no. 1 (2018): 21–35. doi:10.1080/02684527.2017.1316956.

Power, M. *Organized Uncertainty: Designing a World of Risk Management*. Abingdon: Routledge, 2012.

Ruggie, J. G. "Reconstituting the Global Public Domain: Issues, Actors, and Practices." *European Journal of International Relations* 10, no. 4 (2004): 499–531. doi:10.1177/1354066104047847.

Schneier, B. *Data and Goliath: The Hidden Battles to Collect Your Data and Control Your World*. New York: Norton and Company, 2015.

Schneier, B. "WannaCry and Vulnerabilities." In *Schneier on Security*, June 2 (2017). https://www.schneier.com/blog/archives/2017/06/wannacry_and_vu.html

Simon, S., and D. G. Marieke. "Cybersecurity, Bureaucratic Vitalism and European Emergency." *Theory, Culture & Society* 32, no. 2 (2015): 79–106. doi:10.1177/0263276414560415.

Smith, B."The Need for a Digital Geneva Convention." Keynote address at the RSA Conference, February 14, 2017 https://blogs.microsoft.com/uploads/2017/03/Transcript-of-Brad-Smiths-Keynote-Address-at-the-RSA-Conference-2017.pdf

Smith, B. "The Need for Urgent Collective Action to Keep People Safe Online: Lessons from Last Week's Cyberattack." Microsoft blog, May.

Venturini, T. "Diving in Magma: How to Explore Controversies with Actor-Network Theory." *Public Understanding of Science* 19, no. 3 (2010): 258–273. doi:10.1177/0963662509102694.

Venturini, T. "Building on Faults: How to Represent Controversies with Digital Methods." *Public Understanding of Science* 21, no. 7 (2012): 796–812. doi:10.1177/0963662510387558.

Walters, W., and A.-M. D'Aoust. "Bringing Publics into Critical Security Studies: Notes for a Research Strategy." *Millennium - Journal of International Studies* 44, no. 1 (2015): 45–68. doi:10.1177/0305829815594439.

Weintraub, J. "The Theory and Politics of the Public/Private Distinction." In *Public and Private in Thought and Practice: Perspectives on a Grand Dichotomy*, edited by J. Weintraub and K. Kumar, 1–42. Chicago; London: University of Chicago Press, 1997.

# Spreading intelligence

Adam Diderichsen

**ABSTRACT**
Defining intelligence is not just a terminological but also a political question. Intelligence methods are spreading quickly in the contemporary security landscape, and defining intelligence gives us a clearer idea of what we are in fact spreading, and therefore also of the political and social consequences that this may entail. When using intelligence methods in, say, policing, public administration or immigration services, we import a specific adversarial logic and thereby transform the social relationships that these regulatory and administrative practices support and rest upon. In this paper, I shall propose a new definition of intelligence in order to analyse the social transformations that may be produced by the logical structure implicit in the concept of intelligence.

Intelligence has become a defining, perhaps even dominant, feature of today's security landscape. This is the case not only in the sense that intelligence agencies across the world have grown enormously in both resources and importance but also in the sense that the use of intelligence and intelligence methods has spread over a still larger field, as evident in the use of intelligence in such diverse fields as policing, internal revenue services and immigration control. In this paper, I analyse the kind of thinking that goes with intelligence and that we, willingly or not, are spreading along with the use of intelligence methods. Starting with a critical discussion of the various attempts at defining intelligence that we find in the scholarly literature and drawing on cognitive semantics, I argue that intelligence as a concept is tied to an adversarial logic: Intelligence is something that you gather and use when taking part in a conflict with an enemy or adversary. Intelligence is therefore not a neutral tool but has the capacity to transform the nature of a social relation in an adversarial direction. The widespread use of intelligence methods therefore risks transforming the relation between state authorities and citizens. In the last part of the paper, I trace some of the consequences that such a transformation may potentially have for civil society and the democratic legitimacy of state authorities, focusing in particular on policing.

## Defining intelligence

Intelligence can famously be defined as both an activity – the act of collecting, analysing and disseminating intelligence – and a product – the various information, assessments, reports etc. produced by the activity.[1] More elaborate definitions add function and use, or the institutional setting of intelligence activities,[2] noting for instance that intelligence is future-oriented and used by decision makers,[3] or underlining that the function of intelligence is to overcome ignorance and uncertainties in order to identify and assess risks and threats so they can become the object of policy interventions.[4] Some definitions also add secrecy as a defining feature of intelligence[5] and whether or not secrecy should be part of a formal definition of intelligence; it seems clear that the professional identity and organizational legitimacy of Western intelligence services are tied to a specific image of the services as being secret. On the other hand, defining intelligence by means of secrecy seems hard to reconcile with the widespread use of open sources in intelligence practices,[6] just as it leaves unexplained why information and intelligence practices are kept secret in the first place. Other scholars refrain from attempting to give a precise definition of intelligence, noting instead that intelligence organizations are characterized by a *security environment, secrecy* and *surveillance*,[7] which seems to imply that we need to analyse intelligence organizations in order to get a solid grasp of the concept of intelligence.[8]

All of these definitions point to important aspects of, or elements in, the concept of intelligence. It may therefore be tempting to propose a comprehensive definition that encompasses all or most of these various elements. A comprehensive list of defining features may on the other hand leave unexplained why the concept of intelligence has exactly this combination of characteristics. Moreover, a list of defining features may cause us to overlook the logical connection between the items on the list. It may for instance be that the function of intelligence explains why intelligence is often kept secret. In other words, some of the items on the list may be more important or essential than others in the sense that they explain other items on the list.

Definitions may serve various purposes. Instead of trying to decide which definition is the correct one in general, we should therefore start by clarifying the purpose to which we hope to use the definition. More precisely, we need to distinguish between several different senses, in which we may be said to define a term:

(1) We may give a *dictionary definition* of a term. That is, we may try to explain what the term means in common parlance, for instance by supplying a list of synonyms or near synonyms and pointing out the main semantic and stylistic characteristics of the term. Such a definition will be particularly useful to language users, who are uncertain of the meaning of the term and need to learn how to use it. Often, we will find that the term can be used in several different, more or less related senses, which we need to distinguish carefully in our dictionary entry (as I am doing now regarding the term 'definition' itself). Moreover, it may be difficult to give a precise, coherent and complete dictionary definition, since language use, especially in everyday language, is often imprecise and rest on implicit rather than explicit rules, to which may be added the fact that languages change over time, just as language users may use language in creative, new and unexpected ways, which may extent or change the previous meaning of a term.

(2) The author of a text may give an *authorial definition*, i.e., he or she may explain how (s)he will use a specific term in the text. In this area, semantic liberty reigns – any author may use linguistic terms the way that (s)he deems best, although of course the end result may be a dense or even incomprehensible text, if terms are used in an idiosyncratic manner far removed from ordinary use.

(3) A term may be given a *technical definition*, i.e., a precise specification of the way that the term should be used within a particular field of knowledge. Whereas an authorial definition is an explication of the ways that an individual author proposes to use a term, a technical definition should reflect the way that the term is used by a group of language users with specific epistemic characteristics. Sometimes, the distinction may be a matter of degree, since technical definitions may be associated with prominent authority figures within a specific discipline and may often be found in textbooks and other key-text in a discipline. But whereas an author may freely decide how to use a term, a technical definition should be shared by a larger group of persons with the required knowledge and training to use the term in a precise and uniform way. So, whereas a dictionary entry may list many different senses (including technical senses) of a term, a technical definition should ideally be univocal. Note also that whereas a dictionary definition is (mainly) descriptive, in that it explains how a term is actually used by language users (although such a description may have normative implications for language users learning how to use

the term), a technical definition is strongly normative: It not only explains how the term is used by the epistemic community in question but also proposes the definition as a rule, which should be followed by community members (mastery of the use may even be considered a prerequisite of [full] membership of the community, as when students are tested in the use of key technical terms).

(4) Sometimes, we may use a definition as a way of clarifying the often-implicit logic and cognitive structure, which is inherent in the use of a specific term. I shall call this a *philosophical definition*. Philosophical texts are often full of technical definitions, including many that serve to establish and define philosophy as an academic discipline. But that is not what I have in mind here. A *philosophical definition*, as I use the term, aims at rendering explicit the conceptual content in a specific term (or perhaps better: the concept denoted by the term) in order to clarify its logical implications and the problems that may arise from taken-for-granted assumptions associated with the term. Often philosophical definitions draw support from dictionary definition, but they aim not at describing actual language use, but at clarifying and perhaps improving our thinking. A philosophical definition may therefore serve as a stepping-stone for various kinds of philosophical enterprises, including not only conceptual clarity but also criticism of the values and assumption implicit in a specific term – or as a way of reminding us what role a specific phenomenon (such as a particular social institution) should play in our life. So, whereas a dictionary definition of, say, science would enlist the various senses, in which this term is used in contemporary English, a philosophical definition of the term would attempt to catch what is important to or essential in science. Such a definition would assist us in accomplishing tasks such as clarifying whether some particular endeavour should be classified as science or rather as pseudo-science, perhaps pointing out that certain uses of the term are problematic or outright inconsistent; or helping us decide whether we should trust science in contrast to other epistemic practices (if there are any), or whether there are questions which science is unable to address.

Often it is very difficult, if not impossible, to provide philosophical definitions, at least if we expect such definitions to be able to provide us with necessary and sufficient criteria for a social practice to count as something (e.g., science). More generally, a recurrent theme in contemporary philosophy has been to criticize the 'essentialism' inherent in much traditional philosophy, aiming at describing the more or less 'eternal' essences defining a specific phenomenon, thereby overlooking or eliminating the historical, social and political processes, if not outright conflicts, that have led to the contemporary phenomenon. This is in particular true of the attempt to define social practices, such as intelligence, since social practices are often relatively stable over time, even as their (alleged) function and supporting rationalities change over time.[9] When giving a precise definition of a social practice, we may therefore overlook the historical development and changing rationalities that reinterpret the practice over time – as has indeed been the case with intelligence, which has been reinterpreted from its original military context to today's much wider use of intelligence in many different contexts.

On the other hand, we need at least a partial grasp of what is important or essential to a given phenomenon, if we want to consider, perhaps in a critical perspective, the contemporary use and misuse of a specific concept, although we may perhaps want to frame such an undertaking in less ambitious terms than traditional metaphysics, aiming not at describing eternal essences, if we can even make sense of such a thing, but rather at capturing important aspects of the contemporary use of a term.

A clarification of the cognitive core of a specific concept is furthermore a precondition for a critical take on the reinterpretation of social practices that may result from the application of the concept outside its original domain. We need to have some sort of grasp of a concept in order to see what the consequences are of stretching the concept to cover new areas and reinterpreting the associated social practices. This is, in sum, what I shall attempt to do in the following by providing a philosophical definition of intelligence focusing on the cognitive content in the concept.

## Cognitive linguistics

I shall use cognitive linguistics as my overall theoretical framework for understanding concepts and their semantical content.[10] According to cognitive linguistics, language use is based on human cognitive abilities more generally. In particular, concepts are tied to a cognitive domain with a specific structure and associated set of experiences. The way that we use a concept thus depends not only on the meaning (or definition) of the concept itself but also on the associated cognitive structures, which are part of a wider cognitive domain. Moreover, the cognitive scheme is often structured around a set of key-examples that instantiate the concept and specify how the corresponding word is used. This explains that even though many concepts cannot be defined in terms of necessary and sufficient criteria, language users still tend to agree when asked to give good examples of the things or phenomena covered by the concept.[11] We may not be able to specify exactly what is necessary and sufficient for something to count as a chair, but we are still able to point to good examples of chairs. The cognitive core of a concept may thus be relatively clear as specified by instantiation, even though its boundaries may be fussy. By contrast, the phenomena in the periphery of the concept may only partially resemble the core examples, and language users may disagree whether the concept apply to these more peripheral examples.

Taking the concept of intelligence as our example, we may thus expect the concept to be structured around a set of core examples, which more or less everyone would agree are good examples of intelligence (say information concerning the whereabouts of enemy troops), intelligence agencies (CIA, MI6) or intelligence activities (surveillance, spying). These core examples will moreover be tied to a set of experiences, other concepts and common ways of thinking associated with the core examples. Around the core, we will find a more or less extended set of phenomena that resemble the core examples in various ways, but which are less clear and perhaps controversial examples of intelligence (say business intelligence, police crime data or telecom metadata).

A fundamental aspect of human cognition is the ability to transfer cognitive structure from one domain to another. By means of such cognitive 'mapping', we are able to think of something in terms of something else. We can thus use the knowledge and experiences that we have in the source domain to think about and understand the target domain. The clearest example of such a mapping is the use of metaphors and other figures of speech. On the cognitive level, a metaphor thus transfers cognitive structure from a source domain to a target domain. A metaphor is therefore not simply a figure of speech, but a cognitive 'folding' (to use a metaphor), allowing us to see the unfamiliar in terms of the familiar.[12] Our understanding of the target domain is thus changed and reformatted, so to speak, by the introduction of cognitive structures that originally belonged somewhere else. So when we for instance use spatial metaphors in thinking and talking about mental states ('being in high spirits') or existential issues ('moving forward in life or in one's carrier'), we important the relevant mental schemata and associated bodily experiences, allowing us to not only understand the metaphor but also use it to draw new inferences about the target domain on the basis of our knowledge about the source domain – since we know from bodily experience that it is more difficult to move backwards than forwards (in the literal sense), we may continue to think along the lines suggested by the spatial metaphor and draw the inference, or take it for granted, that it may be difficult and otherwise problematic to move backwards in life. Sometimes, we may notice the cognitive change that results from the transfer of cognitive structure, as when we notice a particularly striking metaphor. But often the transfer of cognitive structure takes place at an unconscious level, and we may not notice that the transfer takes place nor be able to see clearly what its consequences are.

In the following, I shall analyse the spread of intelligence practices today as a kind of metaphor, which transfers cognitive structure from the source domain of (military) intelligence to other domains.

More precisely, my claim is that the concept of intelligence is structured around an antagonistic social relation as its 'core' example and that the cognitive structure inherent in the concept is therefore tied to this particular type of social relation. Such a definition of the concept of intelligence may not amount to a set of sufficient and necessary criteria for the application of the concept in a specific context. Nor may it allow us to meet the demand for a precise technical definition for use as part of intelligence practices. Nonetheless, it may allow us to understand more clearly the subtle cognitive transformations that may result from the application of that particular concept.

## The adversarial context

Defining intelligence by means of an antagonistic social relation obviously presuppose that we have a conceptual grasp of that type of social relation. More precisely, we need to draw a (crude) distinction between four different types of social relation:

(1) **Cooperative relation.** In this type of relation, the two parties have a common interest in cooperating and are often known as *partners*. Working relations and trade could be examples. Coercion, threats, deception and secrecy are incompatible with this type of relation, since the use of these means would undermine the trust between the partners.

(2) **Competitive relation.** This type of relation is confrontational in the sense that the various parties have conflicting interests and that one party's gain will be a loss to the other. However, in contrast to an antagonistic relation, a competitive relation is characterized by common rules and an overarching institutional framework that limit the conflict, create a basic level of trust between competitors and give rise to a common ethical framework.[13] Think for instance of competitive sports, which take place within a framework of common rules. Although the conflict may be damaging to the parties (or at least to the looser), the competition and its institutional context may furthermore be socially useful, in the sense that it creates incentives for the competitors to behave in ways that are useful to society at large. A competition is thus partly conflictual, partly cooperative in that it serves a common good. An example would be free marked or commercial competition, which leads to lower prices and better quality.[14] Another would be the competition between prosecutor and defence in court, creating, or at least contributing to, a just legal process. Note that the common institutional framework limits the types of actions that the parties may take in pursuit of their interest, industrial espionage is for instance illegal, just as the use of force is strictly forbidden. The same is true of deception, and although secrecy plays an important role in protecting commercial interests, there may be rules forbidding the parties from hiding certain kinds of information or even requiring them to make certain information public.

(3) **Conflictual relation.** In a conflictual relation, there is no shared goal or common good, which is served by the conflict. However, there is still common normative framework, although the opponents may disagree on the content, the interpretation or the application of common rules in a specific context. Conflicts may therefore be solved or at least handled by a third party that has the authority to interpret the common rules. Sometimes, the third party is accepted by both opponents (a mediator[15]), sometimes the third party is simply someone who has the necessary power to impose her will on both parties.

(4) **Adversarial or antagonistic relation.** This type of relation is characterized not only by conflict between two or more parties but also by an absence of common rules and a comprehensive institutional framework that would allow mediation of the conflict and create some amount of trust between the parties, with the exception perhaps of very loose and open normative principles, such as the rules of war and the various international treatises on warfare. In such contexts, the adversary is often known as the *enemy*, and since there are no common rules, the behaviour of the enemy must be influenced by the use of threats, coercion and the use of force. Very often, we describe these social relations in

terms of warfare, in either a literal or a metaphorical sense (or sometimes in a sense, which seems to lie somewhere in between the literal and the metaphorical sense of the term, as when we talk about *war on drugs, war on crime* or *war on terror*).

In the following, I shall argue that intelligence as a social practice is intrinsically linked to adversarial relations (Type 4 in the above classification). This is true historically as a consequence of the tight link between intelligence and warfare: intelligence practices have their root in warfare and the use of military force. Information about the enemy has of course always been important for warfare, but the political and military importance attributed to intelligence surged during and after the Second World War, leading to what may be termed the classical period in the history of modern intelligence during the Cold War. This, I suppose also explains why militaristic language, concepts and metaphors come so readily to mind when talking about intelligence practices. Warner, for instance, notes that intelligence can be both offensive and defensive,[16] drawing thereby on a militaristic terminology, which is very hard to decide whether it is literal or metaphoric. So, if militaristic language feels so natural in relation to intelligence, it may be because the application of the concept of intelligence to something is already to think of that something in terms of warfare.

## Intelligence – a definition

Intelligence can be defined as *information useful in an adversarial relation*, i.e., information, which can or could be used against an adversary. It is thus the use (the purpose) and the adversarial context that defines the information as intelligence, and otherwise innocuous information may become intelligence the moment it is used in an adversarial context.[17]

In this section, I shall substantiate this claim by showing that the features often cited as defining or characteristic of intelligence can be explained as flowing from the role that intelligence play in this particular type of social relation. The adversarial nature of the social relation is, as it were, the piece that makes all the other pieces fall into place. In the remaining part of the paper, I then turn to the implications and consequences that the use of the concept of intelligence outside antagonistic relations may have.

Let me start by pointing something out, which may seem trivial, but which I think is important, namely, that *you cannot have intelligence about yourself*. Setting aside the thorny question of self-knowledge and whether the notion of information can meaningfully be applied in the realm of self-knowledge, we all have information about ourselves, which we would like to keep private, either because its public disclosure would have unwanted consequences for ourselves or because we simply think that the information in question is no one else's business. It would however be a bit weird to use the notion of intelligence to talk about such information. A person does not have intelligence about his or her own medical history, love life or political affiliation. Such information may possibly be *used as intelligence* by other persons or agencies, say an intelligence agency talking an interest in the medical history of a foreign leader or the romantic life of a foreign state official. But it is (does not function as) intelligence for the person him- or herself. In other words, the social relation is essential, since the concept of intelligence presupposes that the information in question is about someone else. Furthermore, the social relation needs to be adversarial in nature. We would for instance not normally say that a medical doctor has intelligence about the medical history of one of her patients. This seems to be because she is expected to use such medical information for the benefit of the patent himself. For the same reason, we would often say that such information is *confidential*, thereby implying that the collection and use of the information presuppose trust between the two parties, i.e., trust on the part of the patient that the medical practitioner will only use the information to the benefit of the patient. In order words, the concept of intelligence can only be applied in the context of an adversarial relation and not in a relation characterized by mutual trust. This, I suggest, is true even in cases where the information in question concerns more problematic, perhaps illegal, matters. Think for instance of a corrupt official trying to cover her paper trail in order to avoid prosecution. This information would not be intelligence for the official herself. The very same information could however function as intelligence for someone else, say someone using it to extort the official, or a police officer building a case against her. Information only becomes intelligence when it has a potential use for adversarial purposes.

Returning to the definitions of intelligence cited above, we may note that many of them underline the importance of secrecy in intelligence practices, both in the sense that the intelligence is kept secret, and in the sense that the gathering of intelligence takes place in secret. The notion of secrecy points to the particular social relation that underlies intelligence practices. In particular, there is no point in keeping something secret, unless there is someone from whom you wish to keep it secret. Secrecy is a social relation, a relation of non-communication as it were, and therefore implicitly refers to the person or group of persons that we do not communicate with. More precisely, the information in question is kept secret because it can be used *against* another person or group of persons, i.e., the enemy or antagonist – or because we are afraid that someone else may use it against us. Secrecy is thus neither sufficient (things can be secret without being intelligence, such as information about oneself or information, which is not useful for adversarial purposes) nor necessary (information may be public but still useful as intelligence [OSINT]) for something to count as intelligence. However, the adversarial context, in which something may function as intelligence, explains why secrecy is often of paramount importance, whether as a precautionary measure or as a condition for the collection and use of the information.

By the same token, it is not just any type of information used by decision makers that would qualify as intelligence. I shall return to the discursive reinterpretation of business information as business intelligence in a moment. Notice however that we would not normally call, say, a sales report for a piece of intelligence, when used by the business organization itself, not even if the report was kept secret. A sales report may of course be valuable intelligence for other persons and organizations, say competitors or tax authorities. But again, it is only when the information is used for adversarial purposes that we would qualify it as intelligence.

Note also the role that the planning and use of power by state authorities play in many of the definitions as the main or exclusive purpose or function of intelligence. This again points to the adversarial nature of the social relation underpinning the concept of intelligence.

For the same reason, intelligence cannot be characterized exclusively in terms of risk and risk management, because it is not every type of risk information that would qualify as intelligence. Information only becomes intelligences if it is related to a specific type of risk, namely a threat stemming from an opponent in the sense of a conscious adversary.[18]

Moreover, antagonistic social relations are also important for understanding intelligence agencies and their organizational culture. It has for instance been noted that intelligence officers often have a 'realist' conception of international relations, focusing on national interest and conflicts.[19] However, securitization and claims about national interest amount to a transformation of a relation in an antagonistic direction. More generally, I believe that the use of the concept of security in relation to intelligence often serves to underline the antagonistic nature of the relation between the intelligence agent or agency and the persons, groups or organizations under surveillance or scrutiny. Security is a concept with many different applications. But the type of security, which is central to the concept of intelligence, is security in the sense of protection against an enemy. It is thus again the notion of an adversarial or antagonistic social relation that lies at the core of the concept of intelligence and that explains that we so readily associate intelligence with 'realism', security and secrecy.

## Intelligence as transformative social action

An adversarial social relation is thus part of the semantic core of the concept of intelligence. However, as other concepts, the concept of intelligence can be stretched in various directions and applied to new phenomena in more or less creative ways. Sometimes, we may be willing to use the term when talking about information which is only loosely related to an adversarial context, say information which is hard to imagine we could use in confronting an enemy, or information which is only about an enemy in a very general sense. Or information, stemming perhaps from mass-surveillance, which may not be useful at all, but which we collect, since it is nice to have a lot of hay if you need to find the colloquial needle in the haystack.[20] There is nothing surprising in this extension of the concept of intelligence to cover things, which somehow resemble intelligence in the classical or adversarial sense; this is simply how language and human cognition function. However, an extended use of a concept does not mean that the cognitive core in the concept loses its importance; on the contrary, the extended use transfers mental schemata associated with the cognitive core to still new phenomena, which the new language use invites us to see as instances of or in analogy with the core conceptual structure.

If, however, the concept of intelligence is tied to antagonistic social relations, it follows that the use of that specific concept in thinking and speaking about a social relation may potentially transform that relation in an antagonistic direction. Applying the concept of intelligence to a social practice is therefore not just an innocent way of talking. By calling something intelligence, we apply not only a word but a cognitive structure to the thing in question. More specifically, the use of that particular concept imports a cognitive structure bound to antagonistic relations and therefore risk transforming other types of relation in an antagonistic direction. When using intelligence methods in, say, policing, public administration or risk management, we are thus importing a specific adversarial logic and thereby transforming the nature of the social relationships founded in and by these various institutions. This is of course even more true if we not only call something intelligence but actively use intelligence methods within the context of a social relation. Wiretapping Angela Merkel's phone transforms the relation between the United States and Germany (even if you're not caught).

Although Agrell is correct in noting that the term 'intelligence' can be used for more or less everything, I therefore disagree with his conclusion that the term may end up meaning nothing.[21] We need to draw a distinction between the things designated by the term – which may be just about everything – and then the specific type of social relation, which is implied or at least suggested by the use of that specific term in contrast to other possible designations. Even though the term may designate many different things, perhaps more or less everything, it still carries a specific meaning in the sense of a cognitive structure, which is applied to the things so designated.

In order to analyse the ongoing reinterpretation of social reality produced by the spread of intelligence practices, I shall introduce the concept of a transformative social action: Social practices often not only take place within social reality but actively transform it, recreating, so to speak, reality in their own image.

Drawing loosely on Hart's distinction between first and second order legal rules,[22] I shall distinguish first and second-order social action, i.e., social actions that operates within the conceptual boundaries of a specific type of social relation, and actions that transform the very nature of the social relation in question. So, we may distinguish intelligence practices that are first-order social actions in the sense that they operate within a social relation, which is already antagonistic in nature, and second-order intelligence practices that transform a social relation in a specific (antagonistic) direction. My claim will be that we often tend to think about and justify intelligence practices in terms of first-order social actions only, i.e., as something that targets an enemy, which we take for granted exists and is known to be our enemy. However, what often takes place is a reconfiguration of social relations in an antagonistic direction by means of the concept of intelligence, i.e., intelligence practices have become a second-order social action. We do not only apply the concept of intelligence to a still larger range of phenomena, we actively recreate social reality in its image.

Scholars have previously argued that intelligence is not simply a neutral rendering of the world, but a way of actively constructing or reconstructing the world, in which the state acts and sees itself.[23] I would add that this reconstruction takes places, because the re-description of a non-antagonistic social practice in terms of intelligence transforms the nature of the social action in question by transferring cognitive structure from the intelligence cognitive domain, structured around antagonistic social relations, to a target domain, which was not previously structured in this manner.

Note in particular that the distinction drawn above between different types of social relation gives us a clue as to how the transformation may take place. If we for instance start out with a Type 2 relation, that is to say a competitive relation, it may seem tempting to stretch the concept of intelligence, from its original source domain structured around a Type 4 relation so that it also covers the Type 2 relation, because these two relations resemble one another in a certain aspect. It makes sense to think of, say, commercial competition in terms of intelligence, because we face an opponent or rival in both competitive and antagonistic social relations. The fact that both relations are in a wide sense confrontational therefore invites a transfer of cognitive structure from the domain of antagonistic social relations to the domain of commercial competition. It is precisely this type of transfer that the metaphor of business intelligence establishes. Talking about business intelligence is therefore not simply a fashionable way of taking (although it may also be that) but also a way of transforming our conception of commercial competition, aligning it with warfare.

But clearly, understanding a social relation in analogy with warfare may have quite wide-ranging consequences for the nature of the relationship itself. It may for instance invite us to think that everything is permitted and that there are no rules or limits for what you may do to the other person (or company) as part of your struggle to win. If market competition is a type of warfare, as suggested by the business intelligence metaphor, you may use all the means at your disposal in order to win, just as a war faring nation is allowed to do almost anything permitted by the very general laws of war. But that is another way of saying that the metaphor – business is war using information as intelligence – may transform market competition in such a way that it stops being a metaphor and becomes a literal description of the social relation in question. Transformative social actions reconstruct social reality itself, and what's starts out as a metaphor may end up being a literal description of the nature of the social relation as transformed by the metaphorical transfer of cognitive structure.

## In conclusion

In this section, I shall analyse some of the consequences and pathologies of the transformation of the intelligence metaphor into social reality. I shall focus in particular on the use of intelligence methods in policing, and more precisely on the consequences for 'ordinary' policing, both crime control and order maintenance. Using Brodeur's distinction between 'high' and 'low' policing,[24] we may perhaps say that we are witnessing a reformatting of 'low' policing in the image of 'high' policing – a realignment of policing along national security lines. And the metaphor – if that is what it is – of intelligence-led policing plays a key role in this process.

Intelligence-led policing is one of the major 'new' paradigms of policing[25] that have been disseminated throughout the Western world, including both the Anglo-Saxon countries and continental Europe.[26] In particular, it has been raised to the level of national policing model in the United Kingdom (the National Intelligence Model)[27] and recently also in Norway. Often, intelligence-led policing is introduced in response to a real or perceived crisis of legitimacy in policing, as the Norwegian case illustrates, where intelligence-led policing plays a key-role in the so-called quality reform that aims to restore public confidence in the police after the Breivik attack.

Intelligence-led policing thus often implies a certain securitization of policing, as is clear from the connection with anti-terrorism. However, intelligence-led policing is often legitimized as a response to organized crime rather than terrorism.[28] But whether we are talking about terrorism or organized crime, these are clearly examples of high-policing, i.e., policing that targets an enemy, using high-tech, military-like equipment and tactics. In other words, the two central cases used to justify intelligence-led policing are both cases of antagonistic relations, where we face (or think we face) a relatively well-defined and hostile enemy. However, the moment intelligence-led policing is introduced as a general policing model, it is used in a much more general way in dealing with a whole range of problems and social issues that may not so easily adopt to the antagonistic pattern. When intelligence-led policing becomes a general policing model, high-policing becomes the standard for dealing also with low policing issues.

This however means that intelligence-led policing may amount to a transformation of the relation between citizens and the police. We may note for instance that the use of surveillance and other intelligence methods in policing leads to a 'widening of the net' in the sense that it draws the attention of the police to ordinary citizens who may not otherwise have been the subject of policing. Although surveillance is legitimized as an effective way of combatting serious crime, it thus draws the attention of the authorities to a wider range of citizens, many of which would previously have been considered normal rather than deviant.[29] The use of Automatic Number Plate Recognition technologies in detecting social fraud or deciding whether a family lives in the catchment area of a specific school may for instance have large implications for the legitimacy of state authorities, because such a use questions the distinction between 'real' criminals and 'ordinary' citizens.[30] Although intelligence-led policing is often introduced in response to a crisis of legitimacy, it therefore risks undermining the legitimacy of the police,[31] since it transforms the relation between police and citizens in an antagonistic direction, using information gather for one purpose for other adversarial purposes. Note also that the introduction of new technologies, such as Automatic Number Plate Recognition, is often justified by its use in high policing, say in fighting organized crime, even though the technology in question may end up being used for low policing purposes.

Using intelligence methods in policing also means that all sorts of contact between citizens and police may (and will) be reinterpreted as an occasion for gathering intelligence. This in particular means that standards of confidentially will be undermined, since anything a citizen say to a police officer can and will be used as intelligence in attaining police objectives, including objectives which are unrelated to the issues raised in and by the original contact. In relation to the handling of major incidents, scholars have for instance noticed that the British police, with its intelligence-driven approach to policing, regard testimonials and other information given to partner agencies by survivors, relatives or witnesses as potential intelligence and therefore do not accept an absolute guarantee of confidentiality.[32] The same pattern occurs in relation to anti-terrorism, where the police tend to see social workers involved in preventive anti-radicalization social work as an important source of intelligence. This means in particular that families from suspect communities lose their confidence in family liaisons, because they fear that information is passed on to the police.[33]

Intelligence-led policing may thus change the ethical framework of policing, since the introduction of intelligence practices in policing potentially transform citizens into (potential) enemies, thereby undermining trust and legitimacy. Defining the concept of intelligence and understanding what the spread of intelligence methods entail is thus first and foremost a political and ethical question.

## Notes

1. Warner, "Wanted: A Definition of 'Intelligence'".

2. Herman, *Intelligence Services in the Information Age*; and Scott and Jackson, "The Study of Intelligence."
3. Wheaton and Beerbower, "Towards A New Definition of Intelligence."
4. Gill and Phythian, *Intelligence in an Insecure World*, 7; and Phythian, "Policing Uncertainty," 195.
5. See note 1 above.
6. Rønn and Høffding, "The Epistemic Status of Intelligence."
7. Walsh, *Intelligence and Intelligence Analysis*, 19–33.
8. My short list of possible definitions of intelligence is not in any way intended to be exhaustive. I only aim to point out at least some of the most important elements that occur in some of the most often-cited definitions of intelligence, and the list could be expanded considerably: In a recent survey of the scholarly literature, Rønn found 30 different definitions of the concept of intelligence (Rønn, "Indledning.")
9. Foucault, "Nietzsche, Genealogy, History."
10. Johnson and Lakoff, *Metaphors We Live By*; and Lakoff, *Women, Fire, and Dangerous Things*.
11. Lakoff, *Women, Fire, and Dangerous Things*.
12. Johnson and Lakoff, *Metaphors We Live By*.
13. Applbaum, *Ethics for Adversaries*.
14. The common goal may, but need not, be shared by the competitors themselves. So, the participants in a commercial competition may or may not be aware of the fact that free marked competition serves a societal goal. They may even take themselves to be engaged in conflictual or adversarial relation (and commercial competition may sometimes feel that way). I only mean to imply that there exists some common goal (shared or not), which is served by the competition and which can therefore be used in legitimizing the competitive social relation.
15. The distinction between competitive and conflictual relations is not completely sharp and a mediator or judge may play a role in a competitive relation as well – as for instance the referee in competitive sports.
16. Warner, "Intelligence as Risk Shifting," 19.
17. The usefulness in an adversarial contest also explains why information needs to be analysed and interpreted in order to count as intelligence. It is not enough to collect information; the relevance of the information in taking defensive or offensive measures against an adversary must be shown.
18. See also Sparrow, *The Character of Harms*; and Sparrow, *Handcuffed* on the importance of conscious opponents.
19. Phythian, "Intelligence Theory."
20. Aradau, "The Signature of Security."
21. Agrell, "When Everything is Intelligence."
22. Hart, *The Concept of Law*.
23. Fry og Hochstein, "Epistemic Communities."
24. Brodeur, *The Policing Web*.
25. See Ratcliffe, *Intelligence-Led Policing*.
26. den Boer, "Intelligence-Led Policing in Europe."
27. Flood and Gaspar, "Strategic Aspects"; and James, *Examining Intelligence-led Policing*.
28. Sheptycki, "Organizational Pathologies."
29. Kearon, "Surveillance Technologies," 424.
30. Ibid., 421–4.
31. James, "The Path to Enlightenment."
32. Davis, "Contextual Challenges for Crisis Support," 12.
33. Hillyard, *Suspect Community*, see also Millie, "The Policing Task."

## Disclosure statement

No potential conflict of interest was reported by the author.

## Bibliography

Agrell, W. "When Everything Is Intelligence - Nothing Is Intelligence." *The Sherman Kent Center for Intelligence Analysis, Occasional Paper*, 2002. doi:10.1044/1059-0889(2002/er01).

Applbaum, A. I. *Ethics for Adversaries*. Princeton, NJ: Princeton University Press, 1999.

Aradau, C. "The Signature of Security: Big Data, Anticipation, Surveillance." *Radical Philosophy* (2015): 21–28.

Brodeur, J. K. *The Policing Web*. Oxford: Oxford University Press, 2010.

Davis, H. "Contextual Challenges for Crisis Support in the Immediate Aftermath of Major Incidents in the UK." *British Journal of Social Work* 43 (2012): 504–521.

Den Boer, M. "Intelligence-Led Policing in Europe: Lingering between Idea and Implementation." In *The Future of Intelligence: Challenges in the 21st Century*, edited by I. Duyvesteyn, J. van Reijn, and B. de Jong, 113–132. New York: Routledge, 2014.

Flood, B., and R. Gaspar. "Strategic Aspects of the UK National Intelligence Model." In *Strategic Thinking in Criminal Intelligence*, edited by J. H. Ratcliffe, 47–65. Annandale, NSW: Federation Press, 2009.

Foucault, M. "Nietzsche, Genealogy, History." In *The Foucault Reader*, edited by P. Rabinow, 76–100. New York: Pantheon Books, 1984.

Fry, M. G., and M. Hochstein. "Epistemic Communities: Intelligence Studies and International Relations." *Intelligence and National Security* 8 (1993): 14–28. doi:10.1080/02684529308432212.

Gill, P., and M. Phythian. *Intelligence in an Insecure World*. Cambridge: Polity Press, 2006.

Hart, H. L. A. *The Concept of Law*. Oxford: Oxford University Press, 1961.

Herman, M. *Intelligence Services in the Information Age*. New York: Routledge, 2001.

Hillyard, P. *Suspect Community: People's Experience of the Prevention of Terrorism Acts in Britain*. London: Pluto Books, 1993.

James, A. *Examining Intelligence-Led Policing: Developments in Research, Policy and Practice*. London: Palgrave Macmillan UK, 2013.

James, A. "The Path to Enlightenment: Limiting Costs and Maximizing Returns from Intelligence-Led Policy and Practice in Public Policing." *Policing* 11 (2017): 410–420.

Johnson, M., and G. Lakoff. *Metaphors We Live By*. Chicago: University of Chicago Press, 1980.

Kearon, T. "Surveillance Technologies and the Crisis of Confidence in Regulatory Agencies." *Criminology and Criminal Justice* 13, September (2013): 415–430. doi:10.1177/1748895812454747.

Lakoff, G. *Women, Fire, and Dangerous Things. What Categories Reveal about the Mind*. Chicago & London: Chicago University Press, 1987.

Millie, A. "The Policing Task and the Expansion (And Contraction) of British Policing." *Criminology and Criminal Justice* 13 (2012): 143–160.

Phythian, M. "Intelligence Theory and Theories of International Relations: Shared World or Separate Worlds?" In *Intelligence Theory: Key Questions and Debates*, edited by P. Gill, S. Marrin, and M. Phythian, 54–72. London: Routledge, 2009.

Phythian, M. "Policing Uncertainty: Intelligence, Security and Risk." *Intelligence and National Security* 27 (2012): 187–205. doi:10.1080/02684527.2012.661642.

Ratcliffe, J. *Intelligence-Led Policing*. Devon: Willian Publishing, 2008.

Rønn, K. V. "Indledning." In *Efterretningsstudier*, edited by K. V. Rønn, 11–42. Frederiksberg: Samfundslitteratur, 2016.

Rønn, K. V., and S. Høffding. "The Epistemic Status of Intelligence: An Epistemological Contribution to the Understanding of Intelligence." *Intelligence and National Security* 28 (2012): 694–716.

Scott, L., and P. Jackson. "The Study of Intelligence in Theory and Practice." *Intelligence and National Security* 19 (2004): 139–169. doi:10.1080/0268452042000302930.

Sheptycki, J. "Organizational Pathologies in Police Intelligence Systems: Some Contributions to the Lexicon of Intelligence-Led Policing." *European Journal of Criminology* 1 (2004): 307–332. doi:10.1177/1477370804044005.

Sparrow, M. K. *The Character of Harms: Operational Challenges in Control*. Cambridge: Cambridge University Press, 2008.

Sparrow, M. K. *Handcuffed. What Holds Policing Back, and the Keys to Reform*. Washington, D.C.: Brookings Institution Press, 2016.

Walsh, P. F. *Intelligence and Intelligence Analysis*. London: Routledge, 2011.

Warner, M. "Wanted: A Definition of 'Intelligence'." *Studies in Intelligence* 46 (2002): 15–22.

Warner, M. "Intelligence as Risk Shifting." In *Intelligence Theory: Key Questions and Debates*, edited by P. Gill, S. Marrin, and M. Phythian, 16–32. London: Routledge, 2009.

Wheaton, K. J., and M. T. Beerbower. "Towards A New Definition of Intelligence." *Stanford Law and Policy Review* 17 (2006): 319–330.

# Deferring substance: EU policy and the information threat

Hedvig Ördén

**ABSTRACT**
The article describes EU cross-sectoral policy work on online information threats, focusing on the intersection between values and 'referent objects'. Examining discussions on strategic communication, censorship, media literacy and media pluralism, two value-perspectives were identified: while abstract procedural values of efficiency and coherence guide content management in the security/defence/internet communities, media/education communities highlight the end-goals of content pluralism and enhanced citizen judgement. In implementation, the former's lack of substantive goals, coupled with an outsourcing of content management, may give rise to hybrid values. The findings highlight the danger of neglecting substance in favor of efficient management of an online 'battlespace'.

Information and communications technologies (ICTs) allow citizens to access and share vast amounts of information as part of their everyday life. Simultaneously, the security-issues arising from this environment have made the communicative aspects of cyberspace an arena for European Union security policy. A 2016 report by the EU Parliament states that the Union, its Member States and citizens are under a 'growing, systematic pressure to tackle information, disinformation and misinformation campaigns and propaganda from countries and non-state actors'.[1] Perpetrators listed include a wide range of different groups who, nevertheless, all appear to have in common the goal of 'distorting truth, provoking doubt and dividing Member States' through communication and (mis)information-sharing.[2] When suggesting methods for countering information risks, policy intellectuals tend to identify and conceptualize a variety of existing and possible threats. Labels used are 'information warfare', 'hybrid war', 'propaganda', 'hostile strategic communications' or (hostile) 'narratives'.[3] The idea of what constitutes security in relation to such threats, however, remains largely unarticulated and underexplored. Threats related to the everyday communicative side of information technology appear difficult to conceptualize in relation to security, which traditionally refers to distinct objects of protection and exceptional circumstances. What does security mean, and what does security-making entail, in a setting where communicative technologies form an intrinsic part of citizens' life?

To throw some light upon this question, this article describes recent policy developments in the EU that attempt to create 'security' in relation to problems and threats related to the communicative side of ICTs. The overarching aim is to map security-related values, as well as to explore the intersection between values and objects of protection, as discernible through observations of EU policy and policy discussions addressing the information threat. The reason for this focus is twofold. First, no equally comprehensive account of developments in this policy field is currently available. While Intelligence Studies addresses the information threat more broadly, discussions in this line of research almost exclusively involve military or operational perspectives on deception, Psychological and Information Operations, rather than everyday communication threats directed at citizens requiring the intervention of political actors.[4] To keep track of what an influential actor, like the EU, does in relation to new threats is thus important for anyone concerned with the normative and political questions of what should be done to combat those threats. Second, the detailed account of EU policy efforts offered here will provide a much-needed basis to further theoretical discussion, or academic debates, on the meaning of security, and potentially changing meaning of security, as political actors face threats posed through new communication technologies. The need to think carefully about what security means in relation to online information threats can be discerned in the failure of existing research to come up with a broadly acceptable conceptual frame to account for such policy efforts.[5] This article thus aims to broaden the scope from the 'hard' or technological side of security commonly addressed within the field of Cybersecurity, to describe the particular challenges that spring from countering a threat related to the communicative side of ICTs.[6]

In studies addressing the information and communication environment more generally, 'hard' and/or technical aspects have often been favoured by scholars investigating topics such as critical infrastructure protection, cyberwar or cybercrime while the 'soft' informational dimension is primarily explored in communication studies or with the help of communication theory.[7] Where the former often links security to referent objects in the physical world and draws on state security discourses, the latter treats security as a backdrop for theoretical explorations into communication rather than a concept to be theorized in its own right. The threat of information has been more thoroughly explored by scholars within strategic and intelligence studies under headings like 'information warfare', 'hybrid warfare' and 'deception'.[8] Nevertheless, the assumed military setting in this type of research tends to leave crucial aspects of the current phenomenon under-theorized. Firstly, the information threat today is a 'complex threat'[9]; a threat which calls into question 'the meaningfulness of differentiating between internal and external security' – a distinction fundamentally underpinning strategic studies.[10] Without the traditional framework of state security, the object of protection in this setting remains unclear. Secondly, the widespread use of ICTs and enhanced digital infrastructures moves contemporary acts of deception, misinformation and disinformation from an outspoken conflict setting into the everyday life of citizens. A central challenge for policymakers here is how, in practice, such a boundless informational threat should be pursued. The envisaged remedies to the information threat in the contemporary political environment are multifaceted, to say the least: whereas privately funded projects provide technological solutions for deleting terrorist content and media companies offer professional 'fact checking' services, state actors work to limit illegal material through law enforcement and education professionals press for enhanced critical thinking. To understand the security-challenges in this context, it is of fundamental importance to address this morass of policy initiatives in empirical detail.

Investigating EU policy on the information threat, the article finds four proposed remedies: strategic communication, censorship, media literacy and media pluralism. The remedies are articulated within four separate EU policy communities: the security/defence, Internet, media and education sectors. These communities, in turn, describe security-related values in two distinct ways. The security/defence and Internet communities outline security-making in abstract procedural terms, emphasising efficiency and coherence. The referent object is the informational space, described as a digital 'battlefield' protected through continuous management: deletion and production of online content. Any articulations of end-values, specific descriptions of content to be deleted or produced, however, are outsourced to independent actors. The media and education communities relate security to the production of pluralistic online content and initiatives teaching citizens to consider different viewpoints. Security-related values implied are perspectivism and, ultimately, independence of judgement, while the object of protection can be described as citizens' independent democratic judgement. Turning to the process of policy implementation, the analysis displays how hybrid value-constellations may arise with the involvement of three independent actors: civil society, professional communicators and the Internet industry. The respective value systems of these actors may work counter to the end-goal of citizens' independent democratic judgement. Overall, the findings point to a danger in disregarding the question of content and pursuing the information threat through defensive strategies alone; a suitable remedy must consider the substantial values we want to protect and constitute, in all steps of the process.

The rest of the article is disposed in five sections. First, the article outlines the advantages of investigating EU policy on the information threat by exploring values and the intersection between values and referent objects though a value-critical policy analysis; second, it introduces the policy communities and the material which provides the basis for the analysis; third, it pinpoints the EU policies on the information threat in relation to the communities countering the threat; fourth, the analysis zooms in on four key policy communities describing two distinct perspectives on security-related values; fifth, using contemporary examples, it considers the potential consequences of involving three kinds of independent actors from a value-critical perspective: civil society, professional communicators and US Internet companies; finally, it sums up the findings and discusses possible implications for pursuing security in relation to the information threat.

## I. Security, objects and values

Critically oriented approaches have shown that security is not a stable concept. Security is always the security of something – it comes with certain assumptions of a 'referent object' worth protecting.[11] The referent object might be regarded as the 'object' (broadly speaking) to be protected against existential threats in a particular security context.[12] Essentially, however, it is linked to how we understand, talk about and propose to counter a specific threat. Within the Copenhagen School the referent object of security is conceived of as constituted through particular 'securitizing' moves by key actors through which an existential threat is established by references to protection.[13] Discourses on national security are most typical in this respect. However, in other settings, such as cybersecurity, the referent object can be more multifaceted.[14] This narrow focus on objects to be protected, and the linkages between them, however, fails to capture less overt aspects of security-making. In relation to the information threat, securitizing moves outlining specific objects of protection are mostly absent. Instead, we face a paradoxical situation where threat-discussions are common, but references to protection are not. In order to capture what security is in relation to the information threat, it is necessary to widen the scope of investigation. This article proposes that, to explore security in relation to the information threat, we need to include a focus on security-related values. As pointed out by Burgess, security always links up to a particular set of human values.[15] That which has no value 'cannot be threatened in the same sense' as that which we hold dear.[16] The focus on values, however, comes with certain methodological demands. Due to their 'fluid and amorphous'[17] nature, the protection of values inevitably involves a process of constitution and re-constitution. In order to map security here, it is thus necessary to take into account the security-related values envisaged and 'implemented' in the process of security-making, but also the intersection between values and objects. In short, values can help constituting certain referent objects as well as to counteract their constitution.

More precisely, the empirical study draws on a value-critical policy analysis.[18] As shown by Bigo, the different 'threat perceptions' of bureaucrats and security professionals can be regarded as one of the main drivers in security governance.[19] To consider the values forwarded in policy and within relevant policy communities is thus key to mapping this emerging security field. Seeing policy-making as a situated meaning-creating practice, the value-critical policy analysis allows the researcher to consider both the role of value guiding policymaking – values related to 'security' – and the 'context nourishing these assumptions'.[20] The result is a mapping of 'local knowledge'[21] in relation to proposed policies – the shared knowledge among a community of policymakers.[22] In selecting material, the aim has been to not only consider the policies themselves, but also focus on how policy actors discuss the issues or, when possible, reading 'what they read'.[23] By paying attention both policy and local knowledge it becomes possible to better understand[24] 'the ultimate ends of public policy – the goals and obligations that policy wants to promote as desirable in their own right'.[25] Finally, by mapping policy on a specific topic in a detailed and systematic manner, the article differs from previous, more theoretical, studies on security and cyberspace[26] in being carefully empirically grounded.

The EU is a central case for investigating the information threat. Recently making cyberspace into a key security priority,[27] the Union is widely regarded as an active and powerful player in the world of Internet governance. Considering the EU as a case, however, inevitably requires some attention to its organizational structure. The world of EU security policy is multifaceted. In relation to complex threats, EU initiatives make up a transnational and transboundary 'protection-oriented policy space', described in recent research as 'civil security'.[28] Contemporary policies on the information threat stretch over a highly diverse set of areas – from security/defence and Internet to education, culture and media policy. From the perspective of policy values, such a 'cross-sectoral' approach may give rise to conflicts.[29] If every sector forms a community relying on its own local knowledge in the policy process, different end-goals may be emphasized within different policy communities.[30] The value-critical approach here helps in pinpointing potential value-conflicts, either between stated end-goals or between policy goals and processes of implementation. Burgess argues that cross-sectoral policy work can give rise to a 'hybridization' of values.[31] Hybrid constellations emerge when different value-systems overlap[32] and become particularly salient with the use of 'non-military instruments' for countering threats and the involvement of professionals not traditionally participating in security work.[33] This complexity highlights the need to take into consideration policy implementation when mapping security in relation to complex threats. The multitude of actors involved in addressing the information threat might understand security in different and, even, conflicting ways which, in turn, can lead to new, unforeseen, interpretations of security-related values.

## II. The policy communities

The analysis of security-related values focuses on material related to the main policy communities involved in countering the information threat: the security/defence, Internet, education and media sectors. Four centrally placed forums serve as entry-points for investigating security-related values: the *EUISS*, the *EU Internet Forum*, the *ET2020* and the *Media Literacy Expert Group*. The forums were selected to represent the local knowledge within each community in the overall cross-sectoral approach employed by the EU. The below section introduces the actors and their role in EU policymaking as well as the material considered.

The *EUISS* is an autonomous agency under the Common Foreign and Security Policy set-up to analyse EU security and defence issues, engage in strategic debate, contribute to the common security culture within the EU. This group is the main producer of policy-relevant knowledge for the security and defence community within the EU, and serves as an entry-point into the local knowledge among policy active in this context. The analysis consults their comprehensive report on strategic communication produced for the European Parliament Committee on Foreign Affairs titled 'EU Strategic Communication with a view to countering propaganda' – the only comprehensive report to date on the information threat.[34] Due to the independent working conditions of the group, internal discussions or meeting summaries are not available. To compensate for this, the analysis takes into account also externally produced material recommended – upon direct request – by the main author of the report. This material consists of an interview with communications scholar Philip M. Taylor (2002) and the report 'Strategic Communications and National Strategy' (2011) by Chatham House; the only source on strategic communication cited in the EUISS report.[35] In addition, the analysis has also considered the 'Fotyga report' adopted by the EU Parliament Committee on Foreign Affairs after the reception of the EUISS report.[36]

The *EU Internet Forum* represents the Internet sector. Launched by the Commissioner for Migration, Home Affairs in 2015, the forum consist of representatives from US Internet companies, law enforcement agencies and government officials. Their main task is to 'stop the misuse of the Internet by international terrorist' through increased coordination between Internet actors and the

EU law enforcement agencies. All meetings of the group take place behind closed doors and unofficial material is overall very limited. As a result, documents from *the EU Internet Forum* consist of official press releases and the 'Code of Conduct on Countering Illegal Hate Speech Online' signed by the IT companies. While this creates certain limitations for the analysis, the lack of material also constitutes a starting-point for further reflection.

The *ET2020* serves as a forum for exchange of knowledge between EU member states in the education sector chaired by the Commission. The aim of each Working Group is to deliver output on policies agreed on by EU education ministers through 'peer learning' and 'good practices'. Members consist of government representatives, stakeholders and international organizations. The analysis here focuses on the 'ET2020 Working Group on promoting citizenship and the common values of freedom, tolerance and non-discrimination through education'[37] set up in 2016 which addresses common challenges identified in the 2015 Paris Declaration[38] – the radicalization and online indoctrination of young EU citizens. The analysis takes into consideration a rich collection of documents such as the official declaration by EU education ministers, a comprehensive summary of the first meeting and follow-up documents mapping the policy progress.

The *Media Literacy Expert Group*,[39] primarily connected to the media sector, is chaired by the EU Commission. The forum consists of a fluid network of different stakeholders from member states, representatives of associations working with media literacy and members of expert organizations in the field. The material here consists of selected transcriptions of one video recorded meeting, two comprehensive meeting summaries and meeting presentations.

In the process of selecting material, other forums and types of material have been considered and dismissed. In the security community, the *Radicalisation Awareness Network* (RAN) plays a central part in addressing the information threat through online counter-narratives. However, since the EUISS is a key forum for knowledge-production in relation to EU security policy, an analysis of the security-related values promoted by this group here will likely give an illustration of values prominent within the security/defence community at large. With regard to the kind of material used, interviews could possibly enrich the analysis – in particular in relation to the sparse material in relation to the Internet sector. Still, since the overall aim has been to consider values anchored in knowledge 'held by policy-related actors together as a group'[40] – not the opinions of individuals – the focus has been on, either official statements agreed upon by the groups, material recommended by officials or referred to in the reports produced.

## III. The policies

This part provides an overview of the EU policy in relation to the information threat to date. The remedies suggested can be summarized into four distinct categories: *strategic communication, education in critical thinking/media literacy, media plurality* and *censorship*. The below section briefly outlines the approaches in relation to the main policy sectors in which they are promoted[41]; a more in-depth discussion follows as part of the analysis.

The suggestion of using *strategic communication* as a remedy for the information threat is most prominent within the security and defence policy sectors. In relation to the contemporary internal threat of violent extremism and radicalization, the EU Security Agenda[42] argues for a strengthening of 'EU strategic communications' and increased attention to the production of 'common narratives and factual representation of conflicts'.[43] In line with this goal for internal security, the RAN, a network of practitioners organized under the Directorate-General of Migration and Home Affairs , has been set up to promote good practices in relation to 'counter narratives' in the online environment. The defence sector suggests strategic communication as an approach towards external information threats. Most notably, the launch of the East StratCom Task Force[44] in October 2015, consisting of 10 full-time communication experts within the European External Action Service (EEAS), introduced strategic communication as a remedy to disinformation specifically coming from eastern actors. According to their 2015 Action Plan, the communicative approach should further 'the EU's overall policy objectives' in the Eastern Neighbourhood Region through 'positive and effective messages regarding EU policies'.[45] Similarly, the 'Joint Framework to Counter Hybrid Threats', adopted by the EU Commission and High Representative in April 2016, highlights the crucial role of strategic communication in relation to information threats from malicious actors. This policy framework calls for the development of coordinated communication mechanisms to counter externally produced disinformation.

Policies aimed to strengthen critical thinking and *media literacy*[46] are promoted within the education and media sectors under the common Directorate-General of Education, Youth, Sport and Culture. Traditionally, education policy is the sole responsibility of nation states. However, current policy initiatives on the EU level urges for increased coordination between Member States in relation to matters of disinformation and propaganda. The Paris Declaration, adopted by EU Education Ministers in 2015, is a key agreement in this respect. The Declaration calls for a strengthening of

> children's and young people's ability to think critically and exercise judgement particularly in the context of the Internet and social media, they are able to grasp realities, to distinguish fact from opinion, to recognise propaganda and to resist all forms of indoctrination and hate speech'.[47]

As part of its implementation, the strategic framework for European Cooperation in Education and Training (ET2020), provides a forum for the exchange of 'best practices' and mutual learning between Member States in the area of education policy. The ET2020 Joint Report[48] from 2015 explicitly connects media literacy with online information threats by listing the enhancement of 'critical thinking' and 'cyber and media literacy' as central priorities. In addition to this, the 2016 meeting of the group focused explicitly on the enhancement of critical thinking as a way of countering online radicalization and other information threats.[49] In addition to this, the Directorate-General of Communications Networks, Content and Technology (DG CNECT) has launched the *Media Literacy Expert Group* – a network of EU stakeholders from member states and experts in the field[50] – in order to identify 'good practices' in relation to media literacy.

*Media pluralism* is a strategy promoted within the media sector and part of the security work pursued within the framework of the Digital Single Market.[51] Apart from the *Media Literacy Expert Group*, which emphasizes media pluralism in lieu with media literacy, DG CNECT in 2017 launched the High-Level Expert Group on Fake News, which suggests 'diversity of information' as a key main principle for action in relation to online disinformation.[52] In addition, the Commission funds projects together with the European Centre for Press and Media freedom focusing on media freedom in the Neighbourhood Areas.[53] An older but still ongoing initiative focusing on media pluralism within the EU is the Media Pluralism Monitor – an online tool developed by the European University Institute and funded by the EU Commission in 2009.

Finally, *online censorship* – the removal of extremist content and hate speech online – connects the information threat with both the security and Internet sectors. Two different initiatives exist in relation to online content-removal.[54] First, the EU Internet Forum[55] – a forum for dialogue between EU Interior Ministers, Europol, the EU Parliament, the EU Counterterrorism co-ordinator as well as representatives from US Internet companies launched by the Commission in 2015. The aim of this forum is to encourage the Internet industry to delete undesirable online content through self-regulation. Second, the EU Internet Referral Unit – an entity operating under Europol with the task of 'helping Member States to identify and remove violent extremist content online in cooperation with industry partners', launched the same year.[56] This unit focuses on the detection, review and deletion of terrorist propaganda, recruitment attempts and content in the online space while gathering intelligence on terrorist activities – in particular related to Al Qaeda and Daesh.

This section has provided an overview of the various EU initiatives and sectors involved in countering the information threat. To throw some light upon the security-related values implied in the policy work, however, it is necessary to take into consideration local knowledge. In the below, the values connected to the remedies of strategic communication, media literacy, media pluralism, and censorship are analysed by taking into account policy material and discussions related to four central actors.

## IV. The values and referent objects

Taking into consideration local knowledge, the empirical analysis finds two different sets of security-related values. A sharp dividing line exists between the policy communities active in the security/defence and Internet sectors and the communities linked to media and education: the most notable difference between the two perspectives is the contrastive relationship with end-values. Whereas the EUISS and the EU Internet Forum consistently refrain from discussions or solutions conveying any substantial policy goals and, instead, describe security in relation to abstract procedural values – *efficiency* and *coherence* – those active in the *Media Literacy Expert Group* and ET2020 present a security hinging on *perspectivism* – an instrumental value ultimately aiming to secure *independence* in relation to citizen-judgement. The former two communities, then, emphasize values guiding security-making processes aimed to protect the informational space whereas the latter, instead, outlines citizens' independent democratic judgement a desired out-come of this process: an end-goal for security.

The first set of security-related values and objects is presented in the below under the overall heading of 'Security, Coherence and Efficiency' and, the second, under 'Security, Perspectivism and Independence'.

### Security, coherence and efficiency

Policymakers within the security/defence and Internet communities primarily rely on *strategic communication* and *censorship* to counter the information threat. Taking as a starting-point discussions and policies suggested by the EUISS and the EU Internet Forum, the below section describes how coherence and efficiency become two complimentary techniques for managing the informational space.

On the topic of strategic communication and online censorship, the EU actors emphasize the importance of a unified message. Strategic communication, in the EUISS report, is described as the production of coherent communication disseminated online in relation to widespread threat coming from 'East, south and inside'.[57] Focusing primarily on official EU communication, a central criteria for a successful campaign is, first and foremost, tight 'coordination and consistency'.[58] Strategic communication is communication infused with 'an agenda or a plan' as opposed to open-ended online discussions or scattered initiatives by individual EU agencies.[59] By swiftly producing a 'single coherent set of agreed common narratives', the policy should be used as a form of 'rapid intervention' in response to the information threat.[60] The EU Internet Forum outlines a similar form of informational management when suggesting a combination of strategic communication and censorship to counter hostile content online – here, primarily on social media. The explicit objectives of the Forum are to 'reduce accessibility to terrorist content', but also to 'increase the volume' of alternative narratives online.[61] Speaking at the EU Internet Forum, the Commissioner for the Security Union, for instance, emphasizes the importance of 'reducing accessibility to terrorist material' while simultaneously offering 'persuasive but positive alternative narratives'.[62] The purpose of strategic communications is, according to a piece recommended by the EUISS, to produce so-called 'credible truths'.[63] The core argument here hinges on the basic under-standing that there is 'rarely such a thing as telling the whole truth'.[64] However, by presenting a coherent set of narratives, an argument can be made 'on your truth's behalf'.[65] Hence, both strategic communication and censorship aim to achieve informational coherence and, ultimately, a sense of control over the digital information space though coherent, efficient and timely interventions. Efficiency in terms of time is particularly crucial for the EU Internet Forum. In one of their press releases, they describe the process for removing terrorist content in relation to a 'golden hour' objective.[66] To achieve a timely intervention, the Forum suggests a turn to technology. For instance, automatic detection of undesired content and algorithms pinpointing illegal or offensive messages – sometimes even before such messages appear online – are characterized as desirable remedies.[67] Overall, it is possible to describe the policy documents and published material produced by the EUISS and the EU Internet Forum as founded in two abstract procedural values: *coherence* and *efficiency*.

To flesh out how these values translate into a vision of security, it is necessary to consider the understanding of the threat strategic communication and censorship are to counter. A plausible threat-description embraced by the EUISS is the idea of the 'information vacuum'.[68] In a piece recommended by the EUISS, the information vacuum is described as a black hole in the government communication flow that can be 'vacated by the morass of lies, rumours and disinformation generated by its adversaries'.[69] Hence, unless adequately managed, much like a force of nature, the information vacuum will perpetually fill up by itself. While this threat-description is usually employed to describe the necessity of strategic communication in a context of war, it is here taken to describe everyday information threats online. Commissioner Avramopoulos at the EU Internet Forum, for instance, depicts the entire online space as a new 'battlefield' where terrorist messages become 'infectious, spreading from bogus social media accounts, from one platform to another'.[70] In the informational space, then, the war is potentially ever-present and information requires continuous management. A similar connection between a logic of war and the new information environment is outlined in the report 'Strategic Communications and National Strategy' embraced by the EUISS.[71] This piece makes clear that the lack of a coherent and efficient communications strategy on the part of the authorities not only provides one's enemies with a chance to supply the public with disinformation or propaganda – but it will leave the floor open to a vast miscellany of information. The report underlines: 'we're being "out-communicated" – not only by our enemies but by a wide range of perspectives that are sometimes hostile, sometimes indifferent'.[72] This position is echoed by the Fotyga report, adopted by the Parliamentary Committee on Foreign Affairs, which describes the information threat widely in terms of 'informa-tion, disinformation and misinformation campaigns and propaganda'.[73] Even seemingly unproblematic, 'indifferent', information thus appears to pose a problem online. The information threat does not only involve false information, but a lack of control of online information per se. What is called for here, in short, is an understanding of security as intimately connected with an increased and continuous presence in the online environment on the part of the EU.

The combination of strategic communication and censorship offers a two-pronged approach to manage the information vacuum. Despite this emphasis on content production and deletion, however, the actors rarely elaborate on the substance of the strategic communication disseminated by the EU, or the censored online content. What is more, rather than engaging in such a discussion, the EU Internet Forum argues that the production of positive content should be outsourced to paid independent actors[74]: the 'hundreds of NGOs' and 'CVE partnerships' employed by the Internet companies linked to the EU Internet Forum.[75] The same lack of substance-related discussions are visible in the strategic communication strategies proposed by the EUISS. While consistently underlining the importance of 'positive messages', 'respect' and encouraging 'story-telling', the use of 'real people', 'irony' and 'satire', the comprehensive EUISS report mentions little in the way of substantial content.[76] Clearly, it is impossible to specify narrative content in detail on the strategic level. Nevertheless, the active avoidance of generating substance becomes clear when the EUISS formulates a strategy where content is not a policy-matter at all.[77] Instead, decisions on content production are delegated to 'media operators' and communicators recruited by EU agencies. What is more, and perhaps most notably, the same strategy is partly employed towards deletion of content. While the 'database of hashes'[78] – a shared database of known terrorist content – includes the active involvement of EU law enforcement agencies; the companies related to the EU Internet Forum – Facebook, Twitter, Youtube and Microsoft – have also signed a voluntary agreement to remove 'hate speech' from their platforms without any form of external legal review.[79]

To sum up, then, security in the security/defence and Internet sectors involves managing the information space through positive and negative interventions, rather than filling it with any specific (political) content. The referent object these values aim to protect is the informational space, understood broadly. Still, coherence and efficiency are here, first and foremost, abstract procedural values guiding the process of security-making, rather than end-goals characterizing the substance to be delivered. While the EUISS calls for a coherent narrative, this argument is made – not because they can point to or outline such a narrative – but for reasons of coordination. The ultimate purpose which crystallises here is thus to win the battle over the communicative space, regardless of content.

### Security, perspectivism and independence

The education and media policy sectors suggest two methods for countering the information threat: *media literacy* and *media pluralism*. In short, media pluralism is defined as a heterogeneity of political, cultural, geographical, structural and content dimensions in the media[80] while media literacy refers to 'all the technical, cognitive, social, civic and creative capacities that allow us to access and have a critical understanding of and interact with both traditional and new forms of media'.[81] Applied to the online sphere, the first policy, according to the *Media Literacy Expert Group*, provides citizens within the EU and the Neighbourhood Regions with a healthy miscellany of viewpoints. The second, in the view of ET2020, enhances the critical skills needed to both seek out and process such pluralistic information.

Taking into consideration the policy discussions, it is clear that the information threat pinpoints a need for a new form of citizen-knowledge. More specifically, citizens need skills that take as their blueprint the profession of the traditional journalist. At the 2015 meeting of the *Media Literacy Expert Group*, Aralynn McMane[82] argues: citizens have to learn to 'use reporter-like skills to assess all info to separate fact from fiction', 'make informed judgements as users of information [...] and to become skilful creators and producers of information and media messages in their own right'.[83] Journalistic material is, furthermore, a central backdrop for this form of knowledge. In line with this, media needs to 'promote the freedom of expression and the freedom of the press' also in the digital world by providing the public with 'professional, reliable journalistic content'.[84] Consequently, if strategic communication and censorship goes back to the idea of producing coherency in online space, the proposals for media literacy and media pluralism, instead, emphasize the importance of exercising informed judgement and taking a manifold of viewpoints into account. The key value that the policies of media pluralism and media literacy aim to promote may thus be understood in terms of 'perspectivism'.

To throw some light upon how this perspectivism is linked to security, we might consider the understanding of the perceived threat among the policy intellectuals here. In her welcome address at the 2016 meeting of the *Media Literacy Expert Group*, Lorena Boix Alonso[85] describes a fragile geopolitical situation and a 'radicalized' society.[86] Arguing that, 'in times where people are so upset, it is very important that when they go to vote they know what they are doing, and they are well informed' Boix Alonso furthermore makes a link between perspectivism and democracy.[87] What is specifically required, she argues, is an ability among citizens to 'exercise these democratic choices and tools [put] in their hands by democracy in a wise way, in an informed way'.[88] Similarly, Commissioner Harry Panagopulos underlines that 'significant challenges confront citizens in accessing a plurality of sources of [political] information, particularly across borders, and in terms of their confidence in the information they have access to and the modern media environment'.[89] The main threat appears to be that EU citizens struggle with a vast array of unreliable information. Security, then, entails that citizens acquire the skills to evaluate (the reliability of) such information. Hence, while being exposed to the threat, citizens also form an active part in producing the information threat. Comparing the current situation with the time before the Internet, Boix Alonso states that: 'in the past when people were going to exercise their democratic rights, they were receiving information. With social media, they do not only receive, but they also participate'.[90] Similarly, the ET2020 collection of 'good practices', argues that 'young people are confident but not necessarily competent users of the (new) media'.[91] Whereas the policy sectors of security/defence and the Internet understand the security problem as grounded in an abstract 'information vacuum', policy intellectuals conceive of the threat as rooted in the vast array of unreliable information coupled with the general incompetence of citizens in managing the online environment. As Adian White from the Ethical Journalist Network states: the Internet has been 'taken over by governments, corporations and people who don't understand it'.[92]

The perspectivism forwarded within these communities is clearly linked to a higher value: that of securing the active independent democratic citizen. The ET2020 describe the ultimate outcome of their policies on the information threat in terms of young people learning to 'recognise propaganda and to resist all forms of indoctrination', to decode and analyse 'representations and stereotypes' and recognize messenger bias in relation to a specific goal: to master the tools of democracy.[93] Media literacy, furthermore, is specifically referred to as a new 'civic competency' – a skill 'closely related to active engagement in democratic life'.[94] For instance, in relation to the 'competent' sharing of content, the ET2020 suggests that teachers should encourage their pupils to build and disseminate 'their own narratives' to counter 'hate speech and indoctrination' online.[95] The end-goal of these policies implies an understanding of security as related to a particular form of democracy contingent upon the active and, crucially: independently thinking citizen. If perspectivism is the means, the goal is *independence*. What ultimately is to be protected, the referent object that these policies want to safeguard, can thus be described as a form of independent democratic judgement. Unlike the object forwarded by policymakers within the security/defence and Internet communities, however, this referent object is protected though its very constitution: the policies suggested, in this sense, are meant to provide the fertile ground for citizens' independent judgement to appear.

In sum, forwarding the values of perspectivism and independence as remedies for the information threat, the policy communities understand security as hinging upon a new form of Internet-savy democratic citizen. Safeguarding citizens' independent democratic judgement is thus the overarching end-goal of both media literacy and media pluralism. Finally, whereas the security/defence and Internet sectors turn to independent actors in the production and deletion of content, the media and education communities primarily rely on public authorities and already-active national stakeholders in policy implementation.[96]

## V. Implementation

This section focuses on security-related values in the policy work conducted by independent actors, and aims to throw some light upon the potential output side of EU policies on the information threat. Three kinds of actors suggested by the security/defence and Internet communities are taken into consideration: civil society, professional communicators and the Internet industry. Considering contemporary examples of policy initiatives related to these actors (or presumed actors), the analysis shows that overlapping and potentially conflicting security-related values may arise with the outsourcing of online substance-production. The underlying argument is that, if each actor approaches the process of informational management in according to a value system 'proper to one environment'[97] – civil society, media or the technically-oriented Internet industry – these value-systems may have unfortunate and unforeseen effects on the output side of EU policy. The involvement of these actors, coupled with the lack of specificity in relation to substance on the part of EU policymakers may then, in the end, result in hybrid value-constellations in the implementation phase. In particular, the examples illustrate how the abstract procedural value of efficiency can come to encroach upon the construction of reliable and pluralistic content and, thus, how protecting the informational space though timely interventions might, in fact, counteract the constitution of citizens' independent judgement.

Strategic communication is meant to produce a 'credible truth' online; however, the outsourcing of content to civil society actors may actually work to counter this aim. An example is the *Civil Society Empowerment Programme*, an initiative under the *EU Internet Forum* with the aim to recruit and train civil society actors in order to 'provide a credible voice for counter or alternative narrative campaigns'.[98] Credibility is the foremost criteria for recruitment in their call for applications, which states that: 'Both NGOs and statutory practitioners are welcome, as long as the criteria on being a credible are fulfilled'.[99] While this kind of outsourcing can be in line with the values of independence and perspectivism embraced by the media and education sectors, credibility can also be an instrumental value related to a particular kind of efficiency. The Chatham House report, for instance, underlines that borrowed credibility is, in fact, crucial when 'strategic communications require subtlety of message and where the intended influence and outcome should not be seen as connected in any way to government interests or aims'.[100] By consciously involving external actors and, by 'operating outside government messaging', it is possible to 'depoliticize and demilitarize strategic communications' and thus reach a wider audience.[101] While this may be entirely unproblematic – after all, representatives volunteer to participate with their own projects – the practice of strategically using civil society in order to operate outside of government messaging could also work to hollow out the reliability and independence that they promote. In such a situation, the credibility of the independent actor could be undermined by the desire for communicative efficiency; a credibility which, rather ironically, is the very currency used by the EU in the first place.

The EUISS report calls for an outsourcing of content production to professional communicators – a way of using individuals who 'understand' the Internet to provide reliable information to European citizens.[102] This form of substance-deference is particularly present in the official communication produced by the EU. The *East StratCom Task Force*, created in 2015 with the aim of promoting EU policies towards the Eastern Neighbourhood, can serve as an illustrative example. In this case, the professional communicators recruited to the Task Force, upon their installation, came to play a very active role in creating messages for the EEAS.[103] Interviewing the initiators and practitioners part of the group initial group, Hedling describes how their work quickly came to be guided by the 'reach and exposure' of content.[104] By adopting this form of media logic, however, the professionals made efficiency into a feature of the content itself, rather than an abstract procedural value guiding the organizational setup. As a result, the Task Force ended up producing mainly 'simplified, polarized, spectacularized' messages towards the Eastern Neighbourhood.[105] This kind of professionalized content production, when coupled with the media logic driving communication professionals, thus veer starkly from the values of perspectivism and independence in the media and education policy sector. Rather than producing reliable content or offering a multitude of different perspectives, the communication professionals involved in the Task Force make the abstract procedural value of efficiency into an end-goal in itself. Going back to the image described by Boix Alonso, the Task Force might thus have contributed to the 'radicalized society' online which they were, in fact, recruited to counter.[106]

Finally, there is the question of outsourcing content deletion to US Internet companies; companies which then provide efficient automatic removal, sometimes before the content even goes online. In principle, for a conflict of values not to arise on the policy level, the deference of substance can only be employed towards content production – not content-removal. While content production, in theory, could be pursued in line with the values of credibility and reliability, censorship on behalf of the EU is a legal matter. This gives rise to some questions in relation to the policies forwarded by the EU Internet Forum. In the 'Code of Conduct on Countering Illegal Hate Speech Online',[107] signed by US Internet companies involved in the Forum, the parties accept responsibility for deleting illegal and offensive material on their respective platforms. However, the lack of clarity surrounding whether or not the Commission has requested the US Internet companies to remove content, or whether the agreement is voluntary, is a question yet pending an answer.[108] Clear is, however, that the 'Code of Conduct' does not currently correspond with any specific law on the EU level.[109] What is more, the companies are neither required to consider legal matters before content deletion nor to report deleted content to the legal authorities.[110] Given this, it is possible to regard this setup as a way of outsourcing content deletion to private actors, giving rise to a 'hybrid situation'[111] in which the EU is the initiator of censorship while failing to take any legal responsibility. This move goes against the crucial freedom of expression and independent content production emphasized by the media and education sector and reflects a situation where private companies take over the task of EU law enforcement.

In sum, the outsourcing of content-management to independent actors may – if pursued along these lines – create a situation where efficiency comes into conflict with at least three values connected with the end-goal of security as citizens' independent democratic judgement: credibility, reliability, and freedom of expression.

## Concluding discussion

This article has identified four remedies against the information threat: strategic communication, censorship, media literacy and media pluralism. Situating these remedies in relation to local knowledge, the analysis outlines two distinct value-perspectives: while the security/defence and Internet communities emphasize the procedural values of coherence and efficiency, the education and media sector instead forward perspectivism as a way of achieving independence. In line with this, the latter points to an understanding of the referent object as citizens' independent democratic judgement whereas the former focuses on protecting the digital 'battlefield' of the informational space itself.

Reading the two perspectives as complementary, one may regard continuous management of online space as serving both perspectivism and independence. Indeed, security can involve both a 'secured' online environment and Internet-savy democratic citizens. An active management of hate speech and terrorist propaganda, coupled with accurate official information, provides a crucial foundation for pluralist discussion and independent judgement in digital public space. However, value-conflicts arise when EU policymakers regard the informational space as yet another 'battlefield' for security-making and fail to engage with questions of substance. The outsourcing of content deletion and production leaves the articulation of a 'credible truth' and – crucially – the very articulation of the secured online space itself, to independent actors. The examples of policy implementation highlight that the means applied to protect the online space may counteract the end-goal of securing citizens' independent democratic judgement. While EU policy describes efficiency in rather abstract terms, professional communicators and the Internet industry – driven by media logic and technological solutions, respectively – tend to regard efficiency as a value guiding both content production and deletion. Meanwhile, civil society actors could lose the very credibility that they are to represent if recruited to be efficient messengers on EU's behalf. Involvement of independent actors in content-management, then, could give rise to unforeseen hybrid value-constellations on the output side of EU policy. When constructing efficient remedies for the digital battlefield, substantial values cannot be ignored. For future policymakers, this underlines a clear danger in pursuing the information threat through purely defensive strategies, taking as a single point-of-departure a boundless informational space requiring efficient interventions. If the information threat is a threat to our values, this must be taken into account throughout the entire policy process.

These findings add to previous literature on security and the communicative aspect of ICTs in several ways. In relation to studies on information operations focusing on top-down military-led activities in response to information threats,[112] the cross-sectoral focus of this article illuminates some of the complex issues involved in the more far-reaching task of civil security-management. Overall, the findings should make it clear that relying on traditional preconceptions of security-making which emphasize an efficient response to threats in a pre-defined space may be problematic when applied to the communicative aspects of cyberspace. While technological solutions, or the involvement of independent actors, may provide a more efficient management of the 'battlefield', we must not forget that content, in the end, is what constitutes cyberspace. By focusing on action rather than the substance of action – in particular with regard to online censorship – authorities, in fact, lose control over the communicative aspects of the informational space. Furthermore, unlike in the case of cybersecurity, the information threat does not appear to display a multitude of referent objects. The policy area is, instead, characterized by two rather abstract objects of protection which, in the process of security-making, appear to counteract each other. Whereas the informational space is described as pre-given and thus requires protective measures, citizens' independent judgement can be discerned as an end-goal to be constituted through policy. A more traditional approach to mapping the object of protection would inevitably have failed to see the conflicts between referent objects and proposed approaches for security-making outlined in this article.[113] This finding points to a need for expanding the view of referent objects when investigating the communicative side of information technology and the approach could be applicable to other similar areas of civil security policy.

## Notes

1. Fotyga, "Plenary Sitting," 3.
2. Ibid.
3. EUISS, "EU Strategic Communications"; Fortyga, "Plenary Sitting"; and Cornish, Lindley-French and Yorke, "Chatham House."
4. Bennett and Waltz, *Counterdeception Principles*; Clark and Williams, *Counterdeception*; Bell, "Theory of Deception"; Whaley, "General Theory of Deception." Focusing on everyday threats, there is a growing contemporary literature on 'hybrid warfare'. The view of security, however, remains closely linked to the military-operational perspective (Lancu et al, *Countering Hybrid Threats*) and often focus on the 'hard' aspects of hybrid threats (*Critical Infrastructure Protection*, Niglia).
5. An interesting exception of a scholar addressing the information threat in relation to security, but with a different empirical scope to this article, is Mälksoo's "Countering Hybrid Warfare" which mobilises the concept of 'ontological security' for reading NATO and EU security-making in relation to hybrid warfare.
6. The technological side often focuses on state security related to hacking and system-vulnerabilities. For a focus EU cybersecurity policy, see: Carrapico and Barrinha, "EU Cyber." For critical readings on cybersecurity, see: Hansen and Nissenbaum, "Digital Disaster" or Dunn Cavelty, Cybersecurity and Threat Politics.
7. Deibert, *Hyper-Realities*; and Dunn Cavelty, *Cyber-Security*, 6–7.
8. Bennett and Waltz, *Counterdeception Principles*; Bowyer Bell, "Theory of Deception"; and Whaley, "General Theory of Deception."
9. Boin and Rhinard, "Managing Crises."
10. Burgess, "No EU Security," 318.
11. Buzan, Wæver and Jaap, *Security a New Framework*, 21.
12. Buzan, Wæver and Jaap, *Security a New Framework*.
13. Ibid.
14. Buzan talks of, for instance, "societal security" and "environmental security" (Buzan, Wæver and Jaap, *Security a New Framework*).
15. Burgess, "No EU Security," 309.
16. Ibid., 310.
17. Burgess, "No EU Security," 323.
18. Rein, "Value-Critical Policy Analysis."
19. Bigo, "Internal and External Aspects of Security," 387.
20. Wagenaar, *Meaning in Action*, 82–84.
21. While Rein's value-critical policy analysis speaks of 'frames' when describing taken for granted assumptions in policy and the context in which they are produced (Wagenaar, *Meaning in Action*, 84), Yanow's concept of 'local knowledge' more clearly points to context while 'frames' might also denote a cognitive category (Yanow, *Conducting Interpretive Policy Analysis*, 233).
22. Ibid.
23. Yanow, *Conducting Interpretive Policy Analysis*, 239.
24. Ibid.
25. Rein and Thacher, "Managing Value-Conflict," 460.
26. Hansen and Nissenbaum, "Digital Disaster."
27. Carrapico and Barrinha, "EU Cyber," 1255.
28. Bossong and Hegemann, *European Civil Security Governance*.
29. Yanow, *Conducting Interpretive Policy Analysis*; and Rein, "Value-Critical Policy Analysis."
30. Rein, "Value-Critical Policy Analysis."

31. Burgess, "No EU Security," 322.
32. Burgess point to the intermingling between different value systems when a multitude of professionals, from previously distinct sectors, are required to address the same security issue (Burgess, "No EU Security").
33. Ibid., 321–23.
34. EUISS was commissioned by the European Parliament to produce the report 'EU Strategic Communication with a view to countering propaganda' (2016) after a request by the AFET Committee.
35. The report has been described as 'probably the best thing out there' by EUISS officials (John-Joseph Wilkins, E-mail to author, 3 March 2017).
36. The Fotyga report, written after the reception of the EUISS report, was later adopted by the Committee for Foreign Affairs. As such, it can be taken to reflect the more widely shared views of the EU security/defence community in relation to the information threat.
37. The Working Group consists of government representatives from 36 countries. Apart from member states, Iceland, Norway, Switzerland, Albania, Serbia, Macedonia, Montenegro and Turkey are represented.
38. The declaration was adopted after a meeting between EU education ministers after the terrorist attacks in Paris.
39. The objectives of the group are to: (1) discover, bring to the light, document and extend good practices in the field of media literacy; (2) facilitate networking between stakeholders; (3) explore synergies between different EU policies and media literacy initiatives. Members are: member states, experts nominated by candidate countries and EEA countries, representatives of European associations and foundations active in the field of media literacy, and representatives from international organisations.
40. Yanow, *Conducting Interpretive Policy Analysis*, 233.
41. It should, again, be stressed that this outline provides a sketch of the main policy community involved in *articulating* a specific policy. In the wider action plans, and on a higher level of decision-making, the policies are often described together.
42. European Commission, *European Agenda on Security*, 15 and 4.
43. European Commission, *European Agenda on Security*, 15.
44. There are two teams: The East StratCom Task Force consisting of 10 full-time communication experts focused on the Eastern Neighbourhood Region and the StratCom South Task Force, dedicated to the Southern Neighbourhood Region. In addition, in 2015, the Commission funded the Syria Strategic Communication Advisory Team (SSCAT) in order to produce counter-narratives in Arabic.
45. EEAS, "Action Plan Strategic Communication," 1.
46. European Commission, *European Agenda on Security*, 15.
47. European Commission, "The Paris Declaration."
48. The Joint Report of the Council and the Commission on the implementation of the strategic framework for ET2020' (2015).
49. As a result of this meeting, a group dedicated to the enhancement of critical thinking was set up: The Working Group on 'promoting citizenship and the common values of freedom, tolerance and non-discrimination through education'.
50. Participants come from different public authorities related to culture, education and communication. The UNESCO and the Council of Europe are fixed members. In addition, experts are nominated by member states and the meetings of the Media Literacy Expert Group include stakeholders as well as representatives from the media industry.
51. European Commission, *European Agenda on Security*, 4.
52. The group is chaired by Professor Madeleine de Cock Buning and has representatives from civil society, social media platforms, news media organisations, journalists and academia.
53. Examples of projects funded include the 'Index of Censorship', a non-profit organisation publishing work by censored writers and artists, and 'Wiki4MediaFreedom' aimed at 'boosting the availability of accurate knowledge on media freedom and pluralism on Wikipedia'.
54. European Commission, *European Agenda on Security*, 13.
55. The Forum connects DG HOME and DG JUST.
56. See note 54 above.
57. EUISS, "EU Strategic Communications," 4.
58. Ibid.
59. Ibid.
60. Ibid., 30–31.
61. European Commission, "Press Release Fighting Terrorism."
62. European Commission, "Press Release Curbing Content."
63. Taylor, "Strategic Communications," 439–440.
64. Ibid., 440.
65. Ibid.
66. Ibid.

67. European Commission, "Speech Fighting Terrorism Online"; and European Commission, "Press Release Fighting Terrorism."
68. Taylor, "Strategic Communications."
69. Ibid.
70. European Commission, "Speech Fighting Terrorism Online."
71. Cornish, Lindley-French and Yorke, "Chatham House."
72. Ibid., vii.
73. Fotyga, "Plenary Sitting," 3. my italics.
74. See note 70 above.
75. EUISS, "EU Strategic Communications," 30; and European Commission, "Speech Fighting Terrorism Online."
76. EUISS, "EU Strategic Communications," 30–31.
77. Ibid., 30.
78. The database is maintained in connection with the EU Internet Referral Unit (EU IRU) – a unit set up by the Commission's Justice and Home Affairs Council in 2015.
79. European Commission, "Stepping Up Efforts."
80. European Commission DG-CNTC 2015, "2015 Meeting," 10 and 7.
81. European Commission DG-EAC, "Key Messages PLA," 3–4.
82. The speaker comes from the World Association of Newspapers and News Publishers.
83. European Commission DG-CNTC, "2015 Meeting," 15.
84. Ibid.
85. Boix Alonso is Head of Unit of the 'Audiovisual and Media Services Policy' at the European Commission.
86. Boix Alonso, Streamed Meeting Expert Group.
87. Ibid.
88. Ibid.
89. European Commission DG-CNTC, "Summaries of Presentations," 2.
90. See note 86 above.
91. European Commission DG-EAC, "Key Messages PLA," 6.
92. European Commission DG-CNTC, "2015 Meeting," 9.
93. European Commission DG-EAC, "Key Messages PLA," 3.
94. European Council, "Council Conclusions," 6.
95. European Commission DG-EAC, "Key Messages PLA," 9.
96. The bulk of initiatives are linked to national public authorities or civil society organisations on the national level.
97. Burgess, "No EU Security," 321.
98. European Commission, "Call for Proposals."
99. Ibid.
100. Cornish, Lindley-French and Yorke, "Chatham House," 23.
101. Ibid.
102. See note 92 above.
103. Hedling, "Politics and New Media."
104. Ibid., 156.
105. Ibid., 158–159.
106. See note 86 above.
107. European Commission, "Code of Conduct."
108. EDRi, EU Internet Forum.
109. European Commission, "Code of Conduct," 2.
110. Ibid.
111. The Commission has the status of an initiator of 'of the interference with a fundamental right by private individuals' while simultaneously not taking any responsibility for the implementation and the result is a 'state interference by proxy' (Kuczerawy, "The Code of Conduct").
112. Bennett and Waltz, Counterdeception Principles; and Clark and Williams, Counterdeception.
113. For instance, while engaging in a critical reading of cybersecurity, the article by Hansen and Nissenbaum focuses primarily on the hard aspects of this form of security (Hansen and Nissenbaum, "Digital Disaster").

## Disclosure statement

No potential conflict of interest was reported by the author.

# Bibliography

Baldwin, D. A. "The Concept of Security." *Review of International Studies* 23, no. 1 (1997): 5–26. doi: 10.1017/S0260210597000053

Bell, J. B. "Toward a Theory of Deception." *International Journal of Intelligence and Counterintelligence* 16, no. 2 (2003): 244–279. doi:10.1080/08850600390198742.

Bennett, M., and E. Waltz. *Counterdeception Principles and Applications for National Security*. Boston: Artech House, 2007.

Bigo, D. "Internal and External Aspects of Security." *European Security* 15, no. 4 (2006): 385–404. doi:10.1080/09662830701305831.

Boin, A., and M. Rhinard. "Managing Transboundary Crises: What Role for the European Union?" *International Studies Review* 10, no. 1 (2008): 1–26. doi:10.1111/j.1468-2486.2008.00745.x.

Boix-Alonso, L. (2016). "Streamed Meeting of the Media Literacy Expert Group." Brussels. Accessed 6 April 2018. https://webcast.ec.europa.eu/meeting-of-the-media-literacy-expert-group-meeting-of-15-november-2016.

Bossong, R., and H. Hegemann. European Civil Security Governance: Diversity and Cooperation in Crisis and Disaster Management. New York, NY: Springer, 2015.

Bremberg, N., and M. Britz. "Uncovering the Diverging Institutional Logics of EU Civil Protection." *Cooperation and Conflict* 44, no. 3 (2009): 288–308. doi:10.1177/0010836709106217.

Burgess, J. P. "There is No European Security, Only European Securities." *Cooperation and Conflict* 44, no. 3 (2009): 309–328. doi:10.1177/0010836709106218.

Buzan, B., O. Wæver, and D. W. Jaap. *Security: A New Framework for Analysis*. London: Lynne Rienner Publishers, 1998.

Carrapico, H., and A. Barrinha. "The EU as a Coherent (Cyber) Security Actor?" *JCMS: Journal of Common Market Studies* 55, no. 6 (2017): 1254–1272.

Cavelty, M. D. *Cybersecurity and Threat Politics: US Efforts to Secure the Information Age*. New York, NY: Routledge, 2007.

Cavelty, M. D. "Cyber-Terror—Looming Threat or Phantom Menace? The Framing of the US Cyber-Threat Debate." *Journal of Information Technology & Politics* 4, no. 1 (2008): 19–36. doi:10.1300/J516v04n01_03.

Cavelty, M. D. "Cyber-Security." In *The Routledge Handbook of New Security Studies*, edited by J. Peter, 154–162. New York, NY: Routledge, 2010.

Christou, G., S. Croft, M. Ceccorulli, and S. Lucarelli. "European Union Security Governance: Putting the 'Security' Back In." *European Security* 19, no. 3 (2010): 341–359. doi:10.1080/09662839.2010.526109.

Clark, R. M., and W. Mitchell. *Deception, Counterdeception and Counterintelligence*. Los Angeles: CQ Press, 2018.

Cornish, P., J. Lindley-French, and C. Yorke. *Strategic Communications and National Strategy A Chatham House Report*. London: The Royal Institute of Intentional Affairs, 2011.

Deibert, R. J. "Hyper-Realities of World Politics: Theorizing the Communications Revolution." In *Cyber-Diplomacy: Managing Foreign Policy in the Twenty-First Century*, edited by E. H. Potter, 27–47. McGill-Queen's University Press, 2002.

Dunn Cavelty, M. *Cyber-Security and Threat Politics: US Efforts to Secure the Information Age*. Milton Park, Abingdon, Oxon: Routledge, 2008.

Dunn Cavelty, M., M. Mareile Kaufmann, and K. Søby Kristensen. "Resilience and (In) Security: Practices, Subjects, Temporalities." *Security Dialogue* 46, no. 1 (2015): 3–14. doi:10.1177/0967010614559637.

EDRi. 2017. "EU Internet Forum, Web Page." Accessed 22 August 2018 https://edri.org/launch-of-the-eu-internet-forum-behind-closed-doors-and-without-civil-society/

EEAS. 2015. "Action Plan On Strategic Communication 1. Context. Brussels. Accessed 6 April 2018. http://archive.eap-csf.eu/assets/files/ActionPLan.pdf.

EUISS. 2016. "EU Strategic Communications with a View to Counteracting Propaganda." Accessed 6 April 2018. http://www.europarl.europa.eu/RegData/etudes/IDAN/2016/578008/EXPO_IDA2016578008_EN.pdf.

European Commission. 2015 March 17. "Informal Meeting of European Union Education Ministers, Paris, Tuesday ." Declaration on Promoting citizenship and the common values of freedom, tolerance and non-discrimination through education. Accessed 22 August 2018. http://ec.europa.eu/dgs/education_culture/repository/education/news/2015/documents/citizenship-education-declaration_en.pdf.

European Commission. 2015. "Communication from the Commission to the European Parliament, the Council, the European Economic and Social Committee and the Committee of the Regions: The European Agenda on Security." Strasbourg. Accessed 22 August 2018. https://www.cepol.europa.eu/sites/default/files/european-agenda-security.pdf .

European Commission. *Council Conclusions on Developing Media Literacy and Critical Thinking through Education and Training*. Brussels, 2016. Accessed 22 August 2018. http://data.consilium.europa.eu/doc/document/ST-9641-2016-INIT/en/pdf.

European Commission. 2016. "European Commission - PRESS RELEASES - PRESS Release - EU Internet Forum: A Major Step Forward in Curbing Terrorist Content on the Internet." Accessed 20 August 2018. http://europa.eu/rapid/press-release_IP-16-4328_en.htm .

European Commission. *Code of Conduct on Countering Illegal Hate Speech Online*. Brussels, 2016. Accessed 11 April 2018 https://edri.org/files/privatisedenf/euhatespeechcodeofconduct_20160531.pdf.

European Commission. *European Commission – Press Releases – Press Release – Fighting Terrorism Online: Internet Forum Pushes for Automatic Detection of Terrorist Propaganda*. Brussels, 2017. Accessed 20 August 2018 http://europa.eu/rapid/pres.

European Commission. *European Commission – Press Releases – Press Release – Stepping up the EU's Efforts to Tackle Illegal Content Online*. Brussels, 2017. Accessed 11 April 2018 http://europa.eu/rapid/press-release_MEMO-17-3522_en.htm.

European Commission. 2018. "Call for Proposals for Alternative and Counter Narrative Campaigns Supporting the Prevention of Radicalisation Leading to Violent Extremism – Civil Society Empowerment Programme (CSEP) – ISFP-2017-AG-CSEP – Call for Proposal: Up2Europe." Accessed 11 April 2018. https://www.up2europe.eu/calls/call-for-proposals-for-alternative-and-counter-narrative-campaigns-supporting-the-prevention-of-radicalisation-leading-to-violent-extremism-civil-society-empowerment-programme-csep-isfp-2017-ag-csep_2020.html.

European Commission DG-CNCT. 2016. "*Speakers BIOs and Summaries of Presentations Meeting of The Media Literacy Expert Group*." Brussels. Accessed 6 April 2018http://ec.europa.eu/transparency/regexpert/index.cfm?do=groupDetail.groupDetail&groupID=2541.

European Commission DG-CNTC. 2015. "2015 Meeting of the Media Literacy Expert Group." Brussels. Accessed 6 April 2018. https://ec.europa.eu/digital-single-market/en/news/meetings-media-literacy-expert-group.

European Commission DG-EAC. *Strengthening Media Literacy and Critical Thinking to Prevent Violent Radicalisation: Key Messages from the PLA, the Hague, 20–22 April 2016*. Brussels, 2016.

European Commission. 2017. "European Commission – Speech – Fighting Terrorism Online." Accessed 6 April 2018. http://europa.eu/rapid/press-release_SPEECH-17-5151_en.htm.

Fotyga, A. Elżbieta. "Plenary Sitting on the REPORT on EU Strategic Communication to Counteract Propaganda against It by Third Parties." Brussels, 2016. http://www.europarl.europa.eu/sides/getDoc.do?pu

Guittet, E.-P. "Activities with National Boundaries: The French Case." In *Illiberal Practices of Liberal Regimes: The (In) Security Games*, edited by D. Bigo and A. Tsoukala, 137–166. Paris: L'Harmattan, 2006.

Hansen, L., and H. Nissenbaum. "Digital Disaster, Cyber Security, and the Copenhagen School." *International Studies Quarterly* 53, no. 4 (2009): 1155–1175. doi:10.1111/isqu.2009.53.issue-4.

Hedling, E. "Blending Politics and New Media?" Phd Diss., Lund University, 2018.

Iancu, N., A. Fortuna, and C. Barna, eds. *Countering Hybrid Threats: Lessons Learned from Ukraine*. Vol. 128. Amsterdam: IOS Press, 2016.

Kuczerawy. Aleksandra. 2016. "The Code of Conduct on Online Hate Speech: An Example of State Interference by Proxy? – CITIP Blog." Accessed 11 April 2018. https://www.law.kuleuven.be/citip/blog/the-code-of-conduct-on-online-hate-speech-an-example-of-state-interference-by-proxy/.

Mälksoo, M. "Countering Hybrid Warfare as Ontological Security Management: The Emerging Practices of the EU and NATO." *European Security* 27, no. 3 (2018): 374–392. doi:10.1080/09662839.2018.1497984.

Niglia, A., ed. *Critical Infrastructure Protection Against Hybrid Warfare Security Related Challenges*. Vol. 46. Amsterdam: IOS Press, 2016.

Rein, M. "Value-Critical Policy Analysis." In *Ethics, the Social Sciences, and Policy Analysis*, edited by D. Callahan and B. Jennings, 83–111. Boston: Springer, 1983.

Taylor, P. M. "Strategic Communications or Democratic Propaganda?" *Journalism Studies* 3, no. 3 (2002): 437–441. doi:10.1080/14616700220145641.

Thacher, D., and M. Rein. "Managing Value Conflict in Public Policy." *Governance* 17, no. 4 (2004): 457–486. doi:10.1111/gove.2004.17.issue-4.

Wagenaar, H. *Meaning in Action: Interpretation and Dialogue in Policy Analysis*. New York, NY: M.E. Sharp. Inc, 2011.

Weiss, M., and S. Dalferth. "Security Re-Divided: The Distinctiveness of Policy-Making in ESDP and JHA." *Cooperation and Conflict* 44, no. 3 (2009): 268–287. doi:10.1177/0010836709106216.

Whaley, B. "Toward a General Theory of Deception." *The Journal of Strategic Studies* 5, no. 1 (1982): 178–192. doi:10.1080/01402398208437106.

Yanow, D. *Conducting Interpretive Policy Analysis*. London: Sage Publications, 2000.

# Index

boundaries 28–29; duration of crowds 23; emotion, crowds and 21; ICT and 20, 22–23, 23, 28–29; information gathering by crowds 28; intelligence cycle 20; legitimacy/legality of using information 24; London riots, 2011 24, 26, 28; meanings of intelligence 19–20; as non-neutral 20, 28; Occupy Wall Street 22, 23, 24; Other, the, crowds as 28; passive information providers, crowds as 23–25; performing the crowd 27; politics of 27–29; questions regarding 3; rationality of crowd behaviour 21; resources, globalizing of 22; riots 24; social media intelligence (SOCMINT) 23–24, 28–29; superiority of, belief in 22; surveillance of 27; time and space, transcending 22; typology of 23–27

cyber security: accountability 86; as beyond the state 86–87; controversies over WannaCry 89–93; first responders, companies as 92–93; private sector and 87; public, the, defining regarding 85–86; publics, problem of 88–89; subpolitics of publics 93–94; uncertainty and 86–87, 88–90; vulnerabilities, hunting and hoarding 90–92; WannaCry ransomware attack 85, 89–93

data mining as theme 4; see also crowd-based intelligence; image appropriation; social media intelligence (SOCMINT)
de-monopolization: of intelligence practices 2–5; of secrecy 78–79
DeCew, Judith 53
Deibert, R. J. 87
democracy: awareness, communication as 9; challenge to as theme 4–5; perspectivism and 119; privacy and 54; social media intelligence (SOCMINT) 63
Denmark: awareness, communication as 9–10, 16n32; co-production, communication as 13; SOCMINT cases in 58–59
Diderichsen, Adam 28
digital crowd 22–23; see also crowd-based intelligence
digital footprints 55
discursive communication 14
Dondyuk, Maxim 41
Douglas, Mary 14

East StratCom Task Force 115–116
Education and Training 2020 (ET2020) 115, 116, 120
effectiveness 10–12
emotion, crowds and 21
Ericson, R. V. 55
European Union (EU): censorship, online 116, 117–119; civil society, outsourcing to 121; coherence and efficiency as techniques 117–119, 122; cross-sectoral approach 114; East StratCom Task Force 115–116; Education and Training 2020 (ET2020) 115, 116, 120; hybrid value-constellations 120–122;

information threat, challenge of 112; Institute for Security Studies (EUISS) 114, 117, 118; Internet Forum 114–115, 116, 117, 118; internet industry, outsourcing to 121–122; Internet Referral Unit 116; Joint Framework to Counter Hybrid Threats 116; Media Literacy Expert Group 115, 119; media literacy policies 116, 119–120; media pluralism policies 116, 119–120; outsourcing of online substance-production 120–122; perspectivism and independence as techniques 119–120, 122; policies 5, 115–117; policy communities 112, 114–115; professional communicators, outsourcing to 121; Radicalisation Awareness Network (RAN) 115; referent objects 113; remedies to information threat 112; strategic communication as remedy 115–116, 117–119; value conflicts due to outsourcing 122; value systems of actors 112; values, security-related 113–114, 117–120
expectations and possibilities, gap between 1
expert knowledge, information as 11
'Extraordinary Popular Delusions and the Madness of Crowds' (Mackay) 19

Facebook, Cambridge Analytica's exploitation of data from 52–53
Ferree, M. M. 14
Fleming, Jeremy 12

Gallagher, Ryan 76
George, R. 56, 58, 61

Haggerty, K. D. 55
Higgins, A. 36
Hribar, G. 28
human rights 80

ICREACH 76–77
image appropriation: active actants, images turned into 35, 44–46; agency of the image 35–38, 37, 41, 43–44, 46; amateur/citizen, designation of 44; Atlantic Council's use of soldier photography 41–42; authorship rights as casualty 41; citizen-driven initiatives 39–40; civilian-to-civilian 42–44, 43, 44; CORRECT!V 35–36; dilemmas presented to civilians 44–46; evidence, requirements of images for 38; insecurity, producers facing due to 35–37, 41, 44, 47; lack of consideration to civilians 47; levels of 39–40; Malaysian Airlines Flight 17 (MH17) 35–36, 40, 42–44, 43, 44, 45; by media organizations 39; non-state institutions 40; omnipresence of civilian photography 34–35; as rapidly developing practice 35; securitization theory 44; security dilemma 45; silence dilemma 45–46; soldier photos around Debaltseve, Ukraine, 2015 37, 37; spies, civilian 39–40;

Milton Keynes UK
Ingram Content Group UK Ltd.
UK HW051924141024
449569UK00027B/1339